THE FATEFUL ADVENTURES
OF
THE GOOD SOLDIER
ŠVEJK
DURING THE WORLD WAR

presents

THE SAMIZDAT

edition of
the new English rendition of

Jaroslav Hašek's

The Fateful Adventures of

THE GOOD SOLDIER ŠVEJK

During the World War

Book One

Visit our website

**for additional information and enjoyment of the Good
Soldier Švejk, and announcements of future releases of the
remaining Books Two and Three.**

1stBooks-rev. - 4/24/00

ABOUT THE BOOK

Some writers so capture the soul and spirit of a people that they are identified with them forever after. In England, it was Charles Dickens, in the United States, it was Mark Twain. For the Slavic nations, and to some extent for all Central Europeans, it is the Czech writer, Jaroslav Hašek.

Hašek's most important work was centered around a Czech soldier's experiences in World War One. It's actual title is *The Fateful Adventures of The Good Soldier Švejk during the World War*, but it is known by tens of millions of Central Europeans as simply, *The Good Soldier Švejk*. This monumental, humorous, work is acknowledged as ". . . one of the greatest masterpieces of satirical writing" by no less a standard and exalted reference than the *Encyclopedia Britannica*.

One of his biographers, Emmanuel Frynta, writes:

"He was one of that generation which fully fought with the problems of the modern world. He was one of the artists at the start of the century who so splendidly cast light on the question of a live, valid, meaningful art worthy of the time. He was a curious, not easily understood person, too mobile and opaque for portrayal. As a creator, (he was) seemingly careless, natural, (and) spontaneous, . . . but, in reality (he was) sharply discerning and refined in his specific type of non-literariness . . . (he) was working farsightedly in the field of language and style, with something that was to become the shape of (the) speech of the century."

"Hašek's brilliant invention of Švejk, the card-carrying imbecile, and his remarkable adventures, provided many hours of uproarious laughter . . . It is very good to see that classic Eastern European literature is making its way into the culture. Švejk lives!"

- Larry Heinemann, National Book Award winner, fiction, for *Paco's Story* (Farar, Straus & Giroux) in 1986; also the author of *Close Quarters*, FS&G, 1977, and *Cooler by the Lake*, FS&G, 1992.

"Justice is a term rarely found in 'literary' discussions, but Mike Joyce and Zenny Sadlon have sought and delivered exactly that to Jaroslav Hašek and the rest of us.

"This translation of The Good Soldier Švejk comes closer to Hašek's original absurdist protests of war, class systems, and government than the previous English translation tried to convey. Unable to read Czech, I can only put their translation up next to its predecessor and cast my vote.

"In their effort, Joyce and Sadlon remind us that 'justice' in any arena - especially literary - has to be fought for. I believe those who read this book will join the fight."

- Zak Mucha, author of *The Beggars' Shore*,
    Red 71 Press, 1999.

"Jaroslav Hašek's The Good Soldier Švejk is one of the world's great novels, and this is a brilliant new translation.

"Captured here for the first time in the English language is the zany, colloquial audacity of Hašek's wild genius. Švejk is no dainty classic meant to fade quietly into obscurity on the dusty shelves of academia, but a bellowing barroom brawl of a book that will forever have everyday people doubled-up with the painful laughter of recognition.

"Catch 22, Slaughterhouse Five and countless other cherished works owe a great deal to Švejk, and the English-speaking world owes a great deal to Zenny Sadlon and Mike Joyce."

- Don De Grazia, author of *American Skin*, published in the
    U.K. by Jonathan Cape as a hard cover, by Vintage as a

paperback, and in the U.S. by Scribner, teaches fiction writing at Columbia College.

"Just remember: Švejk is actually just a European Forrest Gump. Because Forrest was the same thing. He just kept getting into trouble and managing come out O.K. And it's the same thing Švejk did. I mean, he got into some situations that I thought 'O.K., that's it. The book is gonna end soon now', and somehow he just came out smelling like a rose . . .

"This man is not supposed to make it. And he saw people dying in the hospital, and he was begging for the treatment that they were dying from. And he managed to survive that, not only survive it but get out of it. And everything that happened to him he just managed to overcome it. You're rooting for him, because you really want to make sure that he gets out O.K."

- Ruth Cooper, a retired African-American microbiology technician, avid book reader and a volunteer critic.

"If anyone asks me to pick three literary works of this century which in my opinion will become part of world literature, then I would have to say one of them is Hašek's *The Good Soldier Švejk.*"

Bertolt Brecht

We would like to dedicate this effort to Jaroslav Hašek, a brilliant and magnificent writer for this, or any other, century.

And, we would like to thank him, too. First, for giving the world one of the most significant and enjoyable books of all time. And secondly, for being a trailblazer on the thorny path of modern fiction and marking the way for the 20th century's best writers.

In our fondest daydream, we see him looking down on us with a broad smile on his round, Slavic face. He lifts his frothy Pilsner, gives us a wink, and salutes us with his celestial stein. He is pleased that, at long last, the English-reading world is now able to truly enjoy his modern masterwork.

Zenny Sadlon and Mike Joyce
Chicago, Illinois
April 30, 1997:
The 114th anniversary of
the birth of Jaroslav Hašek

CONTENTS

BOOK ONE

IN THE REAR

NOTE TO THE READER:

In order to join the already wide world of discourse surrounding *The Good Soldier Švejk,* it is essential you learn how to pronounce the good soldier's name.

IN ENGLISH, "ŠVEJK" IS PRONOUNCED "SHVAKE"!
IT RHYMES WITH SHAKE, BAKE AND CAKE

This may look difficult to you, but it really isn't. How do they (the Czechs) get Shvake out of Švejk, you might ask?

Š... That little mark over the S gives it an "sh" sound. Think of the word "shake."

V... The V sound is the same as in English words with the short V sound, like "very" or "value."

EJ.. The E and J combine for a long A sound. You may think this is strange, but we do the same thing in English with the E I combo. We often put those two letters together for the long A sound: for example, in words like "neighbor" and "weigh." How do we get an A sound out of that?

K... Another easy one. It's a "kuh" sound, the same as in English words like "shake," "bake" and "cake."

So, there you have it: Shvake.

Not so strange or difficult after all, was it? And, your efforts might just be worthwhile. After all, someday you might want to join one of the world's Švejk societies, clubs devoted to the study of this character and the book he lives in.

ŠVEJK=SHVAKE
So, now you're ready to ...
ŠVEJK AND BAKE!

INTRODUCTION TO THE NEW ENGLISH EDITION

Some writers so capture the soul and spirit of a people that they are identified with them forever after. In England, it was Charles Dickens, in the United States, it was Mark Twain. For the Slavic nations, and to some extent for all Central Europeans, it is the Czech writer, Jaroslav Hašek.

Hašek's most important work was centered around a Czech soldier's experiences in World War One. It's actual title is *The Fateful Adventures of The Good Soldier Švejk During the World War*, but it is known by tens of millions of Central Europeans as simply, *The Good Soldier Švejk*. This monumental, humorous work is acknowledged as ". . . one of the greatest masterpieces of satirical writing" by no less a standard and exalted reference than the *Encyclopedia Britannica*.

This new translation and rendition of *The Good Soldier Švejk* is our attempt to make this Central European masterwork accessible to the modern reader of English. There have been two other attempts and both are, in our opinion, failures in both practice and spirit. The only attempt at a complete English translation has often been criticized, by those who have read the novel in another language, as a clumsy rendition that left *The Good Soldier Švejk* reading like a hackneyed novel about the British army in the 19th century. We consider this both an injustice to Jaroslav Hašek and a tragedy for those denied the insight and enjoyment of a hilarious and rollicking modern classic.

The book's central character is a quintessential, working-class citizen-soldier, often abused by the fates and the forces of the Austrian empire. In both civilian and military life, Švejk lives by his wits. His chief ploy is to appear witless to those in authority. In fact, he is fond of pointing out that he has been certified to be an imbecile by an official military medical commission. Consequently, he reasons, he cannot be held responsible for his sometimes questionable actions because he's a certified nitwit!

Yet, Švejk is not a coward, nor is he indolent. He is drafted back into the army as cannon fodder to die for an Emperor he despises. His method of subverting the Austrian Empire is to carry out his orders to an absurd conclusion. His is an inspired resistance. He holds the foreign authorities, and their Czech fellow travelers, accountable for their ridiculous platitudes and pseudo-patriotic blather.

The Good Soldier Švejk is as entertaining as any book of the 20th century. And, though it is set in World War One and written shortly thereafter, most readers will find it thoroughly modern. There is good reason for that. Jaroslav Hašek was more than *avant garde*. He was an iconoclastic revolutionary, both in his life and as an artist. The First World War liberated the Czech Lands and Jaroslav Hašek simultaneously. For the first time, he was free to write and create without censorship or fear of imperial reprisal.

Like many great artists, Jaroslav Hašek was a happy confluence of genius, talent, time and place. His talent and genius are widely acknowledged by scholars worldwide. They point to his ground-breaking contribution in transforming and modernizing the novel and making it relevant for our time. And, in the non-English-speaking world, his work has long been loved by legions of regular folks. At any rate, you will soon be able to judge his talent and genius for yourself.

One of his biographers, Emmanuel Frynta, writes:

"He was one of that generation which fully fought with the problems of the modern world. He was one of the artists at the start of the century who so splendidly cast light on the question of a live, valid, meaningful art worthy of the time. He was a curious, not easily understood person, too mobile and opaque for portrayal. As a creator, (he was) seemingly careless, natural, (and) spontaneous, ... but, in reality (he was) sharply discerning and refined in his specific type of non-literariness ... (he) was working farsightedly in the field of language and style, with something that was to become the shape of (the) speech of the century."

And just what is it we have been denied? A host of literary critics acknowledge that Jaroslav Hašek was one of the earliest writers of what we have come to know as modern literature. He experimented with verbal collage, Dadaism and the surreal. Hašek was writing modern fiction before exalted post-World-War-One writers like Hemingway, Fitzgerald, and Faulkner, to name just a few. A literary analyst has pointed out that Hašek is one of the few writers *of all time* to combine political with misanthropic satire. In fact, *The Good Soldier Švejk*, he says, is the only example of this genre in the 20th century.

It seems unconscionable that Hašek's work has been inaccessible to English readers for so long. What if Victor Hugo or Leo Tolstoy had been kept from us? It's hard to imagine literature without them.

Let's reverse the situation. What if you suddenly became aware that, because of some problem with translation or some other oversight, Mark Twain's work had been virtually hidden from Europeans for 75 years? Most Americans would consider that a lamentable travesty. Well, that is what has happened to the Czech people in the case of Jaroslav Hašek. He and his work are practically non-existent in the English-reading world, an influential audience of at least 500 million people.

Finally, literary critics agree that Jaroslav Hašek wrote the granddaddy of anti-war novels. According to one critic, only the first two-thirds of *The Red Badge of Courage* precedes it. *The Good Soldier Švejk* even predated that quintessential First World War novel, *All Quiet on the Western Front*. More familiar to today's readers, perhaps, is Joseph Heller's *Catch 22*, set in World War Two. Hašek's biting satire and humor is its direct ancestor also, as well as that of many others. It might be hard to imagine, but "anti-war" was not "in" before *The Good Soldier Švejk*. And, it should be noted that Hašek's Švejk preceded Joseph Heller's Yosarrian by almost 50 years.

Hašek's talent and genius are obviously well documented. Now, let's look at place. How did location effect Hašek and his work? Obviously, as you will soon read, that place was the city of Prague.

Again, in our opinion, Emmanuel Frynta explains it best:

"...Prague, at the turn of the century, was a collage city. Phenomena torn from different, mutually antagonistic contexts met there and clashed. Stage sets were grotesquely displayed there, set in motion, on the one hand by the natural demands of the advancing modern age, on the other by inert or artificially preserved myths.

We can clearly consider this fact to have been exceptionally worthy of attention both in regards to the works of Franz Kafka and the works of Hašek....Myths and pseudomyths quite undoubtedly influenced these two Prague authors. (These were) myths that substituted in so many ways for objective law and order. (They were) out-of-date, incomprehensible and unacceptable myths.....

"In the concentrated atmosphere of collage-style Prague, right from the very start of this century, political, social, moral and philosophical problems made themselves felt (in Prague) which were only made explicit in the rest of Europe by the (time of the) First World War. This was natural and highly understandable: in societies which were entering the modern age more smoothly, and in a more organic manner, these problems were kept hidden better. They came to the surface less blatantly. Prague (however) was 'Dadaist' and 'surrealist' (and) avant la letter."

By the turn of the century Prague had become a boomtown. Large numbers of people had come to the city from the countryside to participate in the industrial revolution. The rise of a large working class spawned a cultural revolution. The empires of Central Europe ignored these intrinsic changes and became more and more decrepit and anachronistic. As the system decayed, it became absurd and irrelevant to ordinary people. When forced to respond to dissent, the imperial powers did so, more often than not, with hollow propaganda and repression.

The Austrian Empire attempted to conduct the First World War as if it were still a vibrant, viable entity. It expected its subjects to fight, die and foot the bill for what everyday people saw as nothing more than a quarrel among greedy and egotistic rulers. In the empires' Slavic possessions, resentment reigned. And, with good reason.

World War One, amplified by modern weapons and techniques, quickly escalated to become a massive human meatgrinder. It has been eclipsed in many memories by World War Two, the most horrendous conflict of all time. However, if you set that debacle aside, World War One would easily dwarf any other in human history. Fifteen million people died, one million of them Austrian soldiers. Jaroslav Hašek participated in this conflict and examined it in *The Good Soldier Švejk*.

Hašek knew that a momentous, fundamental change in human history was occurring. For Central and Eastern Europe, it was the end of the old order. It was the demise of a social structure that had evolved from prehistoric times and affected every human life. Tribal and clan chieftains had evolved into dukes, counts and lords, and then into monarchs and emperors. These despots caused and lost World War One and suddenly vanished. The decrepit empires were replaced by democratic republics, except in Russia where the bolsheviks instituted their own fatally flawed dictatorship and empire. However, as most historians agree, enough perverse elements and limbic memory of the old order remained in Central Europe to foment and fuel the biggest meatgrinder of them all, World War Two.

So, as you can see, the setting of *The Good Soldier Švejk* is right there on the cutting edge of historical change. It is Jaroslav Hašek's peek, *a la* Charlie Chaplin, at the dawn of truly modern times.

Isn't this great? By reading *The Good Soldier Švejk*, you will get a heavy dose of culture and a glimpse at modern social history in the making. You will have read an important book. And, best of all you'll laugh and have a really good time doing it. How often does a situation like this come along?

Rarely.

What better way to "close the books" on the twentieth century, than by looking back at where it all began?

So, kick off your shoes, make yourself comfortable, and enjoy.

INTRODUCTION

Great times demand great people. There are unrecognized, unassuming heroes, without the fame and history of Napoleon. The results of an analysis of their character would overshadow the glory of even Alexander the Great. Nowadays, you can run into a shabby man in the streets of Prague who himself has no idea of the significance he actually has in the history of the great new era. He modestly walks on his way, not bothering anybody. In turn, he isn't bothered by journalists, who otherwise would be begging him for an interview. If you were to ask him his name, he would answer you with childlike simplicity and modesty: "I'm Švejk . . ."

And this quiet, unassuming, shabby man is indeed the good old soldier Švejk: heroic and valiant, whose name was once upon a time, during the Austrian rule, on the lips of all the citizens of the Czech Kingdom, and whose fame will not fade even in the Republic.

I really very much like the good soldier Švejk, and in presenting his fateful adventures during the World War, I am convinced that all of you will sympathize with this modest, unrecognized hero. He did not torch the temple of the goddess in Ephesus, as did that idiot Herostrates, just to get himself into the newspapers and classroom readers.

And that is enough.

THE AUTHOR

BOOK ONE

IN THE REAR

1

THE GOOD SOLDIER ŠVEJK ACTS TO INTERVENE IN THE WORLD WAR

"So they've done it to us," said the cleaning woman to Mr. Švejk. "They've killed our Ferdinand."

Švejk had been discharged from military service years ago when a military medical commission had pronounced him to be officially an imbecile. Now, he was making his living by selling dogs, ugly mongrel mutants that he sold as purebreds by forging their pedigrees. In addition to this demeaning vocation, Švejk also suffered from rheumatism and was just now rubbing his aching knees with camphor ice.

"Which Ferdinand, Mrs. Müller?" he asked. "I know two Ferdinands. One is the pharmacist Průša's delivery boy, who drank up a whole bottle of hair potion once by mistake. And then, I know one Ferdinand Kokoška, who collects dog turds. Neither one would be much of a loss."

"But Mr. Švejk! They killed the Archduke Ferdinand, the one from Konopiště, the fat one, the religious one."

"Jesusmaria!" yelled Švejk. "That's big! And where did it befall him, the Royal Archduke?"

"They killed him in Sarajevo, Mr. Švejk. They shot him with a revolver as he was riding with that archduchess of his in an automobile."

"There you have it, Mrs. Müller, in an automobile. Well, yes. A lord like that can afford it, so it doesn't even cross his mind that such a ride in an automobile can have an unfortunate ending. And in Sarajevo on top of it. That's in Bosnia, Mrs. Müller. It was probably the Turks who did it. Well, we shouldn't have taken that Bosnia and Hercegovina from them.

"He is then, the Royal Archduke, resting in the truth of the Lord already. Did he suffer long?"

"The Royal Archduke was done for right away, Mr. Švejk. You know, a revolver like that's not child's play! Not long ago, a man from Nusle, near where I live, was also playing with a revolver.

And, he blasted away the whole family. Right on the third floor of an apartment building there. Nusle is truly one of the toughest neighborhoods in Prague! He even shot the resident custodian, who went to take a look at what all the shooting was about."

"Some revolvers, Mrs. Müller, won't go bang no matter what you do. You can lose your mind trying to make them work. There are a lot of such weapons. But, surely they bought something better for the Royal Archduke. You know, taking a shot at a royal archduke is really a tough job. It's not like a poacher taking a shot at the game warden. The problem is how to get to him. You can't go hunting a lord like that in rags. You've got to have a top hat on so the police won't pick you up before you can do it."

"They say there was more than one of them, Mr. Švejk."

"That goes without saying Mrs. Müller," he replied as he finished massaging his knees. "If you wanted to kill the Royal Archduke or the Lord Emperor, then you would surely consult somebody. More people means more brains. This one will advise this, and that one that, and then 'the job will succeed,' just as our anthem says.

"The main thing is to lie in wait for the right moment. Perhaps you remember that anarchist, Luccheni, who ran our Empress Elizabeth through with a file. He was just walking with her. You can't trust anyone! Since then, no empresses will go out for a stroll. And this fate awaits many others. You'll see, Mrs. Müller. They'll even get to that Russian czar and his wife. And could be, God forbid, even to our Lord Emperor himself, since they have already started with his nephew. The old man has a lot of enemies, even more than Ferdinand.

"Just the other day, a fellow at the pub was saying that the time will come that those emperors will be dropping dead, one by one, and that even all the work of their state prosecutors won't be able to save them. However, the thirsty gent saying this didn't have enough to pay his bill, so the pubkeeper called the police. When they tried to arrest him, he punched the pub owner and did a pretty good job on the cop. They had to tie him up and take him away in the police wagon after they knocked him out. Yes, Mrs. Müller, it's hard to believe the things that happen nowadays. It's all a big loss for Austria.

"When I was serving in the army, an infantryman there shot a captain. He loaded a rifle and went to the office. They told him that he had no business there. But, he kept insisting he needed to see the captain. The captain finally came storming out and ordered him confined to the barracks right away. The soldier aimed his rifle and shot the captain right through the heart. The bullet flew out of the captain's back and still managed to do damage in the office. It broke open a bottle of ink that then spilled onto some official documents."

"And what happened to that soldier?" Mrs. Müller asked after a while, as she watched Švejk dress.

"He hung himself with suspenders," answered Švejk, brushing off his felt hat. "And the suspenders weren't even his. He borrowed them from the prison guard by telling him that his pants were falling down. What was he supposed to do? Wait until they shot him?

"You know Mrs. Müller, everyone's head spins in a situation like that. The prison guard was demoted and given six months in jail. But he didn't do all of his time. He ran off to Switzerland and today he is a preacher of some church denomination there.

"Nowadays, there are few straight shooters, Mrs. Müller. I imagine the old Archduke Ferdinand in that Sarajevo misjudged the man who shot him. He saw someone dressed as a gentleman and said to himself: 'There's a fine, upstanding citizen! He's chanting that I should live long.' And then, that properly dressed gentleman blew him away. Did he shoot him once or several times?"

"The newspaper says, Mr. Švejk, that the Royal Archduke looked like a sieve. They emptied the gun and hit him with all the bullets."

"It happens fast, Mrs. Müller, terribly fast. For something like that, I'd buy a Browning. It looks like a toy. But in two minutes you can mow down twenty archdukes, thin ones or fat ones. Although, between you and me Mrs. Müller, you'll hit a fat archduke more likely than a thin one.

"Remember that time in Portugal when they mowed down their own king? He also was fat like that. It's not surprising. After all, you know a king is not going to be skinny.

"I'm going to The Chalice pub now. And, if anybody comes for that pooch I took a down payment for, tell him it's in my kennel in the country. And tell him that I recently clipped the pooch's ears, so it can't be transported right now. It might get sick.

3

"Oh. And please leave my key with the custodian."

There was only one customer sitting at The Chalice pub. He was a neighborhood patrolman named Bretschneider, on loan and working undercover for the state security police. The pub's owner, Palivec, was washing his porcelain coasters and Bretschneider was trying, in vain, to engage him in conversation.

Palivec was well known for his foul mouth. Every other word of his was butt or shit. Still, he was a well-read foul mouth and was currently urging everyone he met to read Victor Hugo's description of the last answer the old guard Napoleon gave to the English at Waterloo.

"We're having a nice summer, aren't we?" asked Bretschneider.

"It's all worth shit," replied Palivec, putting his coasters away.

"They sure did it to us nicely in Sarajevo," Bretschneider continued, hoping to instigate a political discussion.

"What Sarajevo?" asked Palivec. "That wine bar in Nusle? They fight every day there. That's Nusle, you know."

"The Sarajevo in Bosnia, mister pubkeeper, where they shot the Royal Archduke Ferdinand dead! What do you say to that?"

"I don't get myself mixed up in such things," Palivec answered politely, while lighting his pipe. "Everybody can kiss my ass with stuff like that. Getting messed up in stuff like that nowadays can get you hanged. I'm a small businessman. When somebody comes in and orders a beer, then I draw it for him. But some Sarajevo -- politics -- some archduke, that is nothing to me. It holds no promise, except maybe a trip to the Pankrác prison."

Bretschneider quietly stared across the deserted pub. After a while, he said out loud:

"At one time, a picture of our Lord Emperor used to hang here. Right over there where that mirror is now."

"Yeah, you're right," said Palivec, "it used to hang there. And the flies kept shitting on it, so, I put it in the attic. You know that all I would have needed was for some busybody to dare to make some kind of comment. It could have resulted in some unpleasant difficulties. I don't need that kind of trouble."

"It's most likely that business in Sarajevo was pretty nasty, eh Mr. Palivec?"

The crass sneakiness of the patrolman's question prompted the pub owner to answer most carefully:

"You must remember that, around this time in Bosnia and Hercegovina, it is usually terribly hot. When I served in the military there, every so often, we had to put ice on our lieutenant's head."

"Which regiment did you serve with, mister pubkeeper?"

"I don't remember such details. I was never interested in such bullshit and couldn't care less," Palivec replied. "Too much curiosity is detrimental."

The undercover patrolman became silent. His gloomy expression improved only upon the arrival of Švejk, who sauntered into the pub and ordered a dark beer.

"They're sad in Vienna today," said Švejk, hoisting his black-colored beer, "and in mourning, too."

Bretschneider's eyes began to sparkle with hope as he said to Švejk:

"At Konopiště, there are 10 black pennants flying."

"There should be 12 of them," said Švejk, taking another sip from his beer.

"Why do you think 12?" asked Bretschneider.

"To make it fit the count, the dozen" answered Švejk. "It's easier to count. And, in dozens, things always come more cheaply."

Silence reigned again at The Chalice, until Švejk broke it with an audible sigh and began to speak:

"So, he is there already. In the truth of the Lord. May the Lord God give him eternal glory. He did not even live to be the Emperor. When I was serving in the military, one of our generals fell off his horse. He died so calmly, the men didn't even know he was dead. They tried to boost him back into the saddle and were shocked that he was totally dead. He was soon to be promoted to field marshall. It happened during a parade review of the troops. These reviews never lead to any good. In Sarajevo, I hear there was also some kind of troops parade.

"Once, during a parade review, they caught me missing twenty buttons on my uniform. They locked me up in solitary for two weeks because of it. For two days, I was laying still, like Lazarus, with my hands and feet tied up behind my back. But, I agree there has to be discipline in the military, otherwise nobody would take anything seriously, or fear anything. Our lieutenant, Makovec, he would always tell us: 'Discipline must be enforced, you stupid boys! Otherwise, you would all be climbing the trees like monkeys. However, military service will turn you all into humans, you stupid idiots!' And isn't that the truth? Imagine a park. Say, Karlák here in Prague. And, in every tree, you see a soldier without discipline. That's what I always feared most."

"In Sarajevo," said Bretschneider, returning to his favorite subject, "it was the Serbs who killed the Archduke."

"You are mistaken," retorted Švejk. "The Turks did it on account of Bosnia and Hercegovina."

He then expounded on his view of Austria's international policy in the Balkans. In 1912, the Turks, he noted, had lost their territories to Serbia, Bulgaria and Greece. The Turks had wanted Austria to help them maintain control, Švejk explained, and because Austria didn't help them, the Turks shot Ferdinand.

"Do you like Turks?" Švejk asked, turning to Palivec. "Do you like those pagan dogs? Hey, I'm sure you'll say that you don't."

"A guest is a guest," Palivec replied. "He may even be a Turk. For us, who are in a business for themselves, politics has no currency. Pay for your beer and sit in the pub, and babble all you want. That is my principle. Whether it was a Serb or a Turk who shot our Ferdinand, or a Catholic, Mohammedan, anarchist, or Young Czech, it's all the same to me."

Bretschneider was once again becoming discouraged, and losing hope that either of the two could be hooked into disloyal conversation. Still, he tried once again:

"Very well, mister pubkeeper," he ventured. "But, you will admit that it was a great loss for Austria."

Instead of Palivec, Švejk answered:

"A loss it is. That cannot be denied. A terrible loss. Ferdinand can't be replaced by some dimwit. If only he had been a bit fatter than he was."

"How do you mean that?" asked Bretschneider, his hopes suddenly revived.

"How do I mean that?" Švejk echoed the policeman calmly. "Only this: Had he been fatter, he would surely have been hit with a stroke before this. Maybe, when he was chasing after those old broads collecting mushrooms and twigs at his estate at Konopiště. He didn't have to die such a shameful death. Think about it. A nephew of the Lord Emperor and they shoot him dead. Now, that's scandalous. The newspapers are full of it.

"Years ago, by us in Budějovice, during one of those petty arguments in the marketplace, some guys stabbed a livestock dealer named Břetislav Ludvík. He had a son Bohuslav. But, after that, whenever the son came to sell pigs, nobody bought anything from him. Everybody would say, 'That's the son of that shyster who was stabbed. He's got to be a crook, too.' He jumped right into the Vltava River from that bridge in Krumlov. They pulled him out and tried to revive him. They pumped water out of him. They went through all that, but he died anyway in the doctor's arms from an injection he gave him."

"You sure come up with some odd comparisons," Bretschneider said. "You speak first about Ferdinand, then about a livestock dealer."

"But I don't," said Švejk defensively. "God spare me from wanting to compare anybody to somebody else. This pubkeeper knows me. Look, will you tell him that I have never compared anybody to somebody else? I just wouldn't want to be in the skin of the widow left by the Archduke. What is she gonna do? The children are orphans. The Lord's estate at Konopiště is without a master. And to have to be married again to some new archduke? What's in it for her? She'll go with some new archduke to Sarajevo again, and, she'll be widowed a second time.

"Years ago, there was a gamekeeper in Zliv by Hluboká. He had the ugly name of *Pinďour,* Littlepecker. Poachers shot him dead and he left a widow with two children. A year later she married a gamekeeper again. His name was Pepík Šavel and he was from Mydlovary. And, they shot him dead for her, too. She married for the third time. Again, she took a gamekeeper for a husband and said: 'Three times lucky. But, if it doesn't work out this time, I don't know what I'll do.' You bet they did it to her again and shot him dead, as well. By now, she bore, altogether, six children with these gamekeepers.

"She went all the way to the office of the Count of Hluboká to complain that she had suffered nothing but heartbreak with those gamekeepers. So, they recommended Jareš, who worked as a fishpond warden from a cottage at Ražice. And, what would you say if I told you they drowned him while he was fishing out the pond?

She'd had two more children with him. Finally, she married a gelder from Vodňany who whacked her with an ax one night. He turned himself in voluntarily. While they were hanging him at the district courthouse in Písek, he bit off the priest's nose and said he had no remorse for anything. He also said something very ugly about the Lord Emperor."

"Do you know what he said about him?" Bretschneider asked, his voice full of hope.

"I can't tell you that because no one dared to repeat it. But, it was, it is said, something so dreadful and horrible that a court administrator, who was there, lost his mind over it. Until this day, so it is said, they keep him in isolation, so that it won't come out. It was not just a common insult to the Lord Emperor, the kind that is made when someone is drunk."

"And what kind of insult is made to the Lord Emperor when someone is drunk?" asked Bretschneider.

"Gentlemen, please turn the page!" thundered Palivec the pub owner. "You know I don't like it. Someone could blabber out anything and be sorry for it later."

"What kind of insults are made about the Lord Emperor when someone is drunk?" repeated Švejk. "All kinds. Get drunk and have them play the Austrian anthem, and, you'll see what you will start saying. You will make up so much stuff about the Lord Emperor that, if only half of it were true, it would be enough for him to live in shame for the rest of his life. But, the old man really doesn't deserve it.

"Think about it. He lost his young son Rudolf when he was at the height of his manly vitality. His wife Elizabeth, they ran through with a file. He lost Jan Orth. Next, they shot his brother who was the Emperor of Mexico. Shot him dead, up against a wall in some fortress. Now, in his old age, they blast his nephew. Given all that, a man better have nerves of steel. And then, out of the blue, some drunk decides to start calling him names. If something were to break out today, I would volunteer to serve the Lord Emperor until my body was torn to pieces."

Švejk took a long swig of his beer and then continued:

"You think the Lord Emperor will let this go? Then, you don't know him well enough. There must be war with the Turks. They've killed the royal nephew, so we must go and kick their ass. A war is guaranteed. Serbia and Russia will help us in that war. It will be a rumble."

Švejk looked radiant in this moment of prophecy. His simpleton-like face shone brightly. Everything was clear to him.

"Could be," he said, continuing his exposition of the future of Austria, "that, in case of a war with the Turks, the Germans will attack us, because the Germans and the Turks stick together. They are double-crossers without equal in all the world. But, we can unite with France. It has been waiting for an excuse to fight Germany since 1871. And, that'll get things going then for sure. There will be war and I'll say no more."

Bretschneider stood up and proclaimed with both pleasure and gravity:

"You don't have to say anymore. Come with me to the hallway. I'll tell you something there."

Švejk followed the undercover patrolman into the hallway. To his surprise, this friendly man, who had been drinking beer right next to him just moments ago, turned over the lapel of his coat and showed him his "little eagle," the badge of the state security police. He announced that he was arresting him and would immediately take him to headquarters. Švejk tried to explain that there must be some mistake, that he was totally innocent, that he had not uttered one word which could have offended anyone.

Bretschneider told him, however, that he had really committed several criminal offenses, one of which constituted the crime of high treason.

They returned to the pub and Švejk spoke in the direction of Mr. Palivec:

"I've had five beers and a roll with a sausage. Now, give me a quick shot of slivovitz, because I have to go right away. I'm under arrest."

Bretschneider showed Palivec his "little eagle." Then, he stared at him for a moment and asked:

"Are you married?"

"I am."

"And, can your wife run the business during your absence?"

"She can."

"Then, all right, Mr. pubkeeper," Bretschneider said with glee. "Call your wife here. Turn the place over to her, because we'll be coming by tonight to pick you up."

"Don't let it make you feel too bad," Švejk said, attempting to console him. "I'm being taken in for high treason."

"But why me?" lamented Mr. Palivec. "I was so careful."

Bretschneider flashed a wry smile, then victoriously stated:

"You're going in because you said that the flies were shitting on the Lord Emperor. They will, no doubt, manage to knock any such thoughts of the Lord Emperor out of your head."

Švejk left the Chalice pub in custody of the undercover patrolman. Once outside, he asked the following question with a broad, good-hearted smile on his face:

"Should I get off the sidewalk?"

"Why so?"

"I'm thinking that, since I'm under arrest, I don't have the right to walk on the sidewalk."

When they arrived at the gates of the police headquarters, Švejk spoke:

"The time went by quite nicely for us. Do you come to The Chalice often?"

While Švejk was being processed at the police station, Palivec was transferring management of the pub to his weeping wife, and trying to soothe her in his own peculiar way.

"Don't cry, don't bawl. What can they do to me on account of a Lord Emperor's picture being full of shit?"

And, so it was, that the good soldier Švejk intervened in the World War in his own lovable, charming manner. Historians will be interested to know that he saw far into the future. If the situation later developed differently, from how he had predicted it at The Chalice, we have to keep in mind that he hadn't been specifically trained in the diplomatic arts.

THE GOOD SOLDIER ŠVEJK AT POLICE HEADQUARTERS

The Sarajevo assassination filled police headquarters with numerous political victims. They were being brought in one after another.

"That Ferdinand will cost you!" an old inspector in the arraignment office would say with a good-natured voice.

When they locked Švejk in one of the numerous holding rooms on the second floor, he found himself in the company of six people there. Five were sitting around a table, but one, a middle aged man, was sitting in the corner on a bunk, as if he was staying away from them.

Švejk began to ask each why he had been locked up. From the five sitting at the table, he received almost the same answer:

"Because of Sarajevo!" -- "Because of Ferdinand!" -- "Because of the murder of the Lord Archduke!" -- "For Ferdinand!" -- "Because they bumped off the Lord Archduke in Sarajevo!"

But, the sixth one, staying away from the other five, said that he wanted nothing to do with them, lest he fall under suspicion. He said that he was sitting there merely for the attempted robbery and murder of a farmer from Holice.

Švejk sat down with those at the table. They were explaining to each other, for the tenth time, how they had gotten into this mess.

All of them, except one, had been arrested in either a pub, a wine bar or a lounge. The exception was an unusually fat gentleman with glasses, his eyes cried out, who was arrested at home in his apartment. Two days before the assassination in Sarajevo, he had paid the tab for two Serbian engineering students at Brejška's. After that, a detective named Brixi had noticed him drunk with them at The Montmartre on Řetězová Street. He had admitted in a signed statement to the police that he had paid the Serbs' bill there, as well.

He had only one answer to all the questions asked of him during his preliminary interrogation. He kept wailing constantly:

"I have a stationery store!"

To this, he was getting only one answer:

"That doesn't excuse you."

A small gentleman, a history professor, was arrested at a wine bar. He said he had been explaining the history of various assassinations to the wine-bar keeper. He was arrested just at the moment he finished the psychological analysis of these assassinations with the words:

"The idea of an assassination is as simple as the egg of Columbus."

"Just like the fact that Pankrác prison awaits you," added the police commissioner.

The third "conspirator" was the chairman of the charitable club, Dobromil, in Hodkovičky. The day the assassination was carried out Dobromil was hosting a garden party with a concert. The police sergeant came and asked the participants to leave because Austria was in mourning. The chairman of Dobromil replied good-naturedly:

"Wait a moment until they finish playing, 'Rise Up, Slavs!' "

Now, he was sitting with his head down and moaning:

"In August, we're having new board elections. If I'm not home by that time, it could happen that they won't elect me. I'm the chairman for the tenth time around already. I won't live down the shame."

The late Ferdinand had strange fun with the fourth arrestee, a man of sterling character and a spotless record. He had avoided any conversation about Ferdinand for two days. Then, in the evening, he decided to enjoy *mariáš* with some friends, a card game played with tarot cards. While he was trumping the king of 'acorns' with a seven of 'rounds,' he said:

"Seven rounds. Like in Sarajevo."

The fifth man said he too was in jail "because of the murder of the Lord Archduke in Sarajevo." The hair on his head and in his beard was standing on end from fright. He reminded Švejk of a bristle-haired dog, a stable pincher.

He said he hadn't uttered one word at the restaurant where he was arrested. What's more, he said he hadn't even read the newspaper accounts of Ferdinand's murder. He said he had been sitting at a table absolutely alone, when a man came up to him, sat down across from him, and said to him abruptly:

"Have you read it?"

"No, I haven't."

"Do you know about it?"

"I don't."

"And do you know what it's about?"

"I don't, and I don't care about it."

"And yet, it should be of interest to you."

"I don't know. What is it that should be of interest to me? I'll smoke my cigar, drink my few glasses, and have dinner. I don't read the papers. Newspapers lie. What should I get upset for?"

"So, even the murder in Sarajevo is of no interest to you?"

"To me, absolutely no murder is of any interest, regardless of whether it's in Prague, in Vienna, in Sarajevo or London. That's what you have authorities for, the courts and police. If sometime, somewhere, they kill somebody, it serves him right. Otherwise, why would some dimwit be so careless that he lets himself get killed?"

Those were the last words he uttered before his arrest. Since then, he's repeated loudly, in five minute intervals:

"I'm innocent! I'm innocent!"

He screamed those words at the gate of the police headquarters. He repeated them during his transfer to the Criminal Court in Prague. And, with those words, he will be thrown into the hard-labor prison's dungeon.

When Švejk had heard all their dreadful stories, he judged it fitting to explain the hopelessness of their situation.

"It's very bad for us all," he began. "It is not true, as some of you have been saying, that nothing really bad can happen to us. What do we have the police for? For one purpose, to punish us for our bad mouths. If the times are so dangerous that they're shooting archdukes, then nobody should be surprised when they take him to the police station. All of this is done for show, so that Ferdinand will have publicity before his state funeral. The more of us there are here, the better it'll be for us. We can cheer each other up.

"When I was serving in the military, sometimes half the outfit was locked up. And, many innocent people were found guilty. This happens not only in the military, but in the civilian courts too. I remember once some crazy woman was found guilty for having strangled her newborn twins. She swore that she couldn't have strangled twins since she had given birth to only one little girl, whom she had managed to strangle quite painlessly. She was found guilty, nevertheless, of double murder. Or, the innocent Gypsy in Záběhlice who broke into that grocery store on Christmas night. He swore that he went there to warm up. But that didn't help him at all.

"Once a court takes something in hand, it's trouble. But that trouble is necessary. Perhaps, every person is not such a hoodlum as he can sometimes seem to be. But how can you tell the good one from the shyster? Especially today, during such serious times, when even that Ferdinand can be blown away.

"Where I served in the military, in Budějovice, they shot the captain's dog in a forest on the other side of the training ground. When he found out about it, he called us all together and had us stand at attention. He says that every tenth man should step forward. It goes without saying, that I also was tenth. So, we stood at *habacht,* attention, and didn't as much as blink. The captain is walking around us and spouting: 'You hoodlums. You scoundrels. You scum. You spotted hyenas. I would so love to slam you into solitary for that dog, then chop you into noodles. Or blast away. Mow you down and turn you into carp à la blue. Think I'm going soft on you? I'm giving you all two weeks of confinement to the barracks!'

"So there. And, that was just the matter of a doggie. Now, it's the matter of the Royal Archduke. And, that's why there has to be fear, so that mourning for the Archduke will be worth something."

"I'm innocent! I'm innocent!" repeated the bristled-up man.

"Christ the Lord was also innocent," said Švejk. "And they also crucified him. Nowhere, at no time, did an innocent man matter to anybody. *Maul halten und weiter dienen!* Keep your mouth shut and keep on serving! That's what they used to tell us in the military. That is what's best and most admirable."

Švejk laid down on a bunk and fell asleep contentedly.

In the meantime, they brought in two new "conspirators". One of them was a Bosnian. He kept gritting his teeth and pacing around the quarters.

"*Jebem ti dušu*, I fuck your soul," he would constantly curse in Serbian. He was tortured by the thought that his peddler's basket would disappear at the police headquarters.

The other new guest was the pubkeeper, Palivec. He noticed Švejk, woke him, and, with a voice full of tragedy, exclaimed:

14

"Now, I'm here too!"

Švejk shook his hand cordially and said:

"I'm really glad. I knew that the gentleman would keep his word when he told you that they would drive by to pick you up. Being on time like that is a good thing."

Mr. Palivec remarked that being on time in a situation like that is worth shit. He then asked Švejk quietly whether the other prisoners were thieves. If they were, it could be detrimental to him, as a small businessman.

Švejk explained to him that all of them, with the exception of the man who was there for the attempted robbery and murder of the farmer from Holice, were there on account of the archduke.

Palivec was offended. He said that he was not there on account of some stupid archduke, but on account of the Emperor himself. And, because the others seemed interested, he told them the story of how the flies had shit on their Lord Emperor.

"They mucked him up for me, the bitches. And, in the end, they got me thrown in the slammer. I will not forgive those flies for that," he added threateningly.

Švejk went to sleep again, but not for long, They had come to take him to interrogation.

And so, as he ascended the staircase to be interrogated, Švejk carried his cross to the top of Golgotha. He did not, however, take notice of the potential for his own martyrdom.

Having beheld the sign warning that spitting in the corridor was forbidden, he asked the policeman to allow him to spit into a spittoon. Then, beaming with simplicity, he entered the office with these words:

"Gentlemen, I wish to you, one and all, a good evening."

Instead of a reply, somebody poked him under the ribs and pushed him in front of a desk. Behind it sat a man with a cold official face that displayed the features of animal bestiality, as if he had just fallen out of Lombros' book, *On Criminal Types.*

He looked at Švejk with blood in his eye and said:

"Don't look so stupid."

"I can't help it," answered Švejk seriously. "I was released from military service for stupidity, after an examination by the military medical board, and proclaimed to be an imbecile. I'm an official imbecile."

The man with the criminal countenance chattered his teeth, then said:

"The crimes which you are accused of, and which you have committed, indicate that all your five senses are intact."

He enumerated for Švejk a whole line of various crimes, beginning with high treason and ending with offending His Majesty and the members of the imperial house. At the center of the constellation shone the crime of sedition, because it all had happened in a public place.

"What do you say to that?" asked the inquisitor with the features of animal bestiality.

"There's a lot there," answered Švejk innocently. "Too much of anything is bad for you."

"There you go. You recognize it's right."

"I recognize everything. Discipline must be maintained. Without discipline nobody would get anywhere. Just like when I was serving in the military . . ."

"Shut your trap!" the police administrator screamed at Švejk. "And speak only when I ask you something! Understand?"

"How could I not understand?" responded Švejk. "I dutifully report, sir, that I understand and that I am able to grasp all that you desire to say."

"Then, whom do you have contacts with?"

"With my cleaning woman, sir."

"And, you don't have any acquaintance with the local political circles?"

"That I do, kind sir. I buy for myself the afternoon edition of *Národní politika*, National Politics, -- 'little bitches,' looking for stray pooches."

"Out!" the man with the animal visage screamed at Švejk.

When they were taking him out of the office, Švejk said:

"Good night, sir."

Upon his return, Švejk informed the others that this type of interrogation could be fun.

"They scream at you a bit. Then, in the end, they chase you out. In the old days, it used to be worse. I read in a book once that a suspect used to have to walk on red hot iron and drink molten lead to determine whether or not he was innocent. Or, they put his feet in the Spanish boots and jacked him up on the rack, when he didn't

16

want to confess. Or, they burned his sides with a fireman's torch, like they did to Saint Jan Nepomucký, who they say screamed as if they were lifting him up on the tips of knives. They say he didn't stop screaming until they threw him from the Eliška bridge in a water-proof bag.

"There were many such cases. In those days, they would still quarter a man, or impale him on something somewhere by the Museum. When they decided to only throw him into the hunger pit, such a man felt like he was being given a new lease on life.

"Nowadays, it is easy and fun to be locked up," Švejk continued with delight. "No quartering, no Spanish boots. We have bunks, a table, and a bench. We're not crammed together. We get soup. They give us bread. They bring us jars of water. The toilet is right under our nose. You can see many improvements. In all this you can see there is progress. True, it's a little bit too far to go to be interrogated, all the way across three corridors and one floor up. But, on the other hand, the corridors are clean and full of life.

"They take one here, another there; a young one, an old one, a male, and even a female. You're glad that at least you're not here alone. Everybody goes contentedly on his way. He doesn't have to fear that the officials will tell him: 'We consulted one another and, tomorrow, you'll be quartered, or burned at stake, according to your own wish.' That would certainly be a tough decision to think about. In a moment like that, gentlemen, I think that many of you could easily be frustrated until you're groggy. Nowadays, the conditions have improved so much, it's to our benefit."

He had just finished defending the modern incarceration of citizens, when a guard opened the door and yelled out:

"Švejk! Get your coat on! You're going to interrogation."

"I'll go without objection," answered Švejk. "But, I'm afraid that there's some mistake. I was already kicked out of interrogation. And, I'm afraid that the rest of these gentlemen might be angry with me. Here I'm going to interrogation twice in a row, and they haven't been there this evening, not even once yet. They could become jealous of me."

"Crawl out of there and stop blathering!" was the answer to Švejk's gentlemanly concern.

Švejk soon found himself again in front the official who looked like a criminal. Without any further introductions, the inquisitor asked him toughly and inescapably:

"Will you admit everything?"

Švejk gazed intently with his good blue eyes at the merciless man and said softly:

"If you wish, sir, for me to confess, then I'll confess. That can't be too unfavorable for me. I'll do whatever you say. So, if you say: 'Švejk, don't admit anything!' I'll deny everything until my body is torn to pieces."

The stern gentleman wrote something in a document. He handed Švejk a pen, and challenged him to sign.

Švejk signed the document. It was a denunciation by Bretschneider, with this addendum:

All of the above shown accusations against me are based on truth.
Josef Švejk

After he signed, he turned to the stern official:

"Am I to sign anything else? Or, should I come back in the morning?"

"In the morning, they will drive you to the Criminal Court," was the answer he received.

"At what time, sir? So I don't -- heaven help me -- oversleep."

"Out!" the official screamed at Švejk for the second time that day.

"Everything here goes just like it's been greased," Švejk told the policeman who accompanied him to his new home behind bars.

As soon as the door closed behind him, his fellow prisoners showered him with various questions. Švejk had only one reply:

"I've just admitted that, perhaps, I've killed the Archduke Ferdinand."

Six of the men curled up in fright under their lice-infested blankets.

Only the Bosnian saluted him: "*Dobro došli*. Welcome."

Laying himself down on the bunk, Švejk said:

"It's too bad they don't sound reveille for us here."

Even without a reveille, by six o'clock the next morning, Švejk was being driven to the regional Criminal Court in a "Green Anton" police wagon.

As the "Green Anton" drove through the gate of the police headquarters, Švejk announced to his fellow passengers:

"A morning bird gets to hop farther."

3

ŠVEJK BEFORE THE COURT PHYSICIANS

The clean, cozy, little rooms of the Regional Criminal Court impressed Švejk most favorably: whitewashed walls and window bars painted black. Even Mr. Demartini, the head prison guard, proudly wore purple epaulets and a purple border on his government-issue cap. Purple was the prescribed standard color, not only there, but during religious ceremonies, such as Ash Wednesday and Good Friday.

Here, the grand history of Roman rule over Jerusalem was being repeated in 1914. The guards took the prisoners to the main floor and introduced them to the Pilates of a new era. These examining magistrates, instead of washing off their hands honorably, sent for paprika chicken and Pilsner beer from Teissig's, then quickly turned their charges over to the State Prosecutor's Office.

Here logic mostly disappeared and the articles of law prevailed. Here, the stipulations of the law strangled, laughed, threatened, and killed. The articles of the law were unforgiving. The law was going nuts: spluttering. The magistrates were jugglers of statutes, eaters of the letters of law books and devourers of the accused. They were tigers of the Austrian jungle, measuring the distance before jumping on their victims, all according to the clauses in some statute.

However, there were several gentlemen (just like at police headquarters) who didn't take the law quite so seriously. After all, one can find stalks of wheat among the weeds everywhere.

They brought Švejk to one such magistrate for interrogation. He was an older gentleman of good-hearted visage who, when interrogating a notorious killer named Valeš, had never failed to say: "Please, be so kind to sit down, Mr. Valeš. It just so happens that there is one chair still free."

When they brought in Švejk, the congenial magistrate instinctively asked him to sit down and said:

"So, you are then, *this* Mr. Švejk?"

21

"I think, merciful sir, that I must be, since even my father was a Švejk, and my mom a Mrs. Švejk. I could not shame them by denying my own name."

A kind smile fluttered across the face of the magistrate:

"But, you have messed up pretty good. You are responsible for quite a lot."

"I'm always responsible for quite a lot, sir," Švejk said, smiling even more kindly than the court administrator.

"That's evident from what you have signed," the amiable magistrate replied, in an equally kind tone. "They didn't pressure you in any way at the police station?"

"Oh no, your eminence. I myself asked them if I should sign it. And, when they said that I should sign it, I did as they said. You don't want me to get into a brawl on account of my own signature, do you? I sure wouldn't help myself by that. Order must be maintained."

"Do you feel completely healthy, Mr. Švejk,?"

"No, not exactly completely healthy, your eminence. I have rheumatism, and I rub myself down with camphor ice."

The old man smiled kindly again: "What would you say if we were to send you to be examined by court physicians?"

"I don't think that I'm so bad off that those gentlemen should be wasting time on me unnecessarily. Some doctor at police headquarters has already examined me to see if I have gonorrhea."

"I think, Mr. Švejk, we will try another examination, after all. We'll assemble a nice commission, have you put in custody, and you'll rest nicely in the meantime. Just one more question: You were, according to the protocol, stating and disseminating that war will break out sometime soon?"

"If it please your eminence, I said that it will break out as soon as possible."

"Do you have seizures once in a while?"

"No merciful sir, I don't. Once, I was almost seized by some automobile at Karlovo Square, but that was a few years ago."

When the interrogation was finished, Švejk shook the hand of the kindly court administrator and was returned to his little room. He reported to his neighbors:

"So, on account of the murder of the Royal Archduke, the court will now have its physicians examine me."

"I also have been examined by the court physicians," said a young man. "It happened back when I had to face a jury on account of some carpets. They found me to be feebleminded. This time, I absconded with a steam thresher, and they can't do anything to me. My lawyer told me, just yesterday, that since I've been pronounced feebleminded once already, I have to benefit from it for the rest of my life."

"I don't trust those court physicians at all," remarked another man, who appeared to be intelligent. "One time, back when I was forging checks, I also attended the lectures of Doctor Heveroch, just in case they might come in handy. When they caught me, I pretended to be paralytic, just the way Doctor Heveroch described it. But, during the commission's proceedings, I bit one of the physician's legs and drank up all the ink in an inkwell. Then, if you will excuse me, I relieved myself in the corner of the room, in front of the whole commission. However, because I also bit a hole clear through the calf of one of them, they found me to be absolutely healthy, and I was done for."

"I don't fear an examination by those gentlemen at all," declared Švejk. "When I was serving in the military, I was once examined by a veterinarian and it turned out quite well."

"Court physicians are sons-of-bitches," said a small man, crouching as if trying to disappear. "Not too long ago, due to circumstances, they dug a skeleton out of my meadow. The court physicians said that the skeleton had been killed by blows to the head, with some blunt object, forty years ago. I am only thirty-eight. But, here I am locked up anyway, even though I have a certified copy of my birth certificate, a certified copy of my record of entry, and my domicile certificate."

"I think we should try to be fair," Švejk said. "Anybody can make a mistake. The more he's thinking about something, then he almost has to make a mistake. Court physicians are people, and people have their flaws.

"Just like once in Nusle. A gent came up to me at night, while I was returning from Banzets', right by the bridge across the Botič. He whacked me with a blackjack across my head. And, when I was laying on the ground, he shined a light on me and said: 'There's been a mistake. It's not him.' He got so mad at the fact he had made a mistake, that he whacked me again across the back. After all, a man will make mistakes until his death. That's just human nature.

"Just like the fellow who found a half-frozen, rabid dog one night and took him home with him. He shoved it in his wife's bed. As soon as the dog warmed up and got comfortable, he bit the whole family and devoured the youngest one in the crib.

"Or, I can tell you of another case. It's about how a lathe operator in our building made a mistake. He opened some little church in the Podolí neighborhood with a key, thinking it was his home. He took off his shoes in the sacristy, because he thought it was his kitchen. Then, he laid down on the altar, because he thought it was his bed. And, he covered himself with some of those cloths with holy inscriptions. Under his head, he put the gospel and some other sanctified books, to keep his head up high.

"In the morning, the church custodian found him. The lathe operator told him, quite good-naturedly, when he came to, that he'd made a mistake. 'A nice, big mistake,' says the church custodian. 'Since, on account of your mistake, we'll have to have the church sanctified all over again.' So, the lathe operator was examined by the court physicians. They proved to him that he was absolutely sane and sober. They said if he was drunk, he would not have been able to put the key in the lock of the church door. That lathe operator eventually died while serving his sentence at Pankrác prison.

"I'll also give you an example of how, in the city of Kladno, a police dog made a mistake. It was a German Shepherd that belonged to a well-known, mounted police captain named Rotter. Captain Rotter was breeding those dogs. He was training them by having them sniff out itinerant bums. Naturally, all the itinerant bums started avoiding Kladno. So, he gave an order for the police to bring in someone suspicious, one way or another.

"They brought him a quite properly clothed man they found in the Lány forests, sitting on some tree stump. Right away, Captain Rotter had them cut off a piece of the man's coat and gave it to the dogs to sniff. They then took the man to some brick yard, outside of the town, and set the trained dogs on his trail. The dogs found him and brought him back again. Then, he had to crawl up a ladder into an attic, jump over a wall, and jump into a pond with the dogs chasing after him. In the end, it turned out that the man was a radical Czech deputy of the Austrian parliament who went walking in the Lány forests when he'd had enough of the parliament.

"That's why I say that people make errors, they make mistakes. Whether someone is learned, or is a stupid, uneducated idiot. Even government ministers make mistakes."

*

The commission of court physicians met to decide whether Švejk was, or was not, capable of the crimes with which he was being charged. The panel consisted of three unusually serious gentlemen with differing views. Three separate scientific schools of psychiatry were represented. The views of each physician differed markedly from the view of either of the other two.

However, in Švejk's case, an absolute agreement arose quickly among these diametrically opposed scientific camps. It can only be explained by the stunning impression Švejk made on the whole commission. When he entered the room, he noticed a picture of the Austrian monarch hanging on the wall and immediately yelled out: "Gentlemen, long live the Emperor! Franz Josef the First!"

Suddenly, his case was completely clear. Švejk's spontaneous utterance had made a whole number of questions disappear. However, some very important questions remained. And, they could only be answered by Švejk. They began to question him based on the method espoused by psychiatrists Kallerson and Heveroch, and even the Englishman, Weiking.

"Is radium heavier than lead?"

"I have, forgive me, not ever weighed it," answered Švejk with a charming smile.

"Do you believe in the end of the world?"

"First, I would have to see the end of the world," Švejk answered in a carefree manner. "But, definitely, I will not get to see it tomorrow."

"Can you calculate the Earth's diameter?"

"That, forgive me, I cannot do," answered Švejk. "But, I myself would like to pose a riddle to you, gentlemen: There is a three-story building. In that building, there are eight windows on each floor. On the roof, there are two dormers, and two chimneys. On each floor, there are two tenants. Now, tell me gentlemen, in what year did the resident custodian's grandmother pass away?"

The court physicians gave one another meaningful looks. Nevertheless, one of them felt it necessary to pose another question:

"Would you know the greatest depth in the Pacific ocean?'

"That, forgive me, I don't know. But, I think that, definitely, it'll be greater than under the Vyšehrad rock in the Vltava River."

The chairman of the commission tersely asked his colleagues: "Enough?"

One of the members still insisted on this final question:

"How much is 12,897 times 13,863?"

"729," answered Švejk, without batting an eye.

"I think that will be absolutely sufficient," said the chairman of the commission. "Please take the accused back to his old spot."

"Thank you, gentlemen," Švejk said deferentially. "It's sufficient for me, as well."

After his departure, the three physicians agreed that, according to all the natural laws invented by psychiatric scientists, Švejk was a blatant imbecile, and an idiot.

Their report to the interrogating judge said, among other things, the following:

"The undersigned court physicians attest to the total mental dullness and congenital cretinism of the aforementioned Josef Švejk, who has been presented to this commission. He expressed himself by articulating expressions, such as: 'Long live the emperor, Franz Josef I.' This utterance is totally sufficient to shed light on the mental state of Josef Švejk as a notorious imbecile. The undersigned commission therefore recommends:

1. The investigation of Josef Švejk be stopped.

2. Josef Švejk be sent to the psychiatric clinic to be observed, in order to determine to what extent his mental state is dangerous to other people."

While this report was being drafted, Švejk was telling his fellow prisoners:

"They paid no mind to Ferdinand and talked to me about even stupider things. In the end, we told one another that we had talked enough, and we parted company."

"I don't trust anybody," remarked the cringing little man in whose meadow they had dug up the skeleton. "It is all thievery."

"Even thievery must exist," said Švejk, laying himself down on a straw mattress. "If everyone was always honest with one another, then they would soon smash each other out of existence."

4

THEY THREW ŠVEJK OUT OF THE MADHOUSE

When Švejk would later talk about life in the madhouse, he would do so with unusual praise: "I really don't know why the nuts are upset. One can crawl there naked on the floor, howl like a jackal, be crazy and bite. If one were to do that out in public, then people would be flabbergasted. But, in there, madness is mundanely common. Even the socialists haven't dreamt of such freedom!

"One can even impersonate the Lord God or the Virgin Mary in there. Or the Pope, or the English King, or the Emperor, or St. Wenceslaus. Although the nut, who thought he was the saint, was always bound up, naked, and laying down in isolation. There was also a crazy who kept screaming that he was the archbishop. He didn't do anything, except when he was stuffing his face 'til fit. Then, he'd do another thing, which, if you will excuse me, rhymes with it. In there, nobody feels any shame.

"One inmate was actually impersonating the saints Cyril and Method, so that he'd get two portions to eat. And, one gentleman there said he was pregnant and kept inviting everybody to the christening.

"A lot of chess players, politicians, fishermen, Scouts, stamp collectors and amateur photographers were locked up there. One was there on account of some old pots that he called the ash cans. One was kept constantly in a straitjacket, calculating when the world will end. I also met several professors in there. One of them kept telling me that the cradle of the Gypsies was in the Krkonoše, the Giant Mountains. Another would explain to me that inside this planet's globe, there is yet another, much larger one.

"Everybody there can say what he wants. He can say whatever just happens to come to his tongue with his saliva, as if he was in the parliament. Sometimes, they would tell one another fairy tales and get into a brawl, if some princess came to a very bad end. The one raging the most was a gentleman who presented himself as the 16th volume of Otto's Encyclopedic Dictionary. He was begging everybody to open him and find the entry: 'Cartonage stapler.'

Otherwise, he said, he'd be done for. He calmed down only when they put him in a straitjacket. He took great pleasure in it, thinking he had been put into a printing press. He was begging they give him a modern book-binder's trim.

"All-in-all, living there was like being in paradise. You can holler all you want in there. Or, you can scream, sing, weep, bleat, shriek, jump, pray, do somersaults, crawl, skip on one foot, run in a circle, dance, hop around, squat all day or climb the walls. Nobody will come up to you and say: 'You can't do this, sir, it is not proper. You should be ashamed. How can you call yourself an educated man?'

"For instance, there was an educated inventor who kept digging in his nose. Once a day, he'd say: 'I've just discovered electricity.' As I said, it was very nice there. The few days that I've spent in the madhouse belong among the most beautiful moments of my life!"

And surely, the welcome they gave Švejk, after they drove him from the court to the madhouse for observation, surpassed even his lofty expectations. First, they stripped him naked and gave him a long gown. One of the attendants amused him by telling him a joke about Jews. Another grabbed him intimately under his arms, and led him to his bath. They submerged him in the bathtub under warm water. Then, they dragged him out and stood him under a cold shower. They repeated this procedure three times. Afterward, they asked him how he liked it. Švejk explained that he loved to take baths and that this was better than the spa near the Karlův Bridge.

"If you also cut my hair and nails, there will be nothing to stand in the way of my total happiness," he added, smiling pleasantly.

Even this wish was heeded. They then rubbed him down thoroughly with a sponge, wrapped him in a sheet and carried him to a bed in the first ward. There they deposited him, covered him with a blanket and asked him to fall asleep.

To this day, Švejk relates the story with feelings of genuine tenderness:

"Imagine: they actually carried me all the way. I was, at that moment, in a state of total bliss."

Once on the bed, he also blissfully fell asleep. Later, they woke him up and gave him a cup of milk and a braided bun. The bun was already cut into little pieces. While one of the attendants held both

Švejk's hands, the other dunked the pieces of bun in the milk. They fed him, just like they might feed a goose with fattening balls. After they had fed him, they supported him under his arms and brought him to the bathroom, where they asked him to please satisfy both number one and number two physical needs.

Švejk speaks even of this delicate moment with extreme fondness. And, I'm sure I don't have to repeat his description of what they did with him next. I'll mention only that Švejk says:

"While they attended to me, one of them was holding me in his arms."

They brought him back, put him in the bed again, and asked him to please go back to sleep. However, shortly after he did so, they woke him up and took him to the examination room. There Švejk stood, totally naked, in front of two new doctors. It reminded him of that glorious day he was drafted in the army. Suddenly, he involuntarily blurted out:

"*Tauglich.* Fit for duty."

"What did you say?" asked one of the doctors. "Take five steps forward, and five back."

Švejk took ten.

"I told you, didn't I," grumbled the doctor, "to take five steps, not ten."

"I'm not a stickler about a couple of steps," said Švejk.

The doctors then asked him to sit in a chair and one began knocking on his knee. He told the other one that Švejk's reflexes were absolutely correct. The other shook his head and started knocking on Švejk's knee, too. In the meantime, the first one forced his eyelids open and examined Švejk's pupil. After that, they both walked to a desk and exchanged several expressions in Latin.

"Listen, can you sing?" one of them finally asked of Švejk. "Would you sing a song for us?"

"No problem, gentlemen," answered Švejk. "I don't have a voice, or a musical ear, but I'll try to satisfy your wish, since you want to be entertained."

So, Švejk let them have it:

"Why's the young monk in that armchair,
His forehead into his right hand bowing.
Two bitter, burning tears

31

Down his pale cheeks are rolling . . .

"I don't know the rest of it," admitted Švejk. "But, if you want me to, I'll sing another little song for you:

What loneliness round my heart,
That heavily, painfully, lifts up my breast.
When I'm sitting silently, and into the distance gazing
There, there into the distance, my desire . . .

"And I don't know the rest of this one either," sighed Švejk. "But, I do know the first stanza of *Where My Home is*, the Czech anthem. Also, I know *General Windishgrätz and the Military Lords Started a War at Sunrise*, and a couple of other national folk songs like *Preserve Us, Lord God*, and *When We Marched to Jaroměř*, and *A Thousand Times We Hail Thee Virgin Mary* . . .

Both physicians exchanged looks. One of them asked Švejk a question: "Has your mental state ever been examined?"

"In the army," answered Švejk ceremonially and proudly. "The military's own gentlemen physicians officially found me to be a notorious imbecile."

"It seems to me that you are a malingerer!" the second physician started screaming at Švejk.

"I, gentlemen," said Švejk in his own defense, "am no malingerer. I am a real imbecile. You can check with the office of the 91st Regiment in České Budějovice or with the Reserves Command in Karlín."

The older of the physicians waved his hand as if Švejk were hopeless, pointed to him, and told the attendants:

"Return this man's clothes and lock him up in the third-class ward for the indigent in the first corridor. Then, one of you take all his files to the office. And, tell them to process him quickly, so that we won't be stuck with him here for too long."

The physicians again began looking at Švejk, who deferentially shuffled backwards to the door, bowing continuously. One of the attendants asked him why he was moving so stupidly. He answered:

"Because I'm not dressed. I'm naked and I don't want to show the gentlemen anything. So they wouldn't think that I'm impolite or vulgar."

From the moment the attendants received the order to return Švejk's clothes, they stop showing any signs of care for him, whatsoever. They ordered him to get dressed, and one of them took him to the third class ward. It was there, during the several days the office took to process a written order to boot him out, that Švejk had the opportunity to carry out his many madhouse observations.

The disappointed physicians diagnosed him as a "malingerer with a feeble mind." However, because of the time of day that they released him, a minor incident arose:

Švejk loudly protested. He insisted that when they kick someone out of a madhouse, they cannot throw him out without first giving him lunch.

The subsequent disturbance was brought to an end when the madhouse doorman called the police. A patrolman then brought Švejk to the district police station in Salmova Street.

5

ŠVEJK AT THE DISTRICT POLICE STATION IN SALMOVA STREET

After his beautiful sunny days in the madhouse, Švejk now suffered hours full of persecution. Police Inspector Braun set the stage for his meeting with Švejk with the cruelty of a Roman henchman from the time of that charming Caesar, Nero. In those days, they used to say: "Throw that hoodlum Christian to the lions!". Inspector Braun now said, "Put him behind the iron gate!"

He said not one word more, nor less. However, when he gave the order, the eyes of police inspector Braun flashed with peculiar, perverse pleasure.

Švejk bowed and said proudly:

"I am ready, gentlemen. I think that 'the iron gate' must mean the same as segregation. Well, that's not that bad."

"Don't stretch out and get too comfortable here," warned one of his jailers.

Švejk quickly responded:

"I am absolutely modest and grateful for everything that you'll do for me."

In the segregation cell-block, a gentleman sat on a plank bunk, lost in thought. He sat there apathetically. When the key screeched to open the gate, it was clear from the way the man looked that he didn't believe that the door to freedom was opening for him.

"I bend my knee, honorable sir," said Švejk, while taking a seat next to him on the bunk. "About what time might it be?"

"Time is not my master," responded the man lost in thought.

"It's not bad here," said Švejk casually. "This plank bunk was made of sanded lumber."

The pensive man didn't answer. He stood up and started walking quickly in the small space between the locked door of the segregation cell and the bunk, as if he were in a hurry to save something.

In the meantime, Švejk was observing the graffiti on the walls with interest. There was an inscription in which an unknown prisoner promised heaven he would wage a life-or-death struggle with the police. The text read: "You'll get it." Another prisoner wrote: "Dry up and blow away, pigs." Yet another simply stated a fact: "I was sitting here doing time on June 5th, 1913, and I was treated well. Josef Mareček, trader from Vršovice."

There was also an inscription that was jolting in its angst:

"Mercy, great God . . ."

But, underneath it was written: "Kiss my a." The letter "a" was crossed out, however. Beside it was written, in capital letters, COAT TAILS. Next to that, some poetic soul wrote in verse:

"I'm sitting so sadly by the brook.
The sun is taking refuge behind the mountains
And I'm gazing to the hills that reflect a glow.
There, where my dear lover dwells."

Švejk's cell-mate was still running between the door and the bunk, as if he wanted to win a marathon. Finally, he stopped, out of breath. He sat down in his old spot, put his head in his hands and suddenly screamed:

"Let me out!"

He answered himself by saying:

"No, they won't let me out. They won't and they won't. I've already been here since six o'clock this morning."

He stood up straight and asked Švejk:

"You don't, by chance, have a belt on you, so that I could end it all?"

"Glad that I can be of service," answered Švejk, unbuckling his belt. "I've never yet seen a man hang himself with a belt in segregation. -- Only, it's a pity," he continued while looking all around, "that there's no hook here. The window handle won't hold you. All you can do is hang yourself from the bunk by curling up your knees, just like that monk did in the Emmaus Monastery. He hanged himself that way with his crucifix pendant, on account of some young Jewess. I like people who commit suicide very much. So, just go ahead with gusto."

Švejk slipped the belt into the gloomy man's hand. He looked at the strap, threw it into a corner and started to weep. He smudged the tears on his face with his black hands, and shrieked:

"I have kiddies! I'm here because of drunkenness and immoral life! Jesusmaria, my poor wife! What will they say at the office? I have little ones! I'm here because of drunkenness and immoral life!"

He kept going on like that for an eternity.

After a while, he did calm down a little. Then, he went to the door and began kicking it and banging on it with his fist. Soon, steps could be heard approaching in the corridor. They stopped, and a voice asked:

"What do you want?"

"Let me out!" the melancholy man screamed, as if he were left with nothing to live for.

"Where to?" was the question that came from the other side.

"To the office," replied the unfortunate father, husband, office worker, drunkard and immoral man.

Laughter, horrible laughter broke the silence in the corridor, followed by the sound of steps departing.

"It looks to me like that gentleman hates you, since he's laughing at you so," said Švejk, as the hopeless man sat down next to him again. "A policeman like that, when he's angry, can do a lot of harm. And, if he gets even angrier, he's capable of anything. So, just keep sitting here peacefully. Since you don't want to hang yourself, just wait to see how things will unfold. If you're an office worker, are married and have little children, it is, I admit, horrible. You're convinced they'll fire you from your job at the office, if I'm not mistaken?"

"I can't tell you that for sure," he sighed, "because I don't remember all the silly things I did. I only know that they threw me out of some place, and that I wanted to go back in there to light up my cigar.

"Actually, the evening began quite nicely. The chief of our department was celebrating his name's day and invited us to a wine bar. After that place, we all went to a second, a third, a fourth, a fifth, a sixth, a seventh, an eighth, a ninth . . ."

"Don't you want me to help you count?" asked Švejk. "I'm quite familiar with this type of counting. One night, I visited 28

37

different tap-rooms. But, to my credit, nowhere did I have more than three beers."

The unhappy subordinate of the chief who had celebrated his name's day in such a grand manner continued:

"Well, to make a long story short, after we went through about a dozen of those little dives, we noticed that we had lost the chief. Despite the fact that we had tied a string on him and dragged him with us everywhere, like a dog on a leash. But, when he turned up missing, we had to go back to every place again, to look for him. In the end, we all lost each other. Finally, I found myself in one of those all-night coffee houses in the Vinohrady neighborhood. It was a very proper establishment. But, I remember drinking some liqueur straight from the bottle.

"What I did after that, I don't remember. I just know that when they brought me here, both of the policemen reported that I got drunk. They said I behaved immorally, beat up a lady, took somebody else's hat off a rack and cut it with a pocket knife, dispersed a female band, and accused the head-waiter, in front of everybody, of stealing a 20-crown bill. Then, they said I broke the marble top off of the table I was sitting at and spat intentionally into the black coffee of a man sitting at the next table. I don't think I did any more, at least that I can remember. But, believe me, I'm usually such a proper, intelligent man. I don't think of anything else but my family. I'm no hoodlum breaking the peace! What do you say to all that?"

Instead of answering, Švejk asked with interest:

"Did it take a lot of work before you broke the marble top, or did you break it all at once?"

"At once," the intelligent man responded.

"Then, you're done for," Švejk said thoughtfully. "They'll prove in court that you'd been getting ready for that through diligent exercise. And, the stranger's coffee that you spat into, was it with rum, or without rum?"

Without waiting for an answer, Švejk explained:

"If it was with rum, then it'll be worse, because it's more expensive. In court, everything gets counted and added up, so that what you're charged with will climb to at least a felony."

"At the court . . . ," the conscientious father of a family whispered feebly. He then bowed his head and fell into an unpleasant state in which a man's conscience devours*[1] him.

"Do they know about this at home?" asked Švejk. "Do they know that you're locked up, or are you gonna wait until it's in the papers?"

"You think it will be in the papers?" the victim of his boss' name's day asked naively.

"That's more than a sure thing," was Švejk's straightforward answer. It had never been his habit to hide something from another.

"This story about you will give the readers of the newspapers enormous pleasure. I, too, like to read about drunks and their breeches of the peace. Not long ago, at The Chalice, one customer did nothing wrong except to break his own head with a stein. He threw it up in the air and stood under it. They loaded him up and drove him away. And, first thing in the morning, we were already reading about it in the paper. One time in Bendlovka, I slapped an undertaker and he slapped me one back. In order for us to reconcile, they had to arrest both of us. And, right away, the story was in the small afternoon edition.

"And, in that coffeehouse, At the Corpse, an office administrator broke two coasters. Do you think that they spared him? He was in the newspaper right away the next day. The only thing you can do from prison is send a correction to the newspaper, saying that the news item published about you has nothing to do with you. And, that you're not related to the gentleman named in the paper, nor associated with him in any way. But, you can write home to have them cut out the news item about you and save it, so that you can read it when you have sat through your sentence.

"Aren't you cold?" asked Švejk sympathetically, noticing the intelligent gentleman was shivering. "We're having a rather cold end of summer this year."

"I'm finished," moaned Švejk's companion. "There goes my promotion."

---

[1] (Author Jaroslav Hašek's footnote:) * Some writers use the expression "conscience gnaws." I do not view this expression to be exactly fitting. Even a tiger devours a man, rather than gnaws on him.

"You're right about that," Švejk eagerly concurred. "After you have served your sentence, if they don't take you back at the office, I don't know whether you'll find another job that soon. Even if you want to be a carrion collector's assistant, everybody will demand you produce a certificate of moral intactness. Indeed, a moment of indulgent pleasure, like the one that you've allowed yourself, does not pay. Does your missus have anything to live on during the time you'll be sitting in jail? Or will she have to go out begging and teach the kiddies various vices?"

The sound of sobbing rang out:

"My lost babes! My desperate wife!"

The indolent penitent stood up and started talking about his children. He had five. The oldest was twelve and a Boy Scout. He drank only water, which should have been an example to his father. However, it must be noted that his father had done this for only the first time in his life.

"A son with the Scouts?" exclaimed Švejk. "I love to hear about those Scouts! Once in Mydlovary, near Zliv, county of Hluboká, in the police district České Budějovice, the farmers from the area went hunting in the village forest and had themselves a Scout chase. We, the ninety-firsters, were having military exercises there.

"They said those Scouts had multiplied in there like jack-rabbits. They caught three. When they were tying up the smallest one, he wailed, squealed and moaned so much, that even we veteran soldiers couldn't watch it. So, we chose to step aside.

"Three other Scouts bit eight of the farmers as they were being tied up. After being tortured by the mayor with a cane, they confessed that there wasn't one meadow in the area that they hadn't flattened while catching some sun.

"They further confessed that they had also accidentally burned a field of standing rye near Ražice, just before harvest, while roasting a doe on a spit. They had hunted it down with knives in the village forest. More than 100 pounds of poultry and game bones were found, picked clean, in their Scout den in the forest. There was also a stunning volume of cherry stones, a lot of apple cores and other good things."

The poor father of the Scout was disconsolate.

"What have I done?" he wailed. "My reputation is ruined!"

"It sure is," Švejk said with his native sincerity. "After what has happened, your reputation must certainly be ruined for life. Because, when the people you know read about this in the newspaper, they will add more to the story. That's the way it's always done, but you shouldn't let it bother you. The number of people who have ruined or damaged reputations in this world is at least 10 times the number of those with clean reputations. That's just the way it is."

The sound of resolute steps could be heard approaching in the corridor. Then, the key rattled in the lock, the door opened, and a policeman called out Švejk's name.

"Excuse me," Švejk said in a courtly manner. "I've been here since only 12 o'clock noon. But, this gentleman's already been here since six o'clock in the morning. I'm in no hurry . . ."

Instead of an answer, the strong hand of the jailer pulled Švejk into the corridor. He was then led up the stairs in silence to the second floor.

The police commissioner, a fat, jovial gentleman, sat behind a desk on the second floor. When Švejk entered he asked:

"So then, you are Švejk? Well, how did you end up here?"

"It's so simple, it's silly, sir," answered Švejk.

"I came here escorted by a policeman, because I wouldn't put up with being thrown out of a madhouse without lunch. They treated me like some homeless streetwalker."

"You know what, Švejk? Why should we here at Salmovka station be angry with you?" the kindly commissioner observed.

"Wouldn't it be better to just send you to police headquarters?"

"As the saying goes, sir: you are the master of the situation," Švejk replied contentedly.

"Toward evening, a walk down to police headquarters would be a quite pleasant little stroll."

"I'm glad that we are agreed," the police commissioner said merrily. "Isn't it better when we reach an understanding? That's true, isn't it, Švejk?"

"I also love very much to consult with others," Švejk explained. "Believe me, commissioner, sir, I will never forget your goodness."

He bowed deferentially, and was taken by a policeman down to the guard house. A quarter of an hour later, Švejk could be seen at the corner of Ječná Street and Karlovo Square, being escorted by yet another policeman. This one carried a voluminous book under his arm. Its German title read: *Arrestantenbuch.* Arrestee Book.

At the corner of Spálená Street, Švejk and his escort met a band of people pressing around a sign that had just been posted.

"That's the proclamation of the Lord Emperor declaring war," the policeman told Švejk.

"I predicted it," Švejk noted. "In the madhouse, I'm sure, they still don't know anything about it. Although, in there, they should understand it first-hand."

"How do you mean that?" the policeman asked Švejk.

"Because a lot of gentlemen and officers are locked up in there," Švejk explained.

As another group pressed in front of the proclamation, Švejk yelled out:

"Hail to the Emperor, František Josef! This is a war we'll win!"

Someone from the boisterous crowd pulled Švejk's hat down over his ears. He stepped deliberately from the crowd and walked once again through the gate of the police headquarters.

With these words, Švejk bid good-bye to the crowd that had seen him off:

"I repeat it one more time, gentlemen! We'll win this war for sure!"

And somewhere, in the far removed distant parts of history, descending upon Europe was the truth that tomorrow would wreck even the plans of the present.

6

ŠVEJK AT HOME AGAIN, HAVING BROKEN THROUGH THE VICIOUS CIRCLE

The spirit of foreign authority wafted through the police headquarters. The authorities there were charged with finding out to what extent the subject population was enthusiastic for war. There were several exceptions. But, most people didn't deny that they were the sons of a nation that was doomed to bleed itself empty for interests totally alien to them. Police headquarters was also home to the most beautiful gathering of bureaucratic birds of prey. As a means of defending the existence of their convoluted articles of law, they had an affection for the use of hard-labor prisons and the gallows.

However, during this process, they were weighing each word beforehand and handling their victims with caustic kindness.

Švejk was brought to one of these black-and-yellow[2] birds of prey, who said to him:

"I'm very sorry that you fell into our hands again. We thought that you'd straighten out, but we've been disappointed."

Švejk silently nodded his head in agreement. He had such an innocent look on his face that the black-and-yellow predator looked at him quizzically and snapped:

"Don't look so stupid!"

Then, he immediately switched into a kind tone and continued:

"For us, it's certainly very unpleasant to keep you in custody. And, I can assure you that, in my view, your guilt isn't so great, given your little intelligence. There's no doubt that you've been seduced. Tell me, Mister Švejk, who is it, really, who entices you to commit these silly acts?"

Švejk coughed, then spoke up:

"Please forgive me, but I don't know of any silly acts."

---

[2] Black and yellow and the eagle were the colors and the symbol of the Austrian Empire.

"Is it not silliness, Mister Švejk," the inquisitor asked in an artificially fatherly tone, "when, according to the report of the policeman who brought you here, you caused people to gather on a corner in front of a proclamation that was posted concerning the war? Then, did you not incite these people by exclaiming 'Hurrah for Emperor František Josef! This war is won!'?

"I couldn't stay idle," Švejk explained. "I got upset when I saw that they were reading the proclamation and not showing any signs of being glad. No chanting of glory, no hurrahs, nothing at all, mister magistrate."

The goodness in his eyes dissolved the stare of his inquisitor, and Švejk continued:

"It was as if it had nothing to do with them whatsoever. And, there I was, an old soldier from the 91st Regiment. I couldn't stand watching it. So, I proclaimed those sentences. I think that, if you were in my place, you would have done the same. When there is a war, it must be won. 'Glory to the Lord Emperor!' must be chanted. And nobody can talk me out of that."

Outdone and crushed, the black-and-yellow predator couldn't withstand the gaze of this innocent lamb. He lowered his eyes onto the official files before him and said:

"I agree fully with your enthusiasm. But, if it were only shown under different circumstances. A policeman was escorting you. And, you yourself well know that such a patriotic outburst could, and probably did, strike the audience ironically, rather than seriously."

"When somebody is being led by a policeman," Švejk replied, "it is a tough moment in his human life. And, if, in even such a tough moment, a man doesn't forget what the proper thing to do is, especially when there is a war, then I think that such a man is not all that bad."

The black-and-yellow predator growled and once more looked directly into Švejk's eyes.

Švejk's gaze answered his stare with a soft, innocent, unassuming and tender warmth.

For a moment, the two just looked at each other.

"The demons take you, Švejk!" the official finally barked. "If you end up here one more time, then I won't ask you anything more at all. You'll be on your way to the military court at Hradčany. Do you understand?"

Before the official knew what was happening, Švejk stepped up to him, kissed his hand, and said:

"May God repay you for everything. Should you ever need a pure-blooded little dog, please condescend to turn to me. I'm in the business of obtaining dogs for others."

So, Švejk found himself on his way home, free and at-large again. His musing about whether he should stop first at The Chalice pub ended when he found himself opening its front door. This was the very same door from which he had exited some time ago in the custody of undercover patrolman Bretschneider.

Though several guests were sitting there, a grave-like silence reigned at The Chalice. Among the patrons was the church custodian from Saint Apollinaire. All of them were gloomy. Behind the tap-counter sat the pubkeeper's wife, Mrs. Palivcová. She gazed at the beer taps with a dull expression.

"Hey, I'm back!", Švejk called cheerfully. "Give me a stein of beer. Now, where is our Mister Palivec? Is he home already, too?"

Instead of answering, Mrs. Palivcová started weeping. When she finally did answer, she articulated her tragedy with a peculiar staccato, and moaned:

"They -- gave -- him -- ten -- years -- a -- week -- ago."

"Well, there you go," said Švejk. "See, then he's already got seven days behind him."

"He was *so* careful," wept Mrs. Palivcová. "He always said so himself."

The guests in the tap room were stubbornly diffident. It was as if Palivec's spirit was wandering there, exhorting them to even greater caution.

"Carefulness is the mother of wisdom," Švejk said, sitting himself down at a table. "Times are such that they force a man to be careful."

Mrs. Palivcová carried a beer to Švejk and sat it before him on the table. There were little holes in the beer's foamy head, because Palivcová's tears had dripped into the foam.

"Yesterday, we had two funerals," said the custodian from Saint Apollinaire, switching to another subject.

45

"Then, apparently, somebody died," a second guest commented, whereupon a third customer added:

"Did either funeral make use of those ornamental coffin pedestals?"

Švejk then asked:

"What I'd like to know is: what are the military funerals going to be like now, during the war?"

The guests got up, paid, and left in silence. Only Švejk now remained with Palivcová.

"It didn't cross my mind," he said, "that they would sentence an innocent man to 10 years. I've already heard of an innocent man that they sentenced to five years. But, 10 years? That's a little too much."

"My old man confessed!" cried Palivcová. "The things he said in here about those flies and about the picture? He repeated them, both to the police and in court. I was at the trial proceedings as a witness. But, they told me that I was in a familial relationship with my husband, and that I could withhold my testimony. How could I then testify to anything?

"I got so spooked by that familial relationship notion -- God forbid something be made of it -- that I withheld my testimony. And he, the poor old soul, gave me such a look. Until I die, I won't forget those eyes of his. And then, after sentencing, when they were escorting him out, he screamed right there in the corridor, as if he'd been made stupid from it all:

'Long live Free Thought!'[3]

Does Mister Bretschneider come in here anymore?" asked Švejk.

"He's been here several times," the pubkeeper's wife answered. "He has a beer or two, asks me who comes here, and listens to the guests talk about soccer. When they see him, they always talk only about soccer. And, he is always all fidgety, as if at any moment he could go berserk. During all this time, he only got one upholsterer from Příčná Street to swallow his bait."

"It's all a matter of training," remarked Švejk. "Was the upholsterer a dim-witted man?"

---

[3] Free Thought was an international atheistic movement. The Czech branch had been outlawed.

46

"Just about like my husband," she answered, again beginning to weep. "He asked him whether he would shoot at the Serbs. The upholsterer told him that he didn't know how to shoot. He told him he was once at a shooting gallery, and shot up a *crown*.[4] Then, Mister Bretschneider pulled out his notebook and we all heard him say: 'Look here! Again, we have high treason!' Then, he left with the upholsterer from Příčná Street, who has never returned."

"There will be more of those who won't return," said Švejk. "Give me a shot of rum."

Švejk was just having a second shot of rum poured for him, when into the tap-room came Bretschneider. He cast a quick look around and glanced into the empty pub. Then, he sat down next to Švejk. He ordered a beer and waited for Švejk to speak.

Švejk lifted a newspaper from the rack and scanned through the back pages of classifieds, then exclaimed:

"There you have it! This Čimpera fellow in Straškov village, number 5, serviced by the Račiněves post office, will sell a farm with 13 acres of fields. And, there is a school and railway nearby."

Bretschneider nervously drummed his fingers, turned and said:

"I'm surprised that a farm should interest you, Mister Švejk."

"Ah, it's you," said Švejk, extending a hand to him. "I didn't recognize you right away. My memory is very weak. The last time we parted, if I'm not mistaken, was in the intake office of police headquarters. What have you been doing since then? Do you come here often?"

"I came today on your account," said Bretschneider. "I was told at police headquarters that you sell dogs. I need a nice miniature pincher, or a spitz, or something similar."

"I can get you anything," replied Švejk. "Do you wish a pure-blooded animal or something from the street?"

"I think I'll go for a pure-blooded animal," replied Bretschneider.

"And what about ---- wouldn't you like a police dog?" asked Švejk. "The kind that snoops everything out right away and leads you to the trail of crime. A butcher in Vršovice has one that pulls

---

[4] Besides being the headgear of the monarch, it was also the empire's chief monetary unit.

his little wagon. That dog has, as the saying goes, missed his true career."

"I'd like a spitz," Bretschneider said with calm restraint. "A spitz that won't bite."

"Do you want a toothless spitz, then?" Švejk asked. "I know of one. He belongs to a pubkeeper in the Dejvice quarter."

"Then, I better get a little pincher," Bretschneider said indecisively. His knowledge of canines was only in its infancy. If it weren't for a direct order from security police headquarters, he would never attempt to learn anything about dogs.

The order had been specific, clear, and tough: Get to know Švejk better through his dog-selling business. For this purpose, he was given the right to choose assistants and have funds at his disposal for the purchase of dogs.

"The little pinchers come both bigger and smaller," said Švejk. "I know of two smaller ones and three bigger ones. All five can be cradled in your lap. I can recommend them to you with the utmost enthusiasm."

"Then, that's what I would like," decided Bretschneider. "How much would one cost?"

"That depends on size," answered Švejk. "That depends on size. A pincher is not like a calf. With pinchers, it's just the other way around: the smaller, the more expensive."

"I'm inclined to get a bigger one that could be a guard dog," replied Bretschneider, afraid to deplete the secret fund of the state police.

"All right," said Švejk. "I can sell the bigger ones at 50 crowns apiece, and bigger ones yet at 45. However, we've forgotten to discuss one thing. Do you want puppies or older dogs, male dogs or little bitches?"

"It's all the same to me," Bretschneider answered. He was dealing in something he knew nothing about. "Get them for me. And tomorrow, at seven in the evening, I'll come by your place to pick them up. Will they be there?"

"They will," Švejk replied dryly. "But, in this kind of situation, I'm forced to ask you for a deposit of 30 crowns."

"No problem," said Bretschneider, paying out the money. "Now, let's each have a quarter-liter of wine on my account."

They drank it up, then Švejk bought them a quarter-liter on his account. Bretschneider bought yet another round, urging Švejk not to be afraid of him, pointing out that he was off duty, so it was all right to talk to him about politics.

Švejk declared that he never talked about politics in a pub, that the whole game of politics was only for little children.

Bretschneider expressed an even more revolutionary view and declared that every weak state was foreordained to extinction. Then, he asked Švejk to express his opinion.

Švejk declared that he had nothing to do with the state. However, he said he had once cared for a St. Bernard puppy in a weak state, and fed it military biscuits. But, as he recalled, the puppy had croaked anyway.

After they had a fifth quarter-liter of wine each, Bretschneider proclaimed himself to be an anarchist and asked Švejk which organization he should sign up with.

Švejk responded that an anarchist had once bought a leonberger dog from him for 100 crowns, and that he still owed him the last payment.

During the sixth quarter-liter, Bretschneider spoke of revolution and against mobilization. Švejk then leaned toward him and whispered in his ear:

"A customer walked into the pub just now. Be careful that he doesn't hear you, or we might have some unpleasant difficulties from your talk......As you can see, our hostess is already weeping."

Indeed, Mistress Palivcová sat sobbing in her chair behind the tap counter.

"Why are you crying, mistress pubkeeper?" inquired Bretschneider. "In three months, we'll win the war. There will be an amnesty and your husband will return. Then, we'll really wet our whistles in this place. -- Or," he asked, turning to Švejk, "don't you think that we'll win it?"

"Why keep kicking a dead horse," Švejk said. "It must be won, and that's it. But, enough of this. I have to go home already."

Švejk paid his tab and left.

When he returned to his old apartment, his cleaning woman, old Mrs. Müller, was startled to hear a key turn in the lock, and then see Mr. Švejk come striding through the door.

"But sir, I thought you would not be back until years from now," she said with her customary sincerity. "The police have searched the place already three times. And, when they couldn't find anything, they said that you were done for, because you're too cunning. So, in the meantime, I rented your apartment, out of pity, to a doorman from a night club."

Švejk immediately verified for himself that an unknown foreigner had settled in very comfortably. He was sleeping in Švejk's bed, but graciously occupied only half of it. The other half he generously shared with some long-haired creature. She, out of gratitude, had her arms wrapped around his neck as they slept. Various articles of their clothing lay intermingled around the bed. From this chaos, it was apparent that the doorman had returned from the night club with his lady friend in a merry mood.

"Sir," said Švejk shaking the intruder, "don't let yourself be late for lunch. I would feel terrible if you were to tell everyone that I threw you out when it was too late to get something to eat."

The night-club doorman was groggy with sleep and it took a long time before he understood that the owner of the bed had returned home and was laying a claim to it.

In accordance with the custom of all doormen from night clubs, the sleepy man ranted that he would beat up anybody who tried to wake him up. Then, he attempted to keep on sleeping.

In the meantime, Švejk picked up articles of the doorman's clothes and brought them near the bed. After shaking him vigorously, he said:

"If you won't get dressed, then I'll have to try to throw you out into the street just as you are. It would be of great advantage to you to fly out of here dressed."

"I wanted to sleep until eight in the evening," muttered the shocked doorman, pulling on his pants. "I pay two crowns to that woman daily so that I can bring young ladies here from the night club.

"Hey! Tough Mary! Get up!" he yelled to his female companion.

By the time he had put on his collar and knotted his tie, he'd come to his senses enough to assure Švejk that the night club Mimoza was really one of the city's most respectable nighttime establishments, accessible only to ladies whose police registration booklets were in absolute order. He then cordially invited Švejk to come soon for a visit.

In contrast to the doorman, his female companion was in no way satisfied with Švejk's behavior and used several very choice expressions, the most decent of which was:

"You high-priest's punk!"

After the departure of the intruders, Švejk looked through the apartment for Mrs. Müller. He found no trace of her, except for a bit of paper. She had scribbled her thoughts on it in pencil, regarding the unfortunate subletting of Švejk's bed to the doorman of a night club. She expressed herself with uncommon ease:

"Do forgive me, Mr. Švejk, but I won't be seeing you anymore because I'm going to jump from a window."

"She's lying," said Švejk, while waiting for her to return.

A half-hour later, the unhappy Mrs. Müller crept into the kitchen. From the crushed expression on her face, it was apparent that she expected Švejk to offer her some words of comfort.

"If you want to jump out of a window," Švejk said calmly, "go into the bedroom. I've opened the window there. I would not recommend to you that you jump from the kitchen window, because you would fall onto the roses in the back yard. You would crumple the bushes and have to pay for it. From the bedroom window, you could fly down beautifully onto the sidewalk. And, if you were lucky, you would break your neck. If you were unlucky, then you would break all your ribs, arms and legs, and you would have to pay for the hospital."

Mrs. Müller started to whimper, then went silently into the bedroom and closed the window. When she came back, she said:

"There's a draft and it would not be good for your rheumatism, sir."

She made the bed, and was, in general, unusually diligent in putting everything in order. When she returned to Švejk in the kitchen, she had tears in her eyes and remarked:

"Sir, those two puppies that we had in the yard are dead. And the St. Bernard, he ran away when the police were conducting a house search here."

"Oh for-christ-the-lord!" exclaimed Švejk. "That dog has made a lot of trouble for himself. The police will surely be looking for him now."

"He bit a police commander when he was pulling him out from under the bed during the search," continued Mrs. Müller. "One of those policemen said that there was somebody under the bed. So, they commanded the St. Bernard, in the name of the law, to crawl out. When the doggie didn't want to, they dragged him out. Oh, how he wanted to swallow them. Then, he just charged out the door and has never returned.

"They also questioned me. They asked me who came here and whether or not you were getting some money from abroad. They acted like they thought I was stupid, because I had told them that money only seldom came from abroad, the last time from a businessman in Brno.[5] I told them it was a deposit of 60 crowns for an Angora cat you had advertised for sale in the *Národní politika*. I explained that you had sent a blind, fox-terrier puppy to him instead --- in that empty date box.

"After that, they spoke with me very kindly and referred that doorman from the night club to me, the same one you threw out. So that I wouldn't be afraid, they said, all alone in the house . . ."

"I just have bad luck with the authorities, Mrs. Müller," sighed Švejk. "Now, many of them will be coming here to buy dogs. You'll see."

I don't know whether those gentlemen who examined the police archives, after the regime in the Czech Lands changed, ever did decipher those items listed in the secret fund of the state police that read:

B . . . 40K, F . . . 50K, L . . . 80K, etc.

But they were definitely mistaken if they thought that B, F and L were the initials of human men, who for 40, 50, 80 or more crowns, would sell the Czech nation to the black-and-yellow eagle.

B indicated a St. Bernard, *F* stood for fox-terrier, and *L* denoted leonberger. Bretschneider bought all three of these dogs from Švejk, and then brought them to police headquarters. They were ugly mutants and didn't have the slightest trait in common with a pure-blooded breed. Švejk, of course, swore to Bretschneider they had pedigrees.

---

[5] Brno is the largest city and capital of Moravia, the other part of the Czech Lands; NOT a foreign city.

The "St. Bernard" was a mix of mongrel poodle and some stray street pooch. The "fox-terrier" had the ears of a basset and was the size of a butcher's dog. It had twisted legs, as if he had suffered from the angels' bone disease. The "leonberger's" hairy head was reminiscent of a stable pincher's. His tail was chopped off, and he had the height of a basset, but a bare butt, like those famous naked American dogs.

After Bretschneider, a detective named Kalous was sent to buy a dog from Švejk. He returned with a dazed freak that looked like a spotted hyena with the mane of a Scottish sheep dog. So, a new cryptic item was then added to the list in the secret police fund:

D . . . 90 K.

Kalous' mutant beast was now officially playing the part of a (Great) Dane...

However, Kalous did not succeed with Švejk, either. He did only as well as Bretschneider. Švejk managed to deflect the most nimble attempts to engage him in political conversation. Instead, he engaged the cops in long discussions about the treatment of puppy diseases. Even the most inventive of police snares ended with Bretschneider buying another new, amazing, mutant mongrel from Švejk.

The Švejk operation proved to be the end of the famous detective Bretschneider. Eventually, he accumulated seven such mongrel abominations in his apartment. He locked himself up in the back room with them and starved them for so long that they ate him.

Ever the conscientious civil servant, he had saved the state the expense of a funeral.

In Bretschneider's personnel file at police headquarters, under the rubric, "Career promotions," these tragic words are entered:

"Devoured by his own dogs."

When Švejk later found out about this tragic event, he said:

"Only one thing disturbs me: how will they ever put him together again on Judgment Day?"

7

ŠVEJK GOES IN THE MILITARY

It was at the time when the forests along the river Ráb in Galicia saw Austrian troops fleeing across that stream. And down in Serbia, one Austrian division after another was getting a long-deserved kick in the seat of the pants. Then, out of the blue, the Austrian Ministry of Military Affairs remembered Švejk, just in time to help the monarchy out of its current mess.

Švejk just happened to be laying in bed, stricken again with rheumatism, when they brought him the notice that he was to appear in one week for a medical exam at Střelecký Island.

When he received the news, Mrs. Müller was making coffee for him in the kitchen.

"Mrs. Müller," Švejk's called quietly from the bedroom. "Mrs. Müller, come here for a moment."

When the cleaning woman came to his bed, Švejk addressed her in a quiet but mysteriously festive tone:

"Sit down, Mrs. Müller."

When Mrs. Müller did sit down, Švejk suddenly rose up in his bed and declared:

"I'm going in the military!"

"Virgin Mary!" exclaimed Mrs. Müller. "What will you do there?"

"Fight," answered Švejk with a grave voice. "Austria is in big trouble. The enemy is already creeping up on Krakow and down under into Hungary. We're getting threshed like rye wherever we look. And, that's why they're calling me in for military service. Remember how yesterday I was reading to you from the paper that the dear motherland has been surrounded by a bunting of very dark clouds?"

"But you can't even move."

"That doesn't matter, Mrs. Müller. I will ride to military service in a wheelchair. The confectioner around the corner, he has such a wheelchair. He used to push his nasty, paralyzed, old grandfather out into the fresh air in it.

"You, Mrs. Müller, will push me into the military service in that wheelchair!"

Mrs. Müller started crying:

"Oh Mr. Švejk! Shouldn't I just run and get you a doctor?"

"Don't go anywhere, Mrs. Müller. I am, except for my legs, absolutely healthy cannon fodder. And, at a time when it is grim for Austria, every cripple must be at his post. Be calm and keep making the coffee."

Though upset, Mrs. Müller continued to strain the coffee in the kitchen. Meanwhile, the good soldier Švejk started singing from his bed:

> "General Windischgrätz and the military lords
> Started a war at the rising of the sun;
> Jumpity, jumpity, jump!
> A war they started, and cried like this:
> Help us! Christ the Lord and Virgin Mary!
> Jumpity, jumpity, jump!"

Frightened by the dreadful battle song, Mrs. Müller forgot all about the coffee and began to shake all over. The good soldier Švejk kept singing from his bed:

> "With the Virgin Mary and the four bridges
> Build for yourself, Pimont, a stronger advanced guard;
> Jumpity, jumpity, jump!
>
> 'Twas a battle, there 'twas,
> There near Solferino.
> Much blood flowed there,
> Blood up to your knees.
> Jumpity, jumpity, jump!
>
> Blood up to your knees,
> And meat by the wagon full.
> After all, 'twas the eighteenth gang brawling there.
> Jumpity, jumpity, jump!

Eighteenth gang, don't you be afraid of want.
After all, behind you on a cart,
They're bringing money.
Jumpity, jumpity, jump!"

"Your mercy! For-god's-sake, I beseech you!" came the pitiful request from the kitchen. But Švejk was already finishing his war song:

"The money on a cart and the mess in a buggy,
Now, which regiment can manage this?
Jumpity, jumpity, jump!"

When Švejk fell asleep for a nap, Mrs. Müller charged out the door and ran to get the doctor. She came back an hour later.

Švejk was awakened by a pudgy man, who placed his hand on his forehead and said:

"Don't be afraid. I am Doctor Pávek from Vinohrady. Show me your hand --- Put this thermometer under your arm --- Show me your tongue --- Show me again --- Hold your tongue --- What did your father and mother die of?"

And so, at a time when Vienna wished that all the nations of Austria-Hungary would offer to the empire its most exquisite specimens of loyalty and dedication, Doctor Pávek prescribed bromine for Švejk to help combat such patriotic enthusiasm. He also recommended that this brave and good former infantryman think no more about the military:

"Keep laying down and remain calm. Tomorrow, I'll come again."

When he did come the next day, he stopped in the kitchen to ask Mrs. Müller how the patient was doing.

"He's worse, doctor," she answered with true grief. "During the night, his rheumatism flared up, causing him great pain. And he began singing, if you will excuse me, the Austrian anthem."

Doctor Pávek reacted to his patient's new expression of loyalty by increasing his dosage of bromine.

On the third day, Mrs. Müller reported that Švejk was getting worse.

"At midday, doctor, he sent for a map of the battlefield. And by nightfall, he was struck by the delusion that Austria will win a victory."

"He's taking the bromine according to the prescription?"

"He hasn't even sent for it yet, doctor."

Doctor Pávek berated Švejk mercilessly and assured him that he would never again treat a man who refuses medical treatment by bromine.

Only two days were left before Švejk was to appear in front of the draft commission.

In that time, Švejk carried out the appropriate preparations. First, he sent Mrs. Müller to buy a military cap. Second, he sent her around the corner to borrow the confectioner's wheelchair, the one which he had used to drive his nasty, paralyzed grandpa out into the fresh air. Then, he remembered that he needed crutches. Fortunately, the confectioner was also saving a pair of crutches in remembrance of his grandfather.

He was still missing the traditional flowers that a recruit wears in his button-hole. Mrs. Müller even chased those down for him. During this time, the poor woman noticeably lost weight, and was seen weeping wherever she went.

Finally, on that memorable day, a moving display of utmost loyalty appeared on the streets of Prague:

An old woman pushed a wheelchair in front of her. In it sat a man waving his crutches. He wore a military cap with a freshly polished brass "Frankie" pin bearing the Emperor's initials: FJ. On his coat he proudly displayed a recruit's colorful bunch of flowers.

And this man waved his crutches again and again, screaming mightily into the street of Prague:

"On against Belgrade! On against Belgrade!"

A barely noticeable handful of people gathered in front of the building from which Švejk had emerged. But, the crowd kept growing as it followed him. By the time the mob around Švejk's wheelchair reached Václavské Square, it had grown to several hundred.

Švejk was later able to state simply and truthfully that patrolmen standing at an intersection had saluted him.

At the corner of Krakovská Street, the mob beat up a German university student wearing a Teutonic fraternity cap who kept yelling to Švejk:

"*Heil! Nieder mit den Serben!* Hail! Down with the Serbs!"

When the mob reached the corner of Vodičkova Street, the mounted police rode into it and dispersed the crowd.

When Švejk showed the district police inspector his official notice, in black and white, that required him, on that very day, to appear in front of the draft board, the district inspector was a bit disappointed. But, in order to prevent any breech of the peace, he had Švejk's wheelchair escorted by two mounted policemen to Střelecký Island.

An article about the event appeared in the *Prague Official Newspaper*:

Patriotism of a cripple:

Yesterday afternoon, pedestrians at the main Prague thoroughfares witnessed a scene which beautifully speaks of how, in these great and serious times, the sons of our nation can give the most excellent examples of loyalty and devotion to the throne of the dear old monarch. It seems to us that the times of ancient Greeks and Romans have returned, like when Mucius Scaevola had them take him into battle, paying no attention to his burned-off hand. These most sacred emotions and interests were beautifully demonstrated yesterday by a cripple on crutches being pushed in a wheelchair by his old mother. This son of the Czech nation voluntarily, without regard to his being infirm, let himself be drafted into the military service, so that he could give his life and possessions for his Emperor. And, the fact that his call "On against Belgrade!" had such a vigorous reception in the streets of Prague, is only convincing testimony that the inhabitants of Prague provide outstanding examples of love for one's land and the ruling sovereign's house.

The German-boosting *Prager Tagblatt* wrote a similar article. However, that newspaper reported that the cripple volunteer was seen off by a crowd of Germans who wanted to protect him with their bodies from being lynched by Czech agents of the well-known Entente.[6]

Bohemie, a strongly anti-Czech, German daily in Prague, published a piece demanding that the crippled loyalist be rewarded, and announced that it was accepting gifts from German citizens for this unknown patriot in the newspaper's offices.

Though these three journals agreed that the Czech Lands could not offer a more noble citizen, the gentlemen of the draft board did not share that view.

Especially not the chief military physician, Doctor Bautze. He was an obstinate man who diagnosed every condition as a fraudulent attempt to evade military service and avoid the front, the bullets, and the shells.

One of his favorite statements was particularly well known:

"*Das ganze tschechische Volk ist eine Simulantenbande.* The whole Czech nation is a pack of malingerers."

In just ten weeks, he had weeded out 10,999 of 11,000 civilians and labeled them as malingerers. He would have gotten the eleven-thousandth, if that lucky soul hadn't been hit with a fatal stroke when the doctor suddenly screamed at him:

"*Kert euch!* About face!"

"Carry that malingerer away!" barked Bautze, after he had determined the man was dead.

On the memorable day that Švejk and some others were assembled before Bautze, all were fully naked. Švejk attempted to chastely cover himself with the crutches he was leaning on.

"*Das ist wirklich ein besonderes Feigenblatt.* That is really a peculiar fig leaf," said Bautze. "There were no such fig leaves in paradise."

One of his assistants, a master sergeant, looked into Švejk's official papers and remarked to the doctor:

"Discharged for stupidity."

"And what else is wrong with you?" asked Bautze.

---

[6] Members of the alliance against Austria, Germany and Turkey: France, the United Kingdom and Russia. These nations were later joined by Japan, Italy and the United States.

"I dutifully report that I have rheumatism. However, I will serve the Lord Emperor until my body is torn to pieces," Švejk replied modestly. "Though my knees are swollen."

Bautze gave Švejk a horrible look and screamed:

"*Sie sind ein Simulant*! You are a malingerer!"

He turned to the master sergeant and said with icy calmness:

"*Den Kerl sogleich einsparren*! Lock this guy up immediately!"

Two soldiers with bayonets took Švejk to the garrison prison.

As he walked along on his crutches, Švejk began to notice, with horror, that his rheumatism was beginning to disappear.

Meanwhile, Mrs. Müller had been waiting for him with the wheelchair, all alone on the bridge above. When she saw Švejk being led away under bayonets, she started crying and slowly walked away from the wheelchair, never to return to it again.

The good soldier Švejk continued to walk modestly under the careful watch of the armed defenders of the state. Their bayonets glistened in the glow of the sun. Passersby began watching this little parade. When they reached *Malá strana*, the Small Side quarter of Prague, Švejk turned in front of Field Marshall Radecký's memorial statue and yelled to those watching:

"On against Belgrade! On against Belgrade!"

Marshall Radecký was dreamily watching the good soldier Švejk from atop his memorial. He saw him hobbling along on the old crutches, with the recruit's bouquet on his coat, as the distance steadily increased between them.

Meanwhile, some serious gentleman informed the people around him that the guards were escorting a "dezenter" to jail.

8

ŠVEJK AS A MALINGERER

In these momentous times, military physicians took unusual care to exorcise the demon of sabotage out of military malingerers and return them to the womb of the army.

Several degrees of torture were instituted for those suspected of malingering. Many pretended they were: consumptives, rheumatics, or men with a hernia. Others claimed to have kidney disease, typhoid, diabetes, inflammation of the lungs and other illnesses.

The torture the malingerers were subjected to was systematized and the degrees of torture were these:

1. An austere diet was enforced, consisting of only a cup of tea in the morning and evening, for three days. Also, constant doses of aspirin were administered, without regard to the patient's complaint, to guarantee constant sweating.
2. The so-called "Quinine Licking:" quinine was served in copious portions so malingerers would not "think that military service was a bowl of honey."
3. The stomach was flushed out, twice a day, with a liter of warm water.
4. Enemas were administered, using soapy water and glycerin.
5. The subject was wrapped in a bed sheet soaked in cold water.

Some "patients" were courageous, suffered through all five degrees of torture, and let themselves be taken away in a simple coffin to the military cemetery. There were, however, other "patients" of little heart. As soon as they were threatened with an enema, they proclaimed themselves suddenly healthy and said they wished to leave immediately for the front with the nearest march battalion.

Švejk was detained in the hospital building of the garrison prison among just such a group of cowardly malingerers.

"I won't hold up anymore," said a man they had just brought back from having his stomach rinsed out for the second time.

He was feigning shortsightedness.

"Tomorrow I'll be going to the regiment," a malingerer to the left of Švejk decided. He had just received an enema and was pretending to be as deaf as a tree stump.

On the bed by the door lay a dying consumptive, wrapped in a bed sheet soaked in cold water.

"He's the third one this week," remarked a neighbor on Švejk's right. "And, what's wrong with you?"

"I've got rheumatism," Švejk answered.

Hearty laughter erupted all around him. Even the guy who was supposed to have consumption was laughing.

"Don't barge in here with rheumatism expecting to be one of us," a fat man informed Švejk seriously. "Rheumatism has about as much currency around here as corns. I'm anemic. I've lost half my stomach, five ribs are gone, and nobody believes me.

"There was a deaf mute they wrapped in a bed sheet for two weeks, soaking him in cold water every half an hour. Every day they'd give him an enema and pump his stomach. Even all the medics thought he'd won his freedom, that he'd be going home. Then, the doctor prescribed something that made him gag. It could have torn him up. That's when he lost his heart. 'I can't pretend to be a deaf mute anymore,' he told them. 'My speech and hearing have returned.'

"All the guys in the sickbay kept telling him not to doom himself. But, he persevered, insisting he could now hear and speak just like the rest of us. And, that's the way he reported it the next morning during the doctor's rounds."

"He kept it up for quite awhile," remarked a man professing that one of his legs was shorter than the other by four inches.

"He wasn't like the one who pretended that he had a stroke. Three quinine lickings, one enema and a one-day fast were enough. When came the time to pump out his stomach, he confessed. Not even a remnant of the stroke remained.

"The one who said he was bit by a rabid dog held out the longest. He was biting and howling. It's true, he did know how to do that remarkably well. But, he just couldn't whip up foam at his mouth. We tried to help him any way we could. We tickled him constantly for a whole hour before the doctor came by on his rounds. We stopped when he got cramps and turned blue on us. But the foam wouldn't come to his mouth. It just never did. It was something horrible.

"One day during the doctor's rounds, he gave himself up. We felt pity for him. He stood up by his bed, straight as a candle, saluted and said: 'I dutifully report chief medical officer, sir, that perhaps the dog that bit me wasn't rabid.' The chief medical officer gave him such a weird look that his body started shaking all over and he blurted out: 'I dutifully report, chief doctor, sir, that no dog bit me at all. It was just I myself who bit my own hand.'

"After this confession, they investigated him for self-mutilation. They said that he wanted to bite off his own hand, so that he wouldn't have to go into the field."

"All such illnesses, like the ones where you need foam dripping at your mouth," said the fat malingerer, "are hard to simulate."

"Take, for example, falling sickness.[7] There was a guy here once with the falling sickness. He was always telling us that just one seizure would not work. So, he would stage up to 10 of them in one day. He was writhing in those convulsions and clenching his fists. He could bulge his eyes out so far, it looked as if he had them hanging out on stems. He would slam his body around and stick his tongue out, and, in short, I'll tell you, he did an exquisite, and kind of sincere, first-class falling sickness.

"All of a sudden, he got these furuncular boils: two on the neck, two on the back. And that ended his writhing and slamming himself to the floor. He couldn't move his head, nor could he sit or lay. He got a fever and became delirious and told everything on himself during the doctor's visit.

"He really did it to us with those furuncles, because he had to lay down. He lay among us for three days.

"Here's what got to us: they put him on a regular diet. In the morning, he got a braided bun with coffee. For lunch, he had soup, gravy and dumplings. In the evening, he got soup or porridge. And

---

[7] Epilepsy.

65

there we were: hungry, with pumped-out stomachs, and on a starvation diet. Yet, we had to watch that guy feeding his face, smacking his lips, and snorting and burping -- fully satisfied. Three guys claiming they had heart disease were tripped up by that. They all confessed just because of him."

"The best thing one can simulate is lunacy," said one of the group. "In the next room, we've got the best two teachers. One keeps screaming constantly, day and night: 'The pyre of Giordano Bruno is still smoldering! Reopen the trial of Galileo!'

"The other one barks. First, three times slowly, he goes: wharf -- wharf -- wharf. Next, it's five times in quick succession: wharf, wharf, wharf, wharf, wharf. Then, back to three times slowly. And so it goes, without stopping. They've already managed to keep it up for three weeks.

"I originally wanted to pretend to be lunatic myself. I wanted to play a religious nut and preach about the infallibility of the Pope. But, in the end I got myself a nice case of cancer of the stomach from a barber in the *Malá strana*. He charged me 15 crowns for it."

"I know a chimney sweep in the Břevnov neighborhood," remarked another patient. "For 10 crowns, he will give you such a fever that you'll jump out of the window."

"That's nothing," another chimed in. "In the Vršovice section, there is a midwife who, for 20 crowns, will dislocate your foot so bad that you'll be a cripple for the rest of your life."

"Heck, I got a dislocated foot for a tenner," piped up a voice from the row of beds by the window. "For a tenner and three beers."

"My illness has cost me over 200 already," complained the man next to him, a dried-out, little bean-pole. "Name me any poison and you won't come up with one that I haven't used. I am a living warehouse of poisons. I drank sublimate, inhaled mercury vapor, munched on arsenic, smoked opium, drank opium tincture, and sprinkled morphine on bread. I swallowed strychnine, drank a solution of phosphorus in carbon disulfide, and even downed picric acid.

"I've ruined my liver, lungs, kidneys, gall bladder, brain, heart and guts. Nobody knows what illnesses I have."

"The best thing is," somebody declared from somewhere near the door, "to inject kerosene under the skin of your hand. My cousin was really happy when they had to cut his arm off up to the elbow.

66

Today, he's done with the whole damn military and living in peace."

"So, you see, all these things must be suffered for the Lord Emperor," Švejk said. "Even stomach pumping or an enema. When I was serving with my regiment years ago, it was worse yet. They'd bind the arms and legs of a sick man behind his back and throw him in the hole, so that he would get better.

"In those days, there were no nice bunks like these, or spittoons, either. There were just bare planks with sick men laying on them. Once, one of the boys really had a true typhus. And, the one next to him had smallpox. Both were tied with their arms and legs behind their backs. Then, the regiment's doctor kicked them in the stomach, saying that they were malingerers. When both those soldiers died, it got into the newspapers and was mentioned in the parliament. They immediately forbade us to read the newspapers and conducted a search through our footlockers, trying to find hidden ones.

"I always have all the bad luck. Out of the whole regiment, they didn't find anyone with newspapers, except me. So, they put me on regimental report and escorted me to our colonel. Lord God, he was such an ox. He started screaming at me, ordering me to stand straight and tell him who it was who gave the information to the newspapers. Otherwise, he said he'd rip my mouth ear to ear and have me locked up until I turned black.

"Next came the regiment's doctor, swinging his fist under my nose and screaming:

'*Sie verfluchter Hund! Sie schabiges Wesen! Sie unglucklich Mistvieh!* You runaway dog! You shabby beast! You unlucky hunk of barnyard crap! -- You socialist punk!'

"I looked them all sincerely in the eyes and didn't blink. I kept very quiet, my right hand on my cap and my left on the crease of my pants. After they had gone crazy for about half an hour, the colonel ran toward me screaming:

'Are you an idiot?! Or, are you not an idiot?!'

"I replied calmly:

'I obediently report, colonel sir, that I am an idiot.'

"The colonel replied with a long litany:

'Lock him up for idiocy! Confine him to the barracks! Put him in manacles for forty-eight hours! Give him 21 days of strict regimen -- two days of fasting a week! Make sure to lock him up immediately! Make sure no one feeds him! Bind him up and show him that the military doesn't need idiots! We will, you churl, knock that newspaper nonsense out of your head!'

"While I sat there doing my time, wonders were happening in the garrison. Our colonel forbade the soldiers to read anything, even the *Prague Official Newspaper*. In the mess, they couldn't even wrap hot dogs or Limburger cheese in these papers.

"From that time on, our soldiers became big readers. Our regiment became the most educated in the army. They read all the newspapers and, in every company, they composed little verses and songs about the colonel.

"When something would happen, one of the men, some good soul, would always put the story in the newspaper under the title 'Cruel Maltreatment of Soldiers.' And, as if that wasn't enough, they'd write to the parliamentary deputies in Vienna, asking that they stand up for them. Those deputies started making one motion after another, declaring that our colonel was an animal, and more of the like.

"Franta Hencl from Hluboká complained to the deputies in Vienna because the colonel slapped him on the training ground. Some minister of the government sent a commission to investigate. After the commission left, Franta Hencl got two years in prison.

"The colonel had us all fall in, the whole regiment. He said that a soldier is a soldier, that he must shut his trap and keep on serving. If there was something the colonel really didn't like, it was insubordination. The colonel told us:

'So! You hoodlums thought that the commission would help you. Like shit it did. And now each company will march in formation before me and loudly repeat everything I have said.'

"One company after another marched, right-faced, to where the colonel stood. With one hand on the slings of our rifles, we shouted at him:

'So! We hoodlums thought that the commission would help us! Like shit it did!'

"Our colonel laughed so hard that he was grabbing at his gut. That is, until the 11th Company marched by in formation. They came along stomping hard. But, when they reached the colonel: nothing. Silence. Not even a tiny sound. The colonel turned red like a rooster. He sent the eleventh company back and commanded them to do it again as he had ordered. They marched back again in formation, rank after rank, and stared at the colonel just as insolently as before.

"'*Ruht!* At ease!' the colonel said, pacing up and down, lashing at his boots with a riding whip and spitting. All of a sudden, he stops and screams:

'*Abtreten!* Fall out!' He then mounted his old nag and rode out through the gate. We were waiting to see what would happen to the 11th Company. Lo and behold, nothing. We waited for a day, then for a second day, and then for a whole week. Lo and behold, still nothing.

"The colonel didn't show up at the garrison at all. All the men -- all the non-commissioned officers, and all the officers -- were very glad. We got a new colonel and it was rumored that the old one was in some kind of sanitarium because he wrote a letter, in his own hand, to the Lord Emperor accusing the 11th Company of mutiny."

Soon, it was time for the afternoon doctors' rounds. Chief Medical Officer Grünstein went from bed to bed, followed by a medical corpsmen with a records book.

"Macuna?!"

"Here!"

"Enema and aspirin!---Pokorný?!"

"Here!"

"Stomach rinse and quinine!---Kovařík?!"

"Here!"

"Enema and aspirin!---Koťátko?!"

"Here!"

"Stomach rinse and quinine!"

And so it went, one after the other: sharply, mechanically, without mercy.

"Švejk?!"

"Here!"

Dr. Grünstein looked over the new addition.

"What's wrong with you?'

"I dutifully report that I have rheumatism!"

During the course of his medical career, Dr. Grünstein had become accustomed to being subtly ironic with his patients. He found it had a more solid effect than shouting.

"Ah, rheumatism," he said to Švejk. "Then you have a tremendously serious illness. It really must be an accident of chance that you should get rheumatism at a time when there is a world war and you are to serve in the military. I think that this must make you feel terribly sorry."

"I dutifully report, chief medical officer, sir, that I do feel terribly sorry."

"So, I see. He feels terribly sorry about it. That is tremendously nice of you, that you've remembered us with that rheumatism of yours just now. In peace time, the poor guy undoubtedly runs around like a little kid. But, when war breaks out, right away he's got rheumatism. Right away his knees won't serve. Don't your knees ache terribly?"

"I dutifully report that they do ache."

"I suppose that you can't sleep for whole nights at a time. Isn't that true? Rheumatism is a very dangerous, painful and serious illness. We've already had good experience here with people suffering from rheumatism. Our absolute diet and our different manners of healing have proven to work very well. You will get healthier here much faster than in that famous Slovak spa, Píšťany. You'll soon be marching off to a front-line position so well, that only the kicked-up dust will be left behind you to watch you go."

Turning to the medical corpsman, the doctor said:

"Write this: Švejk -- absolute diet. Stomach rinse twice a day. Enema once a day.

"We'll see how it goes from there. For the time being, take him to the consulting room, rinse out his stomach and, when he comes to, give him an enema. And give it to him good, until he calls on all the saints, and that rheumatism of his gets spooked and runs out of him."

He then turned toward all the beds in the room and gave a little speech filled with pithy, terse sentences:

"Don't think that you are looking at some ass who allows himself to be fooled every time. Your behavior will not throw me off balance in any way. I know that you are all malingerers, that you want to desert from the military service. And I am dealing with you accordingly. I've survived and outlived hundreds and hundreds of soldiers such as you.

70

"On these beds have lain a whole lot of men who lacked nothing but military spirit. While their buddies were fighting in the field, they thought that they might roll around in a comfortable bed, getting hospital food, and waiting until the war has blown by. But, they made a damn colossal mistake. And, all of you have also made a damn colossal mistake. Twenty years from now, you'll still be screaming in your sleep when you dream of how you tried malingering while here with me."

"I dutifully report, Chief Medical Officer, sir, that I am healthy already," a faint voice squeaked from a bed by the window. "I noticed last night that my asthma has already disappeared."

"You're name is?"

"Kovařík. I dutifully report, sir, that I'm to get an enema."

"All right, you'll get an enema for the road," decided Dr. Grünstein. "So that you don't complain that you were not getting treatment from us.

"Now, all the sick men whose names I've called follow the medical corpsman so that each will get what he's got coming."

Each did get an honest portion of what was prescribed for him. So what, if some of them tried to influence those executing the doctor's orders. Some simply pleaded with the orderlies. Others threatened to join the medical corps, so that one day maybe these same medical orderlies would fall into their hands.

Švejk, however, held his own with courage.

"Don't spare me," he said, prodding the henchman who was giving him an enema. "Remember your oath. Even if your father or your own brother was laying here, you'd certainly give him an enema without batting an eye. Just think to yourself 'Austria stands on such enemas', and victory is ours."

The next day, during his rounds, Dr. Grünstein asked Švejk how he liked being in the military hospital. Švejk answered that it was an establishment both correct and noble. As a reward, he received the same treatment he had the day before. They put aspirin and three pills of quinine into water and told him to drink them up immediately.

Even Socrates did not drink his goblet of hemlock as did Švejk drink his quinine. Švejk, on whom Dr. Grünstein tried all his stages of trial by torture.

As they were wrapping Švejk in a wet bed sheet the physician asked him if he was enjoying himself.

"I dutifully report chief medical officer, sir, that it is much like being at the municipal swimming pavilion, or at a spa by the sea."

"Do you still have rheumatism?"

"I dutifully report, sir, that it doesn't seem to get any better at all."

Švejk was then subjected to more suffering.

Baroness von Botzenheim, the widow of an infantry general, had gone through a lot of trouble to search out the soldier who was the subject of a news item recently published in the newspaper *Bohemie*. The article had described how this loyal soldier, an invalid, was pushed down the streets of Prague in a wheelchair as he shouted, "On against Belgrade!" This patriotic expression prompted the newspaper to call on its readers to donate money for this loyal hero, who was, after all, an invalid.

Through an inquiry at the police headquarters, it was found that this patriot was Švejk. After that, locating him was easy.

So, the Baroness von Botzenheim summoned her footman and lady companion, gathered a basket of food and gifts, and departed for the Czech Lands' preeminent official site, Prague's most grand and imposing district, Hradčany.[8]

The poor Baroness had no idea what conditions were like in the military hospital of a garrison prison. But, her calling card opened the door of the prison immediately. And, in the office, they treated her with immense kindness.

In five minutes, she knew that *"der brave Soldat,* the good and courageous soldier," Švejk, for whom she inquired, was laying in the third barrack, bed number 17. Dr. Grünstein himself went with her, but he was beside himself, and silly from it all.

---

[8] Dominating the city from a high hill on the west bank of the Vltava River, Hradčany was then the seat of provincial and Imperial power. It was a powerful cluster of edifices containing the central headquarters of the government and military, plus courts, a prison, a palace, a cathedral and the ancient tombs of saints and Czech Kings. Today, it enjoys a similar status and its spires still reach to the clouds and loom above all.

Having endured the usual morning therapy prescribed by Dr. Grünstein, Švejk was just sitting quietly on the bed. He was surrounded by a group of emaciated, starving malingerers, who were tenaciously battling Dr. Grünstein's absolute diet, but had yet to give up.

Anyone listening to them would have had the impression he was in the company of a group of culinary experts, or in an advanced chef's school, or attending a course for gourmets.

"Even lowly suet cracklings are edible, if they're warm," said the one who was supposed to have an inflammation of the stomach. "When the suet is rendered down, the cracklings should be squeezed until dry, then salted, and peppered. I'm telling you that goose cracklings can't equal them."

"Leave goose cracklings out of it," said another, who claimed to have stomach cancer. "There's nothing that tops goose cracklings. Pork lard just doesn't compare. It goes without saying that goose cracklings must be rendered until goldish, like the Jews do it. They'll take a fat goose and strip the fat with the skin when they're rendering it down."

"You know, you're mistaken about pork cracklings," remarked Švejk's neighbor. "Then again, I'm talking about cracklings from home-made lard. So, we're talking home-made cracklings. Not of a brown color, nor a yellow. They must be something between those two hues. Such cracklings can't be either too soft, or too hard."

"They can't be crunchy, or then they're overdone and burnt. They have to dissolve on the tongue. But when they do, you don't want to feel the lard dripping down your chin."

"Who of you has eaten cracklings from horse lard?" somebody called out. Nobody answered him because a corpsman came running in and said:

"Everybody in bed! Some archduchess is coming here! And nobody better show his dirty feet from under the blanket!"

Not even an archduchess could have entered so seriously as did the Baroness von Botzenheim. A whole procession rolled in behind her. The hospital's accountant master sergeant saw in her visit the mysterious hand of an inspection, which might take him from his fat trough in the rear and deliver him to the shrapnel and barbed wire of the front-line positions.

He was pale with worry, but Dr. Grünstein was even more pale. Dancing in front of his eyes was the Baroness' small calling card, prominently proclaiming that she was "a general's widow." To the doctor, this meant she had important connections. Her complaints might get him transferred to the front, or other horrible things.

"There is Švejk," he said, maintaining an artificial calm. He lead the Baroness von Botzenheim to Švejk's bed, and said:

"He is behaving very patiently."

Baroness von Botzenheim sat down on a chair placed next to Švejk's bed for her and said:

"Chekie zauldier, gooht zauldier. Kreepl zauldier, be kahriges zauldier. I luf verie moch zee Chekie Austrian."

As she spoke she caressed Švejk's unshaven cheek.

"I reed ohl in zee paypehr. I breeng you munchie, bitie, smokie, suckie, Chekie zauldier, gooht zauldier. *Johann, kommen Sie her!* Johann, come here!"

Because of his bristly side-burns, her footman reminded many of the famous outlaw, Bábinský. He dragged a big, overflowing basket to the bed. Meanwhile, the old baroness' lady companion, a tall dame with a sad face, sat on Švejk's bed and straightened out the straw pillow under his back. She seemed fixated on the idea that this was the proper thing to do for sick heroes.

In the meantime, the baroness pulled her gifts out of the basket: A dozen roast chickens wrapped in pink silken paper and bound by a black-and-yellow silk ribbon, and two bottles of liqueur with special, war-time labels. The words, *"Gott strafe England!* God punish England!" appeared on one side of the bottle, while the label on the other side bore a picture of Franz Josef holding hands with Kaiser Wilhelm, as if they wanted to play the Czech children's game, "Bunny in his little hollow . . ."

The baroness next pulled out three bottles of wine for the convalescents, and two boxes of cigarettes. She spread everything elegantly on the bed next to Švejk, and added a nicely bound book entitled *Stories from the Life of Our Monarch*. This book was written by the current and esteemed editor-in-chief of the official newspaper, *Czechoslovak Republic*, who saw much of the old monarch, Frankie, in himself.

Then, packets of chocolate were placed on the bed. They were emblazoned with the same inscription on one side as was on the liqueur's label: *"Gott strafe England!"* However, the likenesses of the Austrian and German emperors on the other side were different. In this picture, they were not holding hands. They stood back-to-back, each facing away from the other, and each staying unto himself.

A nice, double-row toothbrush was also presented to the convalescents. It bore Franz Joseph's slogan, *"Viribus unitis.* By united forces," so that everybody who brushed his teeth would think of Austria.

A very fitting and elegant set for cleaning finger and toe nails was also presented. On the box was the picture of a shell bursting. Under it, a man in a cone-shaped Austrian soldier's helmet rushed forward with a bayonet. The inscription underneath read:

"Für Gott, Kaiser und Vaterland! For God, the Emperor, and Fatherland!"

There also was a package of cookies without any picture. Instead the cookies offered a ditty written in German:

> *Österreich, du edles Haus,*
> *steck deine Fahne aus,*
> *lass sie im Winde weh'n,*
> *Österreich muss weig stehn!*

The Czech translation was placed on the reverse side:

> Austria, you noble house,
> hang out your flag,
> let it wave in the wind
> Austria must stand forever!

The baroness' last gift was a hyacinth in a pot.

When all of it lay unwrapped on the bed, Baroness von Botzenheim was so moved she couldn't hold back her tears. The baroness' lady companion, still assisting the seated soldier Švejk, also began to weep. Švejk clasped his hands together and interrupted the church-like silence:

"Our Father who art in heaven, hallowed be Thy name. Thy kingdom come . . . Pardon me, merciful lady, that's not it. I wanted to say: Lord God, heavenly Father, bless us for these Thy gifts, which from Thy bounty we're about to be partaking. Amen!"

After these words, he took a chicken from the bed and tore into it, despite the horrified glare of Dr. Grünstein.

"Ah, the soldier boy is enjoying the taste of it," the old baroness whispered with enthusiasm to Doctor Grünstein in her native German. "He is certainly healthy already and can now go into the field. I am really very glad. This all came just in time for him."

The baroness then went from bed to bed and handed out cigarettes and chocolate pralines. Eventually, she returned to Švejk. She stroked his hair gently, and with the words, *"Behut euch Gott. God protect you all,"* she led her whole procession solemnly out the door.

While Doctor Grünstein accompanied the baroness downstairs, Švejk passed out the chickens, which the patients devoured with great speed. When Doctor Grünstein returned, he found a pile of bones. They were gnawed so clean that it looked as if the chickens had fallen alive into a nest of vultures, been picked absolutely clean, and then blanched for several months by the sun.

The war-time liqueur had disappeared also, along with the three bottles of wine. The package of chocolates, plus the package of cookies, had also disappeared in the stomachs of the patients. Somebody even drank up a vile of nail polish he'd found in the manicure set. Another had bitten into the toothpaste that had been enclosed with the toothbrush.

When Doctor Grünstein returned, he again assumed his fighting stance and made a long speech. It was as if a burden had fallen off his heart when the visitor had left. The pile of bare bones had hardened his view that they were all incorrigible.

"Soldiers, if you had half a brain you would have left all of those gifts alone. You would have known that if you devoured them, the chief medical officer wouldn't believe that you were seriously sick. You have hereby given testimony to the effect that you don't appreciate my goodness.

"I pump your stomachs and give you enemas. I'm trying to make you stick to an absolute diet, and you overstuff your stomachs on me. Do you want to get an ulcer? Well, that won't happen! Before your stomach even tries to digest this food, I'll clean it out of you so thoroughly, that you'll be remembering it as long as you live, even if you were to be the last one to die.

"You'll be telling your children how you once devoured chicken and other various goodies, but that it didn't stay in your stomach for even a quarter of an hour because we pumped it out while it was still warm.

"And so you won't think that I'm an ass like you, but a little bit smarter than all of you put together, you must now follow me out in single file. And, I'm letting you know that tomorrow I'm sending the commission here. I'm siccing them on you because you've been laying around here too long. None of you has anything wrong with you. In just a few minutes, you have managed to mess up your stomachs and turn them into swine-filth very nicely.

"Forward, march!"

When Švejk's turn came, Doctor Grünstein remembered the day's mysterious visit and asked:

"Do you know her ladyship, the baroness, well?"

"She's my stepmother," answered Švejk calmly. "When I was of but a tender age, she abandoned me and now she's found me again..."

Doctor Grünstein ordered tersely:

"Give Švejk an extra enema."

In the evening, sadness reigned in the hospital's bunks. Several hours earlier, they all had various good and tasty things in their stomachs. Now, all they had in them was weak tea and a slice of bread.

From near the window, Number 21 asked his fellow inmates:

"Would you guys believe that I prefer fried over roasted chicken?"

Somebody growled:

"Give him the blanket treatment."

They were all so weak after their ill-fated banquet that nobody moved.

Doctor Grünstein kept his word. Several military physicians from the promised commission came in the morning.

They solemnly went through the rows of beds and nothing could be heard but "Show your tongue!"

Švejk stuck his tongue out so far that his face contorted into a weird grimace and his eyes squinted shut:

"I dutifully report Command Medical Officer, sir, that I can't make my tongue any longer than that."

This prompted an interesting discourse between Švejk and the commission. Švejk claimed that he made the remark because he feared they would think that he was hiding his tongue from them.

The members of the commission differed significantly in their judgment of Švejk.

Half of them insisted that Švejk was "*ein blöder Kerl,* an idiotic guy," while the other half claimed he was a scoundrel who wanted to make light of the military service.

"There'd have to be the devil's thunder in this, if we were not to get the best of you!" the chairman of the commission screamed at Švejk.

Švejk looked at the whole commission with the divine calm of an innocent child.

The Command Chief Physician stepped within an inch of Švejk: "I'd like to know, you sea pig, just what you're thinking now."

"I dutifully report that I'm not thinking at all."

"*Himmeldonnerwetter!* Heaven's thunderstorm!" hollered one of the members of the commission, clanking his saber. "So he doesn't think at all. How come, you Siamese elephant you, that you don't think?"

"I dutifully report that the reason I don't, sir, is that it is forbidden for soldiers in the military service to think. When I was with the 91st Regiment years ago, our captain would always say: 'A soldier must not think on his own. His superiors think for him. As soon as a soldier starts thinking, then he's not a soldier anymore, but some kind of mangy civilian. Thinking doesn't lead. . .'"

"Shut your trap!" the chairman of the commission interrupted furiously. "We've already got the word about you. *Der Kerl meint: man wird glauben, er sei ein wirklicher Idiot.* This guy thinks: they'll believe that I'm a real idiot. . . You're no idiot, Švejk! You're smart. You're cunning. A street punk, a lousy maggot, you understand?!"

"I dutifully report that I understand."

"Didn't you hear me? I've already told you to keep your trap shut."

"I dutifully report that I've heard an order to keep my trap shut."

"*Himmelherrgott!* Heavenly-lord-god! Then obey orders and keep your trap shut! You know well that you're not to talk back!"

"I dutifully report that I know that I must not talk back."

The military chiefs looked at one another and called in the master sergeant. The command chief physician of the commission pointed at Švejk and said:

"Escort this man down to the office and wait there for our report. At the garrison, they'll chase that talking back out of his head. The guy's as healthy as can be. He's malingering. He talks back and makes fun of his superiors. He thinks that they are here just for his amusement and that the whole military is fun, a joke. They will, Švejk, show you at the garrison prison that the military is no shitty joke."

As the master sergeant escorted him across the yard to the office, Švejk hummed this little song :

> *I always thought to myself,*
> *that military service would be fun,*
> *that I'd be there for a week or two,*
> *then home again I'd run. . .*

While the duty officer screamed at Švejk in the office downstairs, yelling that guys like him should be shot, the commission upstairs was purging the malingerers. Of seventy patients, only two saved themselves: a soldier whose leg had already been blown off by a grenade, and another with a real, bone-eating disease.

These were the only two who didn't hear the word "*tauglich,* fit for duty." All the rest, even the three dying of consumption, were declared capable of service in the field.

The command chief physician didn't miss this great opportunity for a rhetorical exercise. His speech was brief, but was interspersed with quite a variety of epithets:

All of them were dumb oxen and piles of manure. Only if they fought courageously for the Lord Emperor would they return to human society. And only after the war would they be forgiven for wanting to get out of military service, and for being malingerers. However, the doctor said he didn't believe they would ever be redeemed. He was sure that the hangman's rope awaited them all.

After his speech, a young military physician, unspoiled and pure of soul, asked the Command Chief for permission to speak. Unlike his superior's speech, this young doctor's was filled with optimism and naiveté. Of course, he spoke in German.

The young physician went on for quite awhile about how all of those leaving the hospital to be with their regiments in the field must become victorious knights.

He said he was convinced that they would be skilled with their weapons in battle, and honest in all matters concerning the war, and in their private lives, as well. They would be invincible warriors. They should remember the fame of heroes like Radecký, and prince Eugen of Savoy.

They would make fertile, with their blood, the monarchy's wide fields of glory. They would victoriously fulfill the role which history had foreordained for them.

With fearless courage, with disdain for their lives, they would rush forward under their regiments' banners, shot full of holes, onward to new glory and new victories.

Once they were in the corridor, the command chief physician told this naive, young man:

"My dear colleague, I can assure you that your speech was all in vain. Not even Radecký, nor your prince Eugen of Savoy could turn those hoodlums into soldiers. Speaking to them in an angelic, or in a demonic manner: it's all the same.

"They're a bunch of gangsters."

9

ŠVEJK IN THE GARRISON PRISON

The last refuge of people who didn't want to go to war was the garrison prison. I knew a substitute math teacher who didn't want to shoot at others with the artillery. He stole a watch from a lieutenant just to get locked up in the garrison prison. He did so with deliberate forethought. The war neither impressed nor enchanted him. Shooting shrapnel and grenades at the enemy and killing equally unlucky substitute teachers and mathematicians on the other side, he viewed as idiocy.

"I don't want to be hated for my aggression," he said, and calmly stole the watch. First, they probed into his mental state. Only when he declared that he wanted to enrich himself did they transport him to the army prison.

There were a few more such people who were doing time in prison for theft or fraud. Idealists and non-idealists. People who viewed the war as a source of income, such as those non-commissioned officers, or NCOs, who worked as accountants. They were committing all kinds of fraud with supplies and with the soldiers' pay, both in the rear and at the front. Then, there were the simple petty thieves, who were a thousand times more honest than those who sent them to prison.

There were other soldiers sitting in army prisons for various other infractions of a purely military nature: breeches of discipline, attempts at mutiny and desertion. There was also a peculiar type, the politicals. Eighty percent of them were innocent, but ninety-five percent of them were found guilty and sentenced.

The apparatus of the military courts was grandiose. Such magnificent machinery is usually present and at the disposal of the government of any country approaching a comprehensive political, economic and moral crash. The limelight of bygone might and glory bolsters these courts, as well as the local police, the state security police, and all whoring informer scum.

In every part of the military Austria had its snoops, ratting on the comrades who shared bread with them on the march and who slept on the same bunks with them at night.

The state security police supplied material for the army's prisons: Messrs. Klíma, Slavíček & Co.[9]

The military censor incarcerated the authors of correspondence between the front and those they left behind in desperation at home. The security policemen even brought in old retired farmers who had sent letters to the front. The farmers had described their domestic misery in an effort to comfort those on the frontlines. For this, the military courts hung the noose of twelve years in prison around each of their necks.

There was a road from the Hradčany prison through the Břevnov quarter of Prague to the Motol military training grounds on the outskirts of the city. In those days, in front of a procession of bayonets would be a man with chains on his wrists. Behind him followed a cart with a coffin on it. After they reached the Motol training ground, a brusque order would be heard:

"*An! Feuer!* Ready-aim! Fire!"

And later, when the regiments and battalions would read aloud the orders of the day, they would announce that a soldier was shot for mutiny. They said that when he was drafted, his wife had clung to him. So, a captain had cut her down with his saber.

At the garrison prison, the trio of Command Warden Slavík, Captain Linhart, and Master Sergeant Řepa, also known as "The Executioner," was fulfilling its role. How many had they beaten to death in solitary?

Yet, it is possible that today Linhart is still a captain, even in this independent Republic. I wish that he would get credit for his years of service in the prison. Slavíček and Klíma, of the state security police, have been given due credit. Řepa has returned to civilian life and continues to perform his job as a masons' foreman. Maybe, he got it because he's a member of various patriotic associations in the Republic.

---

[9] These two state security police officials became rich selling supplies to the army.

Command Warden Slavík became a thief in the Republic and today he's incarcerated. The poor soul has not positioned himself as nicely in the Republic as many other former military bosses have.

It was quite natural that Command Warden Slavík, when he was accepting Švejk into his custody, shot a look full of mute reproach at him and said:

"Your reputation is so wrecked that you made it all the way here into our midst? Well, we will sweeten your stay here, little boy, like we do for all who have fallen into our hands. And those hands of ours are not some nice ladies' hands."

To add weight to his words, he then put his muscular fist under Švejk's nose and said:

"Take a whiff of this, you hoodlum!"

Švejk took a whiff and remarked:

"I wouldn't like to get it in the nose with this one. It has the fragrance of a cemetery."

His calm, deliberate speech struck a chord with the command warden.

"Ha!" he said, poking Švejk in the belly with his fist. "Stand straight. What do you have in your pockets? If you have a cigarette, then you can keep it. Money, you'll turn over. So the others won't steal it from you. You don't have more? Really, you don't? Don't lie! Liars are punished."

"Where are we going to put him?" asked Master Sergeant Řepa.

"We'll put him in 16," decided the Command Warden. "Can't you see what Captain Linhart wrote on his file? *Streng behuten, beobachten!* Watch! Closely guard!. So, put him with those bums who are stripped down to their longjohns.

"Yeah, boy," he said festively to Švejk, "when you deal with scum, you've got to use a scum bag. If somebody is resisting, then we drag him into solitary and break all his ribs for him. We leave him lying there until he dies. We've got the right to do that. Like we did with that butcher. Remember, Řepa?"

"Yeah, he sure made us work, command warden, sir," Master Sergeant Řepa answered. "What a body! I stomped all over him for five minutes before his ribs started cracking and blood poured out of his snout. And, he still lived another 10 days. Almost a perfect diehard."

"So you can see, you hoodlum, how it goes when somebody resists," explained Command Warden Slavík, "or wants to escape. It is then actually a suicide, which we also punish here by us.

"Another thing, you little shithead sonofabitch, God forbid you get an idea to complain about something when there is an inspection. When the inspectors show up and ask: 'Do you have any complaints?' then you must, you putrid stench, stand at attention, salute and answer: 'I dutifully report that I don't and that I'm totally satisfied.' How will you say it, you disgusting ass? Repeat it!"

"I dutifully report that I don't have any complaints and that I'm totally satisfied."

Švejk repeated it with such a lovable expression on his face that the command warden mistook it to be a sincere and honest attempt to comply with his order.

"OK, then strip down to your longjohns. You're going to the 16."

The warden said this amiably, without calling his victim a hoodlum, a disgusting ass or a putrid stench, as he was accustomed.

In number 16, Švejk met 19 other men stripped to their underwear. Their jailers did this to deter them from running away. Like Švejk's, all their files were also labeled:

"*Streng behuten, beobachten!* Watch! Closely guard!"

If their underwear had been clean, and if there were no bars on the windows, you might get the impression, at first glance, that you were in the locker room of some spa.

Švejk was handed over from the master sergeant to the room unit commander, an unshaven man in an open shirt. He wrote down Švejk's name on a piece of paper hanging on the wall and told him:

"Tomorrow, we've got some great theater going on here. They will escort us to the chapel for a sermon. All of us in longjohns must stand right under the pulpit. Wait until you'll see what fun it will be!"

In all jails and penitentiaries, in-house chapels enjoy great popularity. This garrison prison was no exception. It was not that the mandatory visit to the prison chapel would bring the visitors closer to the Almighty. Or that the prisoners would learn more about morality. There can't even be any talk of such silliness. The service and the sermon were merely a nice break from the boredom.

Though the inmates were not interested in getting closer to God, they did have hope of finding a cigarette or cigar butt in the corridors, or maybe somewhere on the way across the yard, laying hopelessly in a spittoon, or just somewhere in the dust. That little stinking object was considered far superior to any thought of God or the salvation of the soul.

Indeed, the sermon did prove to be great entertainment and fun. And why not? After all, the Field Chaplain, Otto Katz, was a delightful man. His sermons were unusual. They were riveting, funny, and refreshing, in stark contrast to the boredom of the garrison prison.

To strengthen the devastated prisoners and ravaged men, he knew how to chatter beautifully about the endless mercy of God. He also knew how to deliver a beautiful tongue-lashing from both the pulpit and the altar. He could scream out his *"Ite missa est,* the Mass is ended," most wonderfully.

He would perform the whole divine service in an original manner, endlessly mixing-up the whole sequence of the Holy Mass. When he was really drunk, he could make-up absolutely original prayers and invent an entirely new Holy Mass, his own rite, something that the world had never seen before.

What fun it was when he slipped and fell with the chalice, or with the exalted sacrament, or with the holy book. Chaplain Katz would loudly accuse the penal company's altar boy of purposefully tripping him. Then, right in front of the very exalted sacrament, he would stop everything and have the unlucky server slammed into manacles and put into solitary.

Even so, the punished man was joyful and proud to have been part of the fun in the convicts' chapel. After all, he had played a great role in the *schtik* and had acquitted himself with dignity.

Field Chaplain Otto Katz, the most perfect of military chaplains, was a Jew. That, by the way, was not at all odd. Archbishop Kohn of Olomouc was also a Jew, and a friend of the great Christian poet, Machar, to boot.

However, Field Chaplain Otto Katz had an even more checkered past than Archbishop Kohn. He studied at the business academy and served in the army as a one-year volunteer. He was so

85

well versed in the laws of bills-of-exchange, and in using these money drafts, that in one year he was able to force the firm of Katz & Co. into bankruptcy. This firm's collapse was famous. And, it was accomplished so well, that his father, old man Katz, left for North America. He had settled with his creditors without the knowledge of either his son, or of his partner, who left for Argentina.

So, the firm of Katz & Co. was unselfishly partitioned and moved to America, both North and South. Otto Katz then found himself in the situation of a man who had absolutely nothing to inherit, who didn't know where he might lay his head, and who must soon go on active duty in the military.

It was at this fateful moment that one-year volunteer, Otto Katz, had a brilliant idea. He made one final trade. He had himself baptized. He turned to Christ, so that He would help him to be successful. He turned to Him with absolute trust. He had made a deal between himself and the Son of God.

They baptized him ceremoniously at the Emmaus Monastery in Prague. Father Alban,[10] himself, dunked Katz in the baptismal font. It was a gorgeous show. A religious major from Otto's regiment was also present, plus an old maid from the institute of the ladies-of-the-nobility of Hradčany. A bulldog-faced representative of the consistory stood up as his godfather.

He scored well on his test to become an officer, so the new Christian, Otto Katz, decided to stay in the military. At first, it seemed to go well. He even signed up to study courses given at command headquarters.

But one day he got real drunk, went to a monastery, turned in his saber, and put on a priest's frock. An archbishop in Hradčany got him into a seminary.

Before his ordination, he got so drunk at a very well known house with female help that he sang in a minor key. This very solid house was located in the alley behind the Vejvodovic pub. He had launched himself right out of a vortex of passionate lust and entertainment straight into his ordination.

---

[10] Alban Schachleitner was a Benedictine monk who later was alleged to have emigrated to Germany and become a Nazi.

After he was ordained, he sought refuge in the protection of his regiment as field chaplain. He then bought a horse so that he could ride through Prague and partake merrily in all the drinking bouts organized by his fellow officers.

Soon, in the hallway of the house where he went to live, the curses of unsatisfied creditors could often be heard ringing out. He constantly brought girls in from the street or would send his military servant to fetch them. He liked to play the card game ferbl very much, and some made suppositions and assumptions that he played with a stacked deck. But, no one ever proved that he had hidden aces in the wide sleeve of his military cassock. In the officers' circles, they called him "Holy Father."

Otto Katz never prepared for his sermons. In this, he differed greatly from his predecessor, a man who suffered from a fixation that troops locked in a garrison prison could be improved from the pulpit. This previous, honorable field chaplain would roll his eyes piously and tell the imprisoned men that the saving of harlots was an absolute necessity.

He also championed reform of the care for unwed mothers. He talked about the problems of bringing up children born out of wedlock. His sermons were of an abstract nature and had no link at all with present reality. They were very boring.

In contrast, Field Chaplain Otto Katz preached sermons which everyone looked forward to.

It was a festive moment when they escorted the inmates of Unit 16 into the chapel. There they stood, 20 angels in white longjohns under the pulpit. Lady luck had given a fleeting smile to some of them, and those lucky souls happily chewed the cigar butts they had found on the way. After all, they had no pockets in which to hide them. The rest of the garrison prison's inmates amused themselves by gawking at the 20 in longjohns, milling about under the pulpit.

The Field Chaplain soon strode into the chapel. Clanking his spurs, Otto Katz climbed the stairs, turned to his flock and yelled:

"Habacht! Attention! Let us pray. All must repeat after me. And you in the back! You hoodlum! Don't blow your nose in the palm of your hand. You are in the temple of the Lord. I can have you locked up for that.

"Could it be, you bums, that you have forgotten your 'Our Father'? No? Then, let's try it................

(Silence.)

"Well, I knew you couldn't do it for me. No, not the 'Our Father'... Maybe two portions of meat and a bean salad...Stuff yourselves....Lay down on your bunks, pick your noses and never think of the Lord God! Am I not right?"

He looked straight down from the pulpit and saw that the 20 white angels in longjohns were tremendously entertained, as was everyone else. In fact, the inmates in the back were playing the bare-butt spanking game called "meat."

"This is all very good," Švejk whispered to the inmate next to him. This prisoner was in jail under the suspicion that, for three crowns, he had cut all the fingers off his friend's hand with an ax, just so his friend could avoid military service.

"The best is yet to come," Švejk's fellow inmate answered. "Today, he is again properly blasted and will soon be preaching about the thorny path of sin."

The Field Chaplain was indeed in an excellent disposition. He was unaware of the danger, but kept teetering on the edge of the pulpit. He could have easily lost his balance and fallen off.

"Sing something boys!" he yelled down. "Or, do you want me to teach you a new song?....all right, then sing along with me!

Of all the most beloved,
I have my love.
I don't go after her alone,
There are many more who also pursue her.
Of lovers, she has thousands,
She is the Virgin Mary----

"You knaves! You will never learn it," Katz said, interrupting his song.

"I am for having you all mowed down by guns. Do you understand me well?! I am declaring it from this divine spot, you scoundrels. God is not afraid of you. He will fix it so you will become dimwits from it all because you hesitate to turn to Christ. You would rather walk down the thorny path of sin!"

"Ah, he's really into it. He's properly tanked," said the inmate next to Švejk.

The Field Chaplain continued:

"The thorny path of sin is, you stupid boys, the path where we must do battle against vices. You are prodigal sons who would rather lay around the solitary than return to the Father. Train your sight farther and higher and into the lofty heavens. You'll be victorious and peace will make a home in your soul, you lousy street punks.

"Now I'm begging -- no, insisting -- that whoever it is in the back, that's snoring and neighing, must stop. He is not a horse, and he is not in a stable. He is in the temple of the Lord. I bring that to your attention, you little darlings of mine.

"So where did I stop? *Ja, über den Seelenfrieden, sehr gut.* Yes, about the peace in the soul. Very good. Remember, you depraved animal, that you are human, and that you have to look through the dark cloud and into distant space. Know that everything is here for a time, but that God is for all the ages.

"*Sehr gut, nicht, wahr, meine, Herren?* Very well, is it not true, my gentlemen? I should be praying for you day and night, so that the merciful God, you stupid jerks, would pour His Soul into your cold hearts. And, with his Holy Grace, He would wash away your sins. So that you would be His forever, so He would love you rascals, always.

"But, you are mistaken! I will not usher you into that paradise."

The Field Chaplain burped.

"I won't," he repeated stubbornly, "I won't do anything for you. It won't even occur to me, because you are all incorrigible scoundrels. You won't be guided in your ways by the goodness of the Lord. The breath of love won't waft through you, because it won't even occur to the beloved Lord God to deal with such bandits. Do you hear me down there? You in those longjohns?"

The 20 in longjohns looked up and said as one:

"We dutifully report that we hear you!"

"It's not enough just to hear," the Field Chaplain said, resuming his sermon. "In the dark cloud of life, a divine smile won't take away your sorrow, you numskulls, because the goodness of God has its limits.

"And, you mule there in the back! Don't look like you're choking with laughter, or I'll have you locked up until you turn black. And, you down there! Don't think that you're in a pub. God is merciful to the utmost, but only for proper people. Not for some outcasts who are the product of human society which is not managed by God's laws. Or even by the *dienstreglamá,* service regulations.

"That's what I wanted to tell you. You don't know how to pray and you think coming to the chapel is some kind of joke, that this is some theatrical production or moving picture show. I'll chase these thoughts right out of your head. Don't think that I'm here to entertain you or to add some joy to your life.

"I'll assign you all to seats in solitary. That's what I'll do with you, you hoodlums! I waste my time with you and I see that all my efforts are in vain. Even if the Field Marshall or the Archbishop himself was here, you wouldn't repent. You wouldn't turn to God. Still, one day you will remember me and know that I intended to do good by you."

In the midst of the 20 longjohns, loud sobbing erupted. Švejk had burst into tears.

Otto Katz looked down and there stood Švejk, wiping his eyes with his fist. All around him could be seen signs of joyous approval.

Pointing to Švejk, the Field Chaplain continued:

"Everyone should use this man as an example. What is he doing? Weeping. Don't weep. I'm telling you, don't weep. You want to change for the better? That you will not accomplish so easily, boy. Now, you're weeping. But, when you return to your cage, you'll be just the same kind of hoodlum as you were before. You must dwell on the ceaseless grace and mercy of God. You must take great care of your sinning soul in order to find the right path in this world, and then walk down it.

"Today, we see that one man of ours has broken down into tears and wants to repent. And, what are the rest of you doing? Nothing at all. That one over there is chewing something, as if his parents were ruminants: cows, maybe. And, over there, they're searching, in the temple of God, for lice in their shirts! Can't you scratch yourselves at home?! Do you have to leave it to do during our very divine services? And you, Command Warden, sir! Don't you even notice these things?

"After all, you're all supposed to be soldiers, not some numskull civilians. You are supposed to behave as soldiers should, even if you are in a church. Get going, goddamit! Search for God and leave your search for lice at home. That's all I have to say to you, you street punks. I'm asking you to behave properly during the Mass. Not like last time, when you were trading government issue· linen for bread in the back, and feeding on it during the elevation of the host."

The Field Chaplain abruptly descended from the pulpit and walked into the sacristy. The command warden hurried after him. A short time later, the command warden reemerged, turned directly to Švejk, pulled him out of the group of 20 in longjohns, and escorted him into the sacristy.

The Field Chaplain was sitting comfortably on a table, rolling a cigarette for himself. When Švejk entered, the Field Chaplain said:

"So here you are. I have already thought everything over. And I think I can see right through you. Do you understand me, man? This is the first time anybody actually ever broke into tears in a church on me."

He jumped off the table and started jerking Švejk by the shoulder. He screamed at him from under a big, gloomy portrait of František Sáleský.[11]

"Admit it, hoodlum! You were bawling like that just for fun!"

František Sáleský gazed quizzically at Švejk from one wall. On the other wall, a dumbfounded martyr stared at Švejk from another picture. Some unknown Roman mercenaries were cutting his butt with a saw. The face of the martyr showed no apparent suffering, or joy, or martyr's glow. He looked only dumbfounded, as if he wanted to ask:

How have I gotten myself into this? What is this, gentlemen? What are you doing to me?

Švejk deliberated carefully and decided to bet everything on one card:

"I dutifully report, Field Chaplain, sir, that I am confessing to God Almighty, and to you, reverend father, who stands in God's place, that I bawled out in the chapel just for fun. I saw that your

---

[11] Saint Francis De Sales.

91

sermon lacked only a reformed sinner and that you looked for one in vain all during your sermon. I really wanted to make you happy. I didn't want you to think that righteous people could not be found anymore. And, for myself, well, I just wanted to have some fun, to lighten my misery."

The Field Chaplain looked quizzically into Švejk's simpleminded face. A ray of sun frolicked on the gloomy picture of František Sáleský and even added a warm glow to the picture of the dumbfounded martyr on the opposite wall.

"I'm beginning to like you," the Field Chaplain said, taking a seat again on the table. "Which regiment do you belong to?"

He began to hiccup.

"I dutifully report, Field Chaplain, sir, that I both belong to, and do not belong to, the 91st Regiment. I don't really know where it is that I actually belong."

"Why is it actually you are sitting here doing time?" asked the Field Chaplain, unable to stop his hiccups.

From the chapel could be heard the sounds of a harmonium, being used in place of an organ. Wailing on it was a musician, a teacher locked up for desertion. He was playing the most nostalgic of church melodies. The Field Chaplain's hiccups began to fuse with the wailing of the harmonium, creating an entirely new Doric scale.

"I dutifully report Field Chaplain, sir, that I really don't know why I'm sitting here. And, I'm not complaining that I'm sitting here. I just have bad luck. I always mean to do everything right, but, in the end, it all turns on me for the worse. Just like that martyr in the picture over there."

The Field Chaplain looked at the picture, smiled, and said:

"I really like you. I'll have to ask the judge advocate about you. But, for now, this conversation is over. God, if I can only get through this Holy Mass and get it off my back!

"Kehrt euch! Abtreten! About face! Fall out!"

When Švejk returned to the group of longjohns under the pulpit, he was peppered with questions about what the Field Chaplain wanted to see him about in the sacristy. He answered them very succinctly:

"He's blasted!"

The Field Chaplain's latest version of the Holy Mass resumed. It was being observed by all with great attention and with open sympathy. Under the pulpit, one prisoner bet another that the Field Chaplain would drop the monstrance from his hand. He bet his whole portion of bread against two slaps in the face, and he won.

It was not the mysticism of the faithful or the religiosity of true Catholics that filled the souls of those watching the rituals of the Field Chaplain Katz. It was more like being in a theater and not knowing the *schtik*. The plot is becoming entangled and we are eagerly waiting to see how it will evolve.

The inmates immersed themselves in the novel images being created for them with great selflessness by the Field Chaplain at the altar. Deep in concentration, they were feasting esthetically on the sight of Otto Katz roaming about the altar with his chasuble, a colorful outer vestment he put on inside out. They watched everything that was taking place at the altar with fervent attention and a high level of excitement.

The red-haired altar boy was now a petty thief operating in the 28th Regiment. He had deserted the Church long ago, but was honestly trying to retrieve the whole process, technique and text of the Holy Mass, from his memory. He was serving concurrently as both an altar boy and a prompter to the Field Chaplain.

Otto Katz was transposing whole sentences with total frivolity. And, instead of reading just the daily Mass, the Field Chaplain had droned all the way to the Advent morning service songs in the priest's book. These he started singing, much to the delight of all in his audience. He had neither a melodic voice, nor a musical ear. So, the squealing and shrieking that reverberated under the vaulting of the chapel, soon began to sound like noises from a pig sty.

"He sure is drunk today," said some of those in front of the altar with full satisfaction and joy. "He's tied one on. Tied one on big. He must've gotten smashed with some broads again, for sure."

At least three times, they heard the Field Chaplain howl from the altar:

"Ite missa est! The Mass is over!"

It sounded like the war cry of the Red Indians. Entire windows were shaking in their frames.

The Field Chaplain looked one more time into the chalice, in case there might be a drop of wine left, gestured as if annoyed, then turned to his listeners:

"All right already, you hoodlums. You can go home now. It's over. And don't think I didn't notice that you're not showing the right piety. You street punks, you're in the presence of the face of the holiest sacrament of the altar. Though you are face-to-face with the Highest God, you're not ashamed to laugh out loud, cough, clear your throats, or shuffle your feet. Even in my presence.

"Me, who represents the Virgin Mary, Christ the Lord, and God the Father, you jerks. If this happens again, I'll nail you all proper. You'll know that there isn't only one hell, the one I preached to you about last time, but that there is also a hell on earth. And you might be able to save yourselves from that first one, but not from the second one. Not from me. *Abtreten!* Fall out!"

The Field Chaplain, who knew how to both explain and practice the damned old thing, so beautifully, did indeed visit with the prisoners. Then, he went into the sacristy, changed clothes and had them pour the church wine from a demijohn into a jug, which he drank right up.

Finally, with the help of the red-haired altar boy, he mounted the cavalry horse he had tied up in the yard, and prepared to leave. But then, he remembered Švejk, dismounted, and went into the office to see Lieutenant Bernis, the military judge advocate.

Judge Advocate Bernis was a social man. He liked company, was a graceful and charming dancer, and a moral degenerate. He was awfully bored at the garrison prison. He wrote German verses for the memorial albums that girls kept in those days, just to have a ready supply on hand at all times.

He was the most important component in the whole machinery of the military court. He had such a horrible quantity of unfinished cases and confused files, that he commanded the respect of the Chief Military Court in Hradčany, the castle district.

He would constantly lose the prosecution's materials, so he was forced to invent new ones. He would switch names, lose the threads of indictments and spin new ones, using whatever notions might occur to him.

He judged deserters for theft and thieves for desertion. He could jumble up even political trials, which he could attract from thin air.

He conducted a wide assortment of hocus-pocus sessions to convict men of crimes they would never commit even in their dreams. He invented insults against His Majesty and would always attribute the made-up, incriminating statements to someone whose indictment or denunciation had been lost in the continuous chaos of his official files and memoranda.

"Greetings," Otto Katz said, extending his hand to the judge advocate. "How is it going?"

"Not too well," Bernis answered. "They have mixed up my material so much that even a demon couldn't find his way through it. Yesterday, I sent material upstairs that had already been processed, regarding a man accused of mutiny. They returned it, saying that the case against him was not mutiny, but for the theft of a can of food. And, I had even put a different number on it. But, how they ever got their hands on it, let God be the judge," the military judge spat.

"Do you still go out and play cards?" asked the Field Chaplain.

"I've lost everything playing cards. The last time I played it was a game of 'makao.' I played with a bald colonel and ended up stuffing all my money down his gullet. But, enough about that. I've got a line on a young gal. What do think, 'holy father?'"

"I need a yeoman," said the Field Chaplain.

"The last one I had was a really old accountant without academic education, and a first-class beast. He whined constantly and prayed for God to protect him. So, I sent him to a marching battalion headed for the front. The word is that batty was completely shredded. Then, they sent me some bum who wouldn't do anything but sit in a pub all day and drink on my account. He was bearable, but his feet sweat. So, I sent him with a marching battalion, as well.

"However, today, during the sermon, I found a man. He broke out in tears on me. Just for the fun of it! I need a man like that. His name is Švejk and he's sitting here in the 16. I would like to know why they locked him up, and whether somehow I could take him out of here."

The judge advocate looked through his drawers for a file on Švejk, but, as usual, he couldn't find anything.

"Captain Linhart's gotta have it," he said after a long search. "Only demons know where all the files disappear to when they're here with me. Apparently, I sent them to Linhart. I'll call over there immediately.

". . . Hello, This is Lieutenant Judge Advocate Bernis, captain, sir. I beg to ask whether you might have files over there on some guy named Švejk?

"Švejk's files have gotta be here with me? I'm surprised. I took them from you? I'm really surprised . . . He's in the 16. I know, captain, sir, that I have the 16. But, I thought the files on Švejk were laying around over there by you somewhere . . . You want me to apologize and stop speaking to you in such a way? You say there's nothing laying around over there? . . .Hello? . . . Hello? . . ."

Judge Advocate Bernis sat down at his desk and angrily decried the disorderly way that investigations were being conducted.

Animosity had long reigned between Bernis and Captain Linhart. Should a file belonging to Linhart get into the hands of Bernis, Bernis would file it so that nobody could make any sense of it. Linhart would do the same with files belonging to Bernis. They were both very systematic. One was constantly losing the other's addenda.*[12]

(Švejk's files were eventually found in the archives of the Military Court, but only after the regime changed. This was noted on his file: "He intended to throw off his hypocritical mask and come out in public against the person of our monarch and against our state." Švejk's files were stuck inside the files of one Josef Koudela. On the jacket was a little cross. Written under it was the word, "Resolved," and the date.)

"So Švejk has disappeared on me," Judge Advocate Bernis noted. "I'll have him called in. If he doesn't confess to anything, I'll let him go and have him escorted to you. You can then talk it over and make a deal with his regiment."

After the Field Chaplain left, the judge advocate sent for Švejk. When Švejk arrived, Bernis left him standing in the doorway while he dealt with an important telegram from police headquarters. The

---

[12] (Author Jaroslav Hašek's footnote:)* Thirty percent of the people who were sitting and doing time in the garrison prison, sat there throughout the whole war without going to interrogation once.

file he had requested, prosecution file number 7267, regarding an infantryman named Maixner, had already been transferred to office number 1, and signed for by Captain Linhart.

While he was waiting, Švejk looked over the judge advocate's office. It did not create a very favorable impression, especially the photographs that adorned its walls. They were pictures of various actions taken by the army in Galicia and Serbia.

They were carefully composed photographs of burnt-out cottages, and of trees with branches straining from the weight of the human bodies hanging from them. Especially cute was a photograph from Serbia featuring an entire family who had been hanged: a small boy, a mother, a father. In the picture, two soldiers with bayonets stood guarding the tree with this entire family hanging in it. In the foreground stood an officer posturing like a victor, smoking a cigarette. In the background, a field kitchen could be seen, hard at work.

"So, how is it with you, Švejk?" the Judge Advocate asked as he put away the telegram. "What is it that you have done? Would you like to confess now, or wait until an indictment against you is composed?

"It can't keep going on like this forever. Don't mistake this for a court where you'd be questioned by some goofy civilians. These are military courts, *k.u.k, Militargericht.* Imperial and Royal, Military Courts. Your only hope of deliverance from a stiff and just punishment is if you confess."

Judge Advocate Bernis had a "special" method he employed when he lost the prosecution material to be used against the accused. As you will see, there was nothing really special about it. Therefore, we must not be amazed that the sum of the results of his investigations and interrogations equaled, any way you figure it, precisely zero.

In these cases, Bernis felt he could rely on his superior and "special" insight. Without having any material against the accused, or knowing what he was charging him with, or why he was doing time in the garrison prison, Bernis merely observed the behavior and the physiognomy of the man brought in for interrogation, and figured out the probable reason they had locked this human being up in the first place.

His insight and his knowledge of people was so great that he once charged a Gypsy (who worked for the storekeeper of a regiment's warehouse) with political crimes. The Gypsy was in jail for stealing several dozen articles of clothing. The Judge Advocate accused him of discussing, in a pub somewhere, the establishment of a new nation-state in the lands of the Czech Crown and Slovakia, with a Slavic king at the helm.

"We have documents," he told the unfortunate Gypsy. "There is nothing left for you but to confess. Tell us when you said it, in which pub you made those statements, and which regiment the soldiers were from who were listening to you."

So, the unlucky Gypsy made up a date, named a pub, and even which regiment was his alleged audience. As he was being escorted away from this bizarre interrogation, the Gypsy bolted and ran away from the garrison prison altogether.

Švejk stood silently before the Judge Advocate and was as mute and unresponsive as a grave.

"So, you don't want to admit to anything?" Bernis probed. "You don't want to tell me why you are here? Why they have locked you up? You could tell me at least, before I'm forced to tell you myself. It would be better for you because it would make the investigation easier, and that mitigates the punishment. In that way, it is the same here as it is in the civilian courts."

"I dutifully report," Švejk's good-natured voice proclaimed, "that I'm here in the garrison prison because I am a foundling."

"How do you mean that?"

"I dutifully report that I can explain it in a tremendously simple manner. There was a coal peddler living on our street who had an absolutely innocent, little, two-year-old boy. Somehow, the boy got all the way from our Vinohrady neighborhood to Libeň, on foot. There a patrolman found him sitting on a sidewalk. He brought the little boy to the police station, and they locked him up, a two-year-old child.

"The little boy was absolutely innocent, and yet he was locked up. If he had known how to speak, and someone were to ask him why he was locked up there, he wouldn't know what to say. With me it is something similar. I am also a foundling."

The wary gaze of the Judge Advocate scanned Švejk's figure and face and then shattered itself against them. Such carefree innocence radiated from the entire being standing in front of Bernis, that he began pacing excitedly around his office. If Švejk had not been promised to the Field Chaplain, only demons would now be able to tell you how Švejk might have ended up. Finally, however, the Judge Advocate stopped pacing and leaned on his desk. Švejk nonchalantly gazed off into the distance.

"Listen up!" Bernis said. "If you cross my path one more time, you'll never forget it. Take him away!"

While they were escorting Švejk back to the 16, Bernis was issuing orders to Command Warden Slavík.

"Until further notice, Švejk is being put at the disposal of Field Chaplain Katz. Prepare his release papers and have two men escort Švejk to the Field Chaplain."

"Should we put him in chains for the trip, Lieutenant, sir?" Slavík asked.

The Judge Advocate hit the desk with his fist:

"You are such a dumb ox! I told you clearly to prepare *release* papers!"

And all that had accumulated throughout this day in the soul of the Judge Advocate, including his dealings with Captain Linhart and Švejk, gushed forth like a wild river, almost drowning the command warden. Bernis finished with these words:

"Now! Do you completely understand why you are indeed the dumbest, vilest, crowned ox of all time?!"

Obviously, this was the sort of title that should be reserved for kings and emperors. But, somehow, it wasn't enough for the uncrowned head of the simple Command Warden. After leaving the Judge Advocate's office, he felt it necessary to kick a prisoner, who was cleaning the corridor, until he curled up into a tight ball.

The command warden then decided that Švejk should spend at least one more night in the garrison prison, so he would have a chance to enjoy still more of what it had to offer.

A night spent at a garrison prison always belongs among the most charming of memories.

Next to the 16 was *ajnclík*: solitary, a gloomy hole. The resounding howl of some poor, locked-up soldier could be heard coming from the hole both day and night, usually because Master Sergeant Řepa had been ordered by Command Warden Slavík to break the prisoner's ribs for some breech of discipline.

When the howling stopped, all that could be heard in the 16 was the cracking of the lice that ended up between the fingers of the soldiers during an inspection.

In an opening on the wall above the door, a kerosene lamp equipped with a protective grille released both a dim light and sooty smoke. The stench of the kerosene blended with the natural vapors of unwashed human bodies. Then there was the bucket of human waste, which hurled another wave of foul odors out into the 16 each time its crusty surface was pushed apart after being used.

Bad nutrition made the process of digesting difficult for everyone at the garrison prison. The majority suffered from the winds they themselves released into the nocturnal silence, and each would answer the other's signals with one of his own, accompanied by various jokes.

The measured pace of patrols could be heard in the corridor and, once in a while, a portal in the door would swing open and a guard would peer at the prisoners through a peep hole.

From the middle bunk Švejk heard this discreet narration:

"I used to be in the number 12. There they put, like, the lighter cases. But that was before I wanted to escape and they put me in here with you.

"Anyway, let me tell you about this man they brought in from somewhere in the country. This charming man got two weeks for letting some soldiers sleep over by his house. First, they thought it was part of some conspiracy, but then the explanation came down that he was just doing it for the money. He was supposed to be locked up with even lighter ones, but because it was all filled up there, they put him in with us.

"You wouldn't believe all the stuff he brought in with him and all that they sent him from home. Somehow, he was allowed to buy his own eats and keep lots of extras with him. He was even allowed to smoke! Whatever a man could want, he kept in two backpacks. He had two hams, giant loaves of bread, eggs, butter, cigarettes and other tobacco.

"And this guy thought he must devour this stuff all by himself. We started begging him to share. But he didn't get the hint that he should share with us, as the others always did when they got something extra. 'No' was all that stingy man could say. He said that the prison cabbage, broccoli and rotten potatoes would ruin his stomach if he had to eat them for the two weeks he was going to be locked up.

"He said he would give us his whole mess portion and his commissary rations. He said he didn't care about them and would let us divide it among ourselves, or take turns, or whatever.

"And, let me tell you, he was such a refined man that he didn't want to sit on the bucket. He waited until we had yard exercise the next day, so he could use the outhouse. He was so spoiled that he had even brought in toilet paper.

"We told him we would piss on that mess portion of his. The man was gobbling down ham, spreading butter on his bread, peeling eggs for himself. In short, he was living it up. We suffered a day, then two, then three. He smoked his cigarettes and wouldn't even give anyone a drag. We must not smoke, he said, because if the guard caught him giving us so much as a drag, they'd lock him in solitary.

"As I said, we suffered for three days. On the night of the fourth day, we acted. When the man woke up in the morning.....Oh, I forgot to tell you: In the morning, and at noon, and in the evening, before he would start stuffing himself, he would always pray. He would pray for a long time.

"So, that particular morning, after he had prayed, he starts looking for his backpacks under the plank bunk. Well, the backpacks were there, but they were shriveled up like dried prunes.

"He started screaming that he had been robbed, that only the toilet paper was left for him. He thought it through again for about five minutes. He decided that we must be playing a hoax on him, that we just hid his stuff here and there. He tells himself sort of joyfully: 'I know that you're little cheats. I know that you'll give it back to me. But, boys, you really got me good!'

"One of our guys was from the Liběn neighborhood. He says: 'You know what? Why don't you just cover yourself with a blanket and count to 10? And then look into that backpack of yours.' The stingy guy covered himself like an obedient boy and began counting: 'One, two, three . . .' The guy from Liběn stops him: 'You must not count so fast. You must go very slowly.'

101

"So, under the blanket, he counts slowly, with pauses: 'One . . . Two . . . Three . . .' When he finished counting to 10, he crawled out of the bunk and inspected his backpacks. 'Jesusmaria, people!" he started screaming. 'They're as empty as they were before.' And, all the while, he has this stupid grimace on his face. We could have ripped ourselves open laughing.

"But the guy from Libeň says: 'Try it one more time.' And would you believe that he was so stupid from it all, that he tried it one more time? When he saw, again, that there was nothing in there, except his toilet paper, he started beating on the door and screaming: 'They've robbed me! They've robbed me! Help! Open up! For christ-the-lord, open up!'

"The guards flew in there right away. Then they called the command warden and Master Sergeant Řepa. To a man, we all said the guy had just gone nuts. We told them that, yesterday, he had been eating long into the night and must have devoured it all.

"He started weeping and kept saying: 'There have to be some little crumbs somewhere.' So, they searched for crumbs. But, they didn't find any. We were too smart for that. What we couldn't down ourselves, we sent on a string up to the second floor. They couldn't prove anything against us. Although that idiot kept whining: 'But the crumbs must be somewhere.'

"He didn't eat anything all that day. And, he was on the lookout to see whether anybody was eating something, or smoking. The next day, at lunchtime, he still didn't touch the mess. But, by the evening meal, the rotten potatoes, broccoli and cabbage were going down good. Except, he wasn't praying anymore, like he used to, before he would attack those ham and eggs. Then, somehow, one of us got some cheap smokes from the outside. That's when he first started to talk to us, asking us to give him a drag. We gave him nothing."

"I was afraid that you would say that you did give him a drag," remarked Švejk.

"You would have spoiled the whole tale. Such magnanimity is to be found only in novels. But, in a garrison prison, under such circumstances, that would have been stupid bullshit."

"You didn't give him a beating under the blanket?" a voice piped up.

"We forgot that."

A quiet debate began about whether the man should have gotten the blanket in addition to all the rest, or not. The majority was for it.

The talk slowly gave way to silence. They were falling asleep. They scratched their armpits, chests and bellies, wherever in their underwear the lice liked to hang on the best. As they fell asleep, they pulled their lice-infested blankets over their heads, so that the light from the kerosene lamp wouldn't disturb them.....

At eight in the morning, Švejk was told he was going to the office. His fellow inmates instructed him:

"By the office door, on the left side, there is a spittoon. They often throw butts in there. Then, on the second floor, you go past another one. They wait until nine to sweep the corridors, so there should be something there, too."

But Švejk was destined to dash their hopes. He returned no more to the 16. The 19 remaining in longjohns were left to speculate and guess about his fate.

Some freckled soldier from the Land Defense, with a wild imagination, spread the story that Švejk had taken a shot at his captain and that they were taking him to the Motol training ground to be executed that very day.

10

ŠVEJK AS MILITARY SERVANT TO THE FIELD CHAPLAIN

I

Once again, Švejk's odyssey began under the honorable escort of two soldiers with bayonets. They were under orders to transport him to Field Chaplain Otto Katz.

His escorts were men who complemented one another. One was a tall beanstalk, the other, short and fat. The beanstalk had a gimpy right leg, the fat one limped with his left. Both were serving in the rear because, at one time, they were both totally exempt from military service.

They walked earnestly along the sidewalk, occasionally stealing sidelong glances at Švejk, who marched smartly down the center of the pavement and saluted just about everyone.

His civilian clothes had been lost by the garrison prison. They even had lost the military cap he'd had Mrs. Müller buy after he was drafted. So, before they released him, they gave him an old military uniform that had previously belonged to someone with a huge belly, and who was at least a head taller than Švejk.

Three more Švejks could have fit into the pants with him. The endless folds of cloth, which reached all the way up to his chest, were causing him to be spontaneously admired by many onlookers. The huge pants hung from his frame like the costume of some circus clown.

A huge, greasy, dirty military blouse, with patches on the elbows, also dangled from Švejk, like a coat hanging from a scare crow. The military cap they had given him in exchange for his own, slid down over his ears.

Švejk answered the smiles of onlookers with his own soft smile and with the warmth and tenderness of his good eyes.

So, the trio set off for the Karlín neighborhood and the apartment of the Field Chaplain, Otto Katz.

The short, fat one was the first to speak to Švejk. They just were in *Malá strana*, the Small Side quarter, way down under the arcades.

"Where are you from?"

"From Prague."

"Aren't you gonna try and escape from us?"

It is a very peculiar phenomenon that short fat ones are mostly good-natured optimists, and that, on the other hand, extruded beanstalks are usually skeptics.

"If he could, he'd run away," the beanstalk remarked, jumping into the conversation. "Now, why would he run?" asked the short fatso. "He's free one way or the other. He's out of the garrison prison. It's all here in the package."

"So, what's in this package for the Field Chaplain?" asked the beanstalk.

"That I don't know."

"There, you see. You don't know, but you talk."

They walked across the Karlův bridge with absolute propriety. On Karlova Street, the short fat one again spoke to Švejk:

"Do you know why we're escorting you to the Field Chaplain?"

"To confession," Švejk said nonchalantly. "Tomorrow they're going to hang me. It's always done like that. It's called comforting the condemned soul."

"And why are they going to, ehm, you know...?" the beanstalk asked carefully, while the fat one cast a consoling look at Švejk.

They both were tradesmen from the country, fathers of families.

"I don't know," answered Švejk, smiling good naturedly. "It's apparently my fate."

"Perhaps you were born on an unlucky planet," the short one commented with the sympathetic knowledge of an expert. "They hanged someone by us, in the village of Jasenná, near Josefov, back during the Prussian war. They came for him, didn't tell him anything, took him to Josefov, and just hanged him."

"In my opinion," the skeptical beanstalk said, "they don't hang a man for nothing. There always must be some cause for it, so that it can be justified."

"When we are not in a war," remarked Švejk, "then hanging must be justified. But in wartime, one man isn't considered that important. Will he fall on the front, or be hanged at home? Will he die on his feet, or by swinging off the back of a cart?"

"Listen, are you some kind of a political case?" asked the beanstalk. From the cadence of his speech, it was discernible that he was beginning to sympathize with Švejk.

"I'm much too political," smiled Švejk.

"Are you a National Socialist?"

Now, the little fat one began to be cautious.

"What do we care?" he interrupted. "There are lots of people around here, and they're watching us. If we could at least go into a passageway somewhere and take these prongs off our rifles, we wouldn't be so conspicuous.

"You aren't going to run away on us, are you? We would be in nasty trouble if you did. Wouldn't we, Toníku?" he asked, turning to the beanstalk, who looked at Švejk and remarked quietly:

"We can take our bayonets off. He's our kind, after all."

The beanstalk had ceased to be a skeptic. His soul filled with sympathy toward Švejk. They searched for a suitable passageway and removed their bayonets. The short one allowed Švejk to walk next to him, and asked:

"You'd like to have a smoke, right? I wonder if . . ."

The short one didn't finish his sentence, because he wanted to say: "I wonder if they will give you a smoke before they hang you." But, he felt saying it might be tactless.

They all had a smoke. The two escorts began telling Švejk about their families in the Králův Hradec region: about their wives, their children, about their fields, about their cow.

"I'm really thirsty," said Švejk.

The beanstalk and the short one looked at each other.

"We would stop someplace for one, too," said the short one, feeling the beanstalk would agree. "But, we've got to go somewhere we wouldn't be conspicuous."

"Let's go to the Kuklík," Švejk suggested enticingly. "You can hide your rifles in the kitchen. Serabona, the pubkeeper, is a Sokol, a real Czech patriot. You don't have to be afraid of him. They have violin and accordion music, and street girls go in there, too. There is all sorts of good company going to the Kuklík that is forbidden to go in proper places like The Representative."

The beanstalk and the short one looked at each other one more time. Then, the beanstalk said:

"All right, we'll go there. It's a long way to Karlín."

Švejk told them a variety of jokes along the way, so they were in a pleasant mood when they entered the Kuklík. They did as Švejk had advised and hid their rifles in the kitchen. As they entered the pub, the violin and accordion filled the room with the sounds of a popular song:

> "At Pankrác, on that little hill, there stands a nice
> double row of trees..."

Some seductress was sitting on the lap of a burned-out young man with a crisp part in his smoothly-combed hair. She sang in a raspy voice:

> "I had a girl all talked up,
> but someone else is romancing her . . ."

Three more young ladies sat on the other side of the pool table, under a mirror, and shouted at a railway conductor:

"Young man! Treat us to some vermouth!"

Over by the band, two guys were arguing about whether Mares was picked up by the patrol the day before. One said he saw it with his own eyes, while the other insisted that she went to Valeš' Hotel with some soldier to sleep with him.

A drunken sardine vendor was sleeping at one of the tables. Every once in a while, he'd wake up, bang on the table with his fist and mumble:

"It won't work."

Then, he'd fall back asleep.

A soldier was sitting with several civilians by the door and discussing the injury he got in Serbia. His hand was bandaged and his pockets were full of cigarettes he'd gotten from the others. He was saying that he couldn't drink any more. But, one of the group, a bald old geezer, kept challenging him:

"Just drink, soldier boy. Who knows if we'll ever meet again? Should I have the band play something for you? Do you like 'A Child Was Orphaned?'"

This was, in fact, the old geezer's favorite tune. Within minutes, the violin and accordion started playing it. Tears came to the old geezer's eyes and he began to sing with a trembling voice:

> "When the babe began to reason,
>   it was asking for its mommy,
>   it was asking for its mommy . . ."

"Keep it to yourself! Go and get stuffed!" yelled the patrons at another table. "Hang it up on a nail! Peel off from here with that orphan!"

Finally, the opposing table trumped the old geezer by singing:

> "Parting, oh sad parting,
>   my heart is altogether broken, broken . . ."

After they had drowned out "The Orphaned Child," they called to the injured soldier:

"Franto! Come and sit with us. Piss on them already. Let them be, over there. And bring those cigarettes with you. What are you gonna do? Entertain those old stuffings?"

Švejk and his escorts watched it all with great interest.

It revived Švejk's memories of how he used to sit at the Kuklík often, before he was drafted. A police commissioner named Drašner used to invade the place for inspections and the prostitutes were afraid of him. To counter their fear, they composed songs poking fun at him.

For instance, one particular day they were all singing this in unison:

"During the reign of Mister Drašner,
There was quite a rumble here.
Tough Mary was oh so drunk,
That Old Drašner she feared not."

Right then, Drašner strode in, followed by his frightful and relentless entourage. It was as if someone had fired a shotgun into a flock of quails. The detectives marshaled everyone into a cluster. Švejk, too, had been snared in the raid. And, it wasn't only his bad luck that got him in trouble. When Commissioner Drašner had demanded Švejk show his identification, he had asked the gendarme:

"Do you have an authorization for this raid from police headquarters?"

Švejk also fondly remembered a poet who used to sit under the mirror. There in the bustle of the Kuklík, he would write his little poems. Then, with singing and the sounds of the accordion in the background, he would read them through to the prostitutes.

Švejk's present escorts, on the other hand, had no such reminiscences. For them, this was all brand new, and they were beginning to enjoy it. The short, fat one was the first to find total satisfaction. That's not surprising because, aside from their general optimism, short fat ones also tend to be Epicurean.

For a while, the beanstalk resisted. But, just as he had lost his skepticism, he began to slowly lose his sense of moderation and prudence. He watched the couples enjoy the stomp dance while he downed five beers.

"I, too, will have a dance," he finally decided.

The short one devoted himself entirely to pleasure seeking. A young lady sat next to him, talking obscenely. And his eyes gleamed playfully with the devil's delight.

Švejk kept drinking. The beanstalk finished dancing and returned to the table with his partner.

The escorts continued to sing and dance and pet their female companions. And in this atmosphere of nicotine, alcohol and love for sale, an old slogan circled inconspicuously:

"After us, let the flood come!"

Sometime past noon, a soldier sat down beside them and offered to give them blood poisoning for a tenner. He said he had a syringe on him and would inject kerosene into their foot or hand*.[13] They would be laid up for at least two months. And, if they kept feeding the wound with saliva, then, perhaps, half a year later, they would be released from the military for good.

The beanstalk, who had already lost his mental balance, had the soldier inject kerosene under the skin of his leg in the bathroom.

When the day was leaning toward evening, Švejk suggested they resume the journey to the Field Chaplain. The short fatso was babbling and trying to convince Švejk to stay a little longer. The beanstalk was also of the opinion that Otto Katz could wait. Švejk, however, was not enjoying himself at the Kuklík anymore and threatened to go on alone if they would not leave with him.

So, the trio set out again, but Švejk had to promise they would stop again somewhere along the way.

Just past the Florence corner, they stopped in a nice little restaurant where the fat one sold his silver watch so that the revelry could continue.

When they left, Švejk had to support both of them under their arms. Their legs constantly buckled from under them. It was a tremendous amount of work. But, they still wanted to stop somewhere else to drink. The short fat one almost lost the package of papers for the Field Chaplain, so Švejk was forced to carry it himself.

Švejk was also forced to constantly alert his escorts whenever an officer or NCO came walking toward them. After a superhuman effort and much exertion, he finally managed to drag them to the Field Chaplain's house on Královská Street.

---

[13] (Author Jaroslav Hašek's note:)* It is a means, rather well proven, of getting oneself into a hospital. But the odor of kerosene, which stays in the swelling, gives one away. Gasoline is better because it evaporates faster. Later, they were injecting ether with the gasoline, and then came other improvements.

Švejk reattached the bayonets to their firearms. Then, he poked them in the ribs, so they would act like they had escorted him and not the other way around.

On the second floor, there was a calling card on the door that read: "Otto Katz *Feldkurat*. Field Chaplain." A soldier opened the door for them. From the room came the sound of voices and the clanking of bottles and glasses.

"*Wir--melden--gehorsam--Herr--Feldkurat.* We are dutifully reporting, Field Chaplain, sir," the beanstalk said haltingly, and with much effort. He saluted the soldier who had opened the door and continued:

"*ein--Paket--und ein Mann gebracht,* bringing in one package and one man."

"Crawl in further," said the soldier. "Where did you get so messed up? The Field Chaplain, he also is....." he grumbled and spat.

The soldier left with the package. They waited in the hallway for a long time. Suddenly, the door opened and the Field Chaplain bounded into the hallway. He had a vest on and in one hand he held a cigar.

"So you're here already," he said to Švejk. "And they escorted you. That is to say. Eh . . . do you have any matches?"

"I dutifully report , Field Chaplain, sir, that I don't."

"Eh? . . . and why don't you have any matches? Every soldier is supposed to have matches so he can light up. A soldier that doesn't have matches is . . . What is he?"

"I dutifully report, sir, that he is a soldier without matches," answered Švejk.

"Very good. He is without matches and therefore he cannot light up anybody. So that would answer one question. And, now for the other. Do your feet stink, Švejk?"

I dutifully report, sir, that they don't."

"Then, that answers the other. And now, a third question. Do you drink the hard stuff?"

"I dutifully report that I don't drink the hard stuff. Only rum."

"All right. Look at this soldier over here. I borrowed him for today from Lieutenant Feldhuber. He's his yeoman, his personal servant, his *putzfleck*, his spotshine. And he doesn't drink anything. He's a t-t-t-teetotaler. And that's why he's gonna go with a marching company. B-b-because, I've got no use for such a man. He is not a yeoman. He is a cow. It also drinks only water and lows like an ox . . . You are a teetotaler!" he spat, turning to the soldier. "Aren't you ashamed, you jerk? You deserve a couple of slaps."

The Field Chaplain focused next on those who brought Švejk to him and who were now tottering and leaning on their rifles in a vain attempt to stand up straight.

"You got d-d-drunk," said the Field Chaplain. "You got drunk on duty, and for that I will have you locked up. Švejk, you will take their rifles from them and escort them to the kitchen. You'll guard them until the patrol comes to take them away. I will immediately call-ca-call the garrison."

And so the words of Napoleon were fully borne out even here:

"In the military, the situation changes with every blink of an eye."

That very morning, two escorts had started out to bring Švejk in under bayonet guard. They feared that he might run away. But ultimately, Švejk was forced to bring his own guards to their destination. And, in the end, Švejk wound up guarding his former escorts himself.

At first, the pair did not realize a turnabout had occurred. Only later did they grasp it, when they were sitting in the kitchen and saw Švejk standing by the door with a rifle and a bayonet.

"I'd like something to drink," sighed the short optimist. The beanstalk again became a skeptic and said that it was all a lousy betrayal. He loudly blamed Švejk for bringing him into this position. He even reproached him for having said that he was to be hanged the next day. It was all clear now that it was a joke, including going to the Field Chaplain for confession before being hanged.

Švejk kept silent and paced by the door.

"We were dumb!" screamed the beanstalk.

In the end, having heard all the accusations, Švejk declared:

"Now, at least you're seeing that military service is no bowl of honey. I am doing my duty. I got into this just like you. But, as they say on the streets: Lady Luck has smiled at me."

"I'd like to drink something," repeated the optimist desperately.

The beanstalk got up and walked to the door with a wobbly step.

"Let us go home," he said to Švejk. "Come on pal, stop the nonsense.

"Back off," answered Švejk. "I must guard you. We don't know one another now."

Otto Katz appeared in the doorway: "Somehow I just can't get through to the garrison on the phone. So, go home. And re-remember: drinking on duty is forbidden. March!"

To the credit of the honorable Field Chaplain, let it be said that he didn't get through to the garrison because he didn't have a telephone in his home. All along he had been talking into his lamp stand.

II

Švejk had been Otto Katz' personal servant for three days. And, in that time, he had seen him only once. On the third day, Lieutenant Helmich's yeoman came with the message that Švejk should come immediately to retrieve the Field Chaplain.

On the way, the yeoman informed Švejk that the Field Chaplain had argued with the Lieutenant and broken an upright piano. He was soused to the gills and didn't want to go home.

Lieutenant Helmich, he said, was also drunk and had thrown Otto Katz out into the hallway. He was now sitting on the floor by the door and was snoozing.

When Švejk arrived, he shook Otto Katz firmly. He growled and opened his eyes. Švejk saluted and said: "I dutifully report, Field Chaplain, sir, that I'm here."

"And what do you want --- here?"

"I dutifully report that I came to get you, Field Chaplain, sir."

"So. You came to get me. --- And where will we go?"

"To your apartment, Field Chaplain, sir."

"And why would we go to my apartment? --- Am I not in my apartment?"

"I dutifully report, Field Chaplain, sir, that you are in a hallway in a stranger's building."

"And -- how -- did -- I -- get here?"

"I dutifully report that you were visiting here."

"I was n-not on a visit. You are mi-mistaken."

114

Švejk slowly lifted his drunken superior and stood him against the wall. Otto Katz was swinging from side to side and rolling up against him.

"I'll fall, that's what I'll do to you," he said, rolling from side to side. "I'll fall," he repeated, smiling like a fool.

With some effort, Švejk managed to press him against the wall. In this new position, Otto Katz again started to doze.

Švejk woke him up.

"What do you want?" Otto Katz said, making a futile attempt to slide down the wall and sit on the ground. "Who the heck are you, anyhow?"

"I dutifully report," answered Švejk, holding him up against the wall, "that I'm your *putzfleck*, your spotshine, Field Chaplain, sir."

"I don't have any *putzfleck*," said the Field Chaplain with great effort again trying to lean on Švejk. "I'm no field chaplain. ---- I'm a pig," he added with the sincerity of a dedicated drinker. "Let me go, sir! I don't know you."

Švejk completely won this little tussle. His victory gave him the opportunity to drag Katz down the stairs and into the carriage-way. Once there, the Field Chaplain resisted being hauled into the street.

"I don't know you, sir," he insisted continuously during his duel with Švejk.

"Do you know Otto Katz? That's me! --- I was at the Archbishop's!" he hollered while hanging onto the gate in the carriage-way.

"The Vatican is interested in me! Understand?"

Švejk shed the "I dutifully report" and began speaking to the Field Chaplain in a rough, familiar tone.

"Let go of that gate!" he ordered. "Or I'm gonna whack you across your paw. We're going home and that's it. No more talk."

Otto Katz let go of the gate and rolled over against Švejk:

"Then let's go somewhere. But not to Šuha's. I won't go there, I owe them money!" Švejk pushed him away from the gate. Then he carried him out of the carriage-way and dragged him along the sidewalk in the direction of his home.

"What kind of a gentleman is that?" asked somebody from among the onlookers on the street.

"He's my brother," answered Švejk. "He's on leave. He came to visit me and got drunk. He's overjoyed, because he thought that I was dead."

Otto Katz caught Švejk's last words and began to hum a motif from an operetta that nobody could recognize. He then rose to face his audience:

"Whoever among you is dead, let him register at the Corps Command within three days, so that his corpse can be sprinkled thoroughly with holy water."

He fell silent, then tumbled toward the sidewalk, almost smashing it with his nose. Švejk grabbed him under his arms and began lugging him towards home.

Otto Katz' head bounced up ahead and his feet dragged behind. He flailed them like a cat with a broken back. The Field Chaplain kept murmuring to himself:

"Dominus vobiscum – et cum spiritu tuo. Dominus vobiscum."

When they reached a cab stand, Švejk sat the Field Chaplain up against a wall and went to negotiate with the carriage drivers over transport.

One of the drivers declared that he knew this "gentleman" very well. He had driven him once and would never drive him anywhere again.

"He puked everything up," the driver said forthrightly. "And he didn't even pay for the ride. I drove him around for over two hours before he found where he lived. A week later, after I'd been to see him about three times, he gave me a lousy five crowns for all of that."

After a long negotiation one of the cab drivers decided that he'd drive them home.

Švejk returned to find Otto Katz sleeping. The Field Chaplain usually went about in civilian clothes. And while Švejk had been negotiating with the drivers, somebody had removed the black felt hat from his head and carried it away.

Švejk woke him up and, with the help of the driver, shoved Katz in the cab. Once inside, the Field Chaplain's brain became numb and he began to believe that Švejk was Colonel Just from the 75th Infantry Regiment.

He repeated several times in succession:

"Don't be angry, buddy, that I address you in the familiar second person singular.[14] I'm a pig."

For a moment, it seemed that the bouncing of the cab over the cobble stones might help him regain his power to reason. He sat up straight and started singing some excerpt from a song that could have only been a product of his imagination:

> *I'm remembering the golden times*
> *When he rocked me in his lap.*
> *We were living at the time*
> *Near Domažlice in Merklín.*

After a while, however, he was again completely delirious. Turning to Švejk and squinting one eye, he asked:

"How are you doing today, ma'am? -- Will you be going anywhere to spend the summer?"

After a short pause, he began seeing everything double.

"You already have an adult son?" he asked, pointing his finger at Švejk.

"Sit!" Švejk screamed as Otto Katz tried to climb out of his seat. "Don't think that I won't teach you what's proper!"

The Field Chaplain turned silent and stared out of the cab with his little piggy eyes, not having any grasp whatsoever of what was actually happening to him.

He had totally lost his sense of reality. He turned to Švejk and said with pining sadness:

"Ma'am, give it to me, first class."

He made an attempt to drop his pants.

"You button up right away, you swine!" shrieked Švejk. "All the cabmen already know you! You've puked once already, and now this to boot. Don't think that you're gonna end up stiffing them like the last time."

---

[14] In Czech, only friends, family members and intimates are addressed in the second-person singular. All others are addressed in the second-person plural. These two forms of address are used in most European languages, unlike in modern English, which uses the word "you" in all instances.

Otto Katz rested his head into the palms of his hands and in a melancholy manner started singing:

"Nobody likes me anymore . . ."

He interrupted his singing immediately, however, and remarked:

"*Entschuldigen Sie lieber Kamerad, Sie sind ein Trottel, ich kann singen, was ich will*. Excuse me dear friend, you are an idiot, I can sing what I want."

He apparently wanted to whistle some melody. But instead he emitted a mighty moan from his lips that sounded a lot like "whoa," and the carriage suddenly stopped.

At Švejk's request, they continued on their way and the Field Chaplain attempted to light up his cigarette holder.

"It won't burn!" he cried desperately after using a whole box of matches. He looked angrily at Švejk and said:

"You're blowing them out! ---- That's what you're doing to me!"

However, he immediately lost his train of thought and started laughing. "That's funny! We're alone in the street car, aren't we, my dear colleague?" He started searching through his pockets.

"I've lost the fare-card!" he shouted. "Stop! The fare-card must be found!"

He then waved his hand in resignation:

"Let them go . . ."

Then he began babbling:

"Often, in most occurring cases . . . Yes, all right . . . In all cases . . . You are mistaken . . . The second floor? . . . That's an excuse . . . Never mind me, but it's you, dear madam whose interest . . . I'd like to pay . . . I've got to pay for black coffee . . ."

Half dreaming, he began to argue with some imagined enemy who was denying him the right to sit in a restaurant at the window. Then, he started to think the carriage was a train. Leaning out, he screamed into the streets in both Czech and German:

"Nymburk Town! Change trains!"

Švejk pulled him back in toward himself and Otto Katz forgot about the train.

He started to imitate various animal sounds. He lingered the longest on the rooster. His "cock-a-doodle do" rang victoriously out of the cab.

For a while, he was really quite lively and restless. He kept trying to dive out of the cab and began abusing all the people they passed. He called them all street punks. He then threw a' handkerchief out of the cab and yelled for the driver to stop, saying he had lost his luggage. He began to narrate:

"In Budějovice there was a military drummer. – He got married. – A year later he died." He broke into laughter. "Isn't that a good joke?"

The whole time, Švejk had been disciplining the Field Chaplain with ruthless strictness.

Otto Katz made various attempts to play little games: like falling out of the cab or ripping out the seat. Švejk gave him one stiff punch under the ribs after another. The Field Chaplain accepted them with unusual apathy.

Only once did he attempt to rebel and actually jump out of the cab. He declared that he wouldn't ride any farther, that he knew that, instead of going to Budějovice, they were going to Podmoklí.

Within a minute, Švejk had quelled this rebellion entirely. He forced Katz to return to his proper position on the seat and made sure that he would not fall asleep on him. The gentlest admonition Švejk made during this time was:

"Don't dare fall asleep on me, you croaking stiff!"

The Field Chaplain was gripped suddenly by a spell of melancholy. He began to shed tears and asked Švejk whether he had a mother.

"I am, folks, forlorn in this world! " he wailed from the cab. "Take charge of me!"

"Don't embarrass me," Švejk reprimanded. "Stop it, or everybody will know that you're a drunken bum."

"I've had nothing to drink, buddy," Otto Katz answered. "I'm totally sober."

All of a sudden, however, he stood up, saluted and said:

"*Ich melde gehorsam, Her Oberst, ich bin besoffen.* I dutifully report, colonel, sir, I am drunk. – I'm a filthy porker," he repeated 10 times in a row with a desperate, sincere hopelessness.

The Field Chaplain turned to Švejk, begging and pleading tenaciously:

"Throw me out of this automobile. Why are you giving me a ride?"

He sat down and growled:

"Around the moon, circles are being formed. – Do you believe, captain, sir, in the immortality of the soul? Can a horse get to heaven?"

He began to laugh loudly. But in a moment, he turned sad and apathetically stared at Švejk.

"Pardon me, sir," he said. "I've seen you somewhere before. Have you been to Vienna? I remember you from the seminary."

A little while later, he amused himself by loudly reciting Latin verses:

"*Aurea prima sata est aetas, quae vindice nullo.* A golden age first arose that did not need judges. – I can't go further," he said. "Throw me out. Why don't you want to throw me out? I won't get hurt. – I want to fall on my nose," he stated resolutely.

"Sir," he continued in a pleading voice. "Dear friend, give me a slap across the back of the head."

"One or several?" asked Švejk.

"Two."

"Here they come . . ."

The Field Chaplain counted the head slaps out loud as he got them and accepted them blissfully.

"It's doing me a lot of good," he said. "It's all on account of the stomach. It fosters digestion and brings on the hunger pangs. Punch my face now!

"–Oh, my heartfelt thanks!" he exclaimed when Švejk quickly obliged him. "I'm totally satisfied. Rip my vest! Please!"

He expressed a variety of other wishes. He asked that Švejk dislocate his ankle, choke him for a while, cut his nails and pull out his front teeth.

He displayed a desire for martyrdom. He asked Švejk to tear off his head, put it in a bag and throw it into the Vltava River.

"Little stars around my head would flatter me," he said. "I'd need 10 of them."

He started talking about horse races and then quickly switched to ballet, unable to talk very long about either.

"Do you dance the czardas?" he asked Švejk. "Do you know the bear dance? Like this . . ."

He wanted to hop, but fell on Švejk, who immediately punched him and laid him down on the seat.

"I want something!" bellowed the Field Chaplain. "But I don't know what. Don't you know what I want?" He hung his head in total resignation.

"What do I care what I want," he said seriously. "And you, sir, it's none of your business, either. I don't know you. How dare you to stare at me? Do you know how to fence?"

For a minute, he became more aggressive and made an attempt to knock Švejk down.

Then, when Švejk was calming him down, while humbling him shamelessly with his physical superiority, the Field Chaplain asked:

"Is today Monday or Friday?"

He was even curious as to whether it was December or June. Katz showed a great ability to pose the most varied questions:

"Are you married? Do you enjoy eating Gorgonzola cheese? Did you use to have bedbugs at home? Are you doing well? Has your dog had rabies?"

He became talkative. He disclosed that he owed someone for riding boots, a whip and saddle. He said that, years ago, he had gonorrhea and treated it himself with potassium permanganate.

"There wasn't the time or opportunity to think about anything else," he said hiccuping. "Maybe it seems to be a rather bitter pill to you. But say, uh, uh, what am I to do, uh? You just have to forgive me already......."

"Autotherm," he continued, having forgotten what he was talking about before, "is a term that designates vessels which keep drinks and meals at their original temperature. What do you think, dear colleague, about the question of which game is more fair: ferbl or 21? --

"Really, I've seen you somewhere before!" he exclaimed, trying to hug Švejk and kiss him with his drooling lips. "We used to go to school together. – You good-natured guy, you," he said gently, caressing his own leg. "How you've grown since last we parted. The joy of seeing you makes up for all the suffering."

He got into a poetic mood and started talking about the return of the sunshine of happy faces and warm hearts.

Then he knelt down and prayed the "Hail Mary," laughing loudly in the process.

When they stopped in front of his apartment, it was very hard to get him out of the carriage.

"We're not in the right spot yet!" he yelled. "Help me! They're kidnapping me. I wish to ride farther." In the true sense of the analogy, he was pulled out of the cab like a boiled gastropod is pulled out of its shell. For a moment, it seemed they'd tear him apart because his feet got entangled under the seat.

"You'll rip me in two, gentlemen," he said, laughing so loudly that it ticked them off. ·

They dragged him roughly down the carriage-way and up the stairs to his apartment. Once inside, they threw him down like a bale of hay onto the sofa. He declared that he would not pay for an automobile he had not ordered. It took over a quarter of an hour before they managed to explain to him that he had been in a horse-drawn cab.

Even then, he wouldn't agree to pay. He objected, saying that he would only ride in a *fiacre*, a small coach, drawn by two horses.

"You want to fool me!" the Field Chaplain proclaimed, winking at Švejk and the driver meaningfully. "We walked."

All of a sudden, in a fit of magnanimity, he threw his wallet to the cabman: "Take it all! *Ich kann bezahlen.* I can pay. I couldn't care less about a *krejcar*."

To be correct, he should have said that he couldn't care less about 36 *krejcary,* because there wasn't any more money in the bag. Fortunately, the cabman subjected him to a thorough search, cursing him and slapping him in the process.

"So hit me then," Otto Katz said. "Do you think that I can't take it? I can take five of your best."

The cabman found a tenner in his vest and accused him of costing him his livelihood. He left cursing both his fate and Otto Katz.

The Field Chaplain put himself to sleep slowly by continuously making up plans. He wanted to undertake all kinds of things: to fry some little fish for himself, to take dancing lessons and to play a piano.

He promised Švejk a sister he didn't have. He also wished to be carried to his bed and laid down. In the end, he fell asleep declaring that he wanted the humanity in him to be recognized as being at least equally as valuable as the pig in him.

III

In the morning, Švejk stepped into the Field Chaplain's living room. He found him laying on the sofa, thinking diligently about how someone could have possibly doused him with glue so that his pants got stuck to the leather sofa.

"I dutifully report, Field Chaplain, sir," said Švejk, "that last night you . . ."

With but a few words, he explained to Katz how terribly mistaken he was in thinking that he'd been doused with glue. The Field Chaplain, whose head felt unusually heavy, was in a depressed mood.

"I can't remember," he said, "how I got from the bed to the sofa."

"You haven't been to bed at all. When we got here, we deposited you onto the sofa right away. You'd go no farther."

"Was I doing silly things? Was I doing any goofy things at all? Or was I just drunk?"

"As God is my judge, -- you were drunk beyond recognition," answered Švejk. "You were totally smashed. A little delirium came over you, Field Chaplain, sir. I hope you will feel better when you change and wash up."

"I feel as if somebody has beaten me up," Otto Katz complained. "And I've got this thirst. Was I fighting yesterday?"

"It could be worse, Field Chaplain, sir. Your thirst today is the consequence of yesterday's thirst. A man can't get over that so soon. I used to know a cabinet maker. He got drunk for the first time on New Year's Eve of the year 1910. And on January first, he had such a thirst, and he felt so sick, that he bought himself a herring and began drinking again. He kept it up daily for four years. Nobody could help him get out of his habit, because on Saturday he would always buy the herrings for a whole week. It was a sort of merry-go-round, as an old master sergeant of the 91st Regiment used to say."

Otto Katz was suffering from a quintessential hangover and was totally depressed. Whoever might have heard him at that moment would have been convinced that he was attending a lecture of Dr. Alexandr Batěk, entitled:

"LET US DECLARE A LIFE OR DEATH STRUGGLE AGAINST THE DEMON OF ALCOHOL, WHICH KILLS THE BEST OF MEN WHO ARE OUR BEST." Or that he was reading Batěk's: "HUNDRED SPARKS OF ETHICS."

It's true, however, that he rearranged Batěk's ideas a little. Otto Katz would put it this way:

"If a man drank some noble drinks like arak, maraschino, or cognac, well fine. But yesterday, I drank *borovičku*, that liquor that tastes like pine wood. I marvel that I can lap up stuff like that. Its taste is repulsive. At least it could have been cherry brandy. People will think up all kinds of swine filth to drink. Stuff like that burns the throat.

"If it had been at least the genuine article, for instance, a distillate from juniper, like the one I drank in Moravia. But this *borovička* was made from some wood alcohol and oils. Take a look at how I'm burping. -- Hard liquor is poison," he decided.

"It must be original and genuine, and not something manufactured at a factory in a cold alley on the way from Jewtown. It's the same with rum. Good rum is a rarity. -- If we had some genuine nut liquor here," he sighed, "that would fix my stomach. Captain Šnábl in Bruska has such a nut liquor."

He started frisking himself and looking through his money pouch.

"All I have is 36 *krejcary*. What if I were to sell the sofa?" he weighed this option.

"What do you think? Will somebody buy a sofa? I'll tell the landlord that I loaned it out, or that somebody stole it on us. No, I'll keep the sofa. I'll send you to Captain Šnábl. He will lend me a hundred crowns. He won at cards the day before yesterday. If you don't succeed there, then you'll go to Vršovice, to the garrison, to Lieutenant Mahler. Should you fail there, you'll go to Hradčany to Captain Fišer. You'll tell him that I have to pay for the horse's fodder because I spent the money on drink. And if you don't succeed there, we will pawn the upright piano.

"Let happen what may. I will write a few lines of introduction in a general vein. Don't let them get rid of you easily. Tell them that I'm in need, that I'm absolutely without any money. Make up anything you want, but don't come back with empty hands or I'll

124

send you to the front. And, ask Captain Šnábl where he buys that nutty liquor and buy us two bottles."

Švejk fulfilled his mission excellently. His simple-heartedness and honest face evoked full trust in him. It was as if whatever he was saying must be true.

Švejk decided that telling Captain Šnábl, Captain Fišer and Lieutenant Mahler that Otto Katz needed money for horse fodder wouldn't work. Instead, he concocted a bolder story. He told them the Field Chaplain needed money to pay alimony to girls.

He got money everywhere he went.

When he returned honorably from the expedition, he had 300 crowns to show the Field Chaplain. Katz, who had washed and changed in the meantime, was very surprised.

"I got it all in one sweep," said Švejk. "So we wouldn't have to chase money again tomorrow, or the day after tomorrow. It went pretty smoothly, but I had to get down on my knees in front of Captain Šnábl. He's a real sonofabitch. But, when I told him that you have to pay alimonies . . ."

"Alimonies?" repeated the horrified Otto Katz.

"Yes, alimonies, Field Chaplain, sir. Disposition payments to the girls. You said I should think something up and I couldn't come up with anything else. At home, a cobbler was paying alimonies to five girls at once, and he was totally desperate from it all. He had to borrow to pay them. Everybody gladly believed that he was in that horrible position. Your officer friends asked me what kind of girls you had to pay. I said one was very pretty and not even 15 years of age. So, they wanted her address."

"You sure executed that nicely, Švejk." Otto Katz sighed heavily and started pacing around the room.

"This is another big embarrassment," he said grabbing his head. "My head is really hurting."

"I gave them the address of an old, deaf woman on our street," explained Švejk. "I wanted to execute it thoroughly, because an order is an order. I didn't let them get rid of me easily. ----- I had to think of something .

"Also, Field Chaplain, sir, they're waiting in the hallway for the upright piano. I brought them along so that they could take it to the pawn shop for us. It won't be so bad when the upright is gone. There'll be more room in here and we'll have more money. We can be carefree for a few days. If the landlord asks what we did with the upright, I'll say that the wires in it were torn up and that we sent it to the factory for repairs. I already told the resident custodian, so that she won't be suspicious when they carry it out and load it in their wagon.

"Also, we have a buyer for the sofa. He's an acquaintance of mine, a trader in old furniture. He'll come here past noon. Nowadays, a leather sofa brings good money."

"You haven't done anything more, have you Švejk?" asked Otto Katz, still holding his head in his hands and looking around desperately.

"I dutifully report, Field Chaplain, sir, that instead of two bottles of nutty liquor, the kind that Captain Šnábl buys, I've brought five bottles, so that we will be well stocked and have something to drink.

"Can they take away the upright piano now? Before they close the pawn shop on us?"

Otto Katz waved his hand hopelessly. A short while later, the upright was loaded on a cart and taken away. When Švejk returned from the pawn shop, he found the Field Chaplain sitting in front of an open bottle of nutty liquor, bitching that the schnitzel he had for lunch wasn't cooked through.

Otto Katz was at it again. He declared to Švejk that, starting tomorrow, he would lead a new life. Drinking alcohol is vulgar materialism, he said, adding that what one needs is to live a spiritual life.

He spoke philosophically for about half an hour. When he opened the third bottle of nutty liquor, the trader of old furniture came by. The Field Chaplain sold him the sofa for next to nothing. Katz tried to insist the furniture dealer join him for a friendly chat. He was very dissatisfied when the trader excused himself to go buy a night stand.

"Too bad I don't have one," Otto Katz said with recrimination. "One doesn't think of everything."

After the departure of the trader of used furniture, the Field Chaplain and Švejk drank up another bottle. They began to have a really good time. Otto Katz' conversation was about his personal relationship with women and cards.

They drank long into the evening, absorbed in friendly conversation.

However, later that night, the Field Chaplain returned to the drunken state he had been in yesterday. He mixed Švejk up with somebody else and told him:

"No, don't leave. Remember that red-haired cadet from the supply company?"

This idyll continued until Švejk told the Field Chaplain:

"I've had enough of this. Now you crawl in bed and snooze, understand!"

"I'm crawling, darling, crawling -- how could I not crawl?" babbled the Field Chaplain. "Remember when we were attending the fifth grade together? And I was doing your Greek language home-work? You had a villa in Zbraslav. And you took the steam boat on the Vltava. Do you know what the Vltava is?"

Švejk forced him to take off his shoes and undress. Otto Katz obliged and protested to unknown persons:

"Gentlemen," he said, addressing the wardrobe and a ficus plant, "see how my relatives treat me . . .

"I don't know my relatives," he decided suddenly, depositing himself in bed. "Even if heaven and earth were to conspire against me, I won't know them . . ."

Soon, the Field Chaplain's snoring resonated throughout the room.

IV

Sometime during the next few days, Švejk decided to pay a visit to his old cleaning woman. Instead of Mrs. Müller, Švejk found her female cousin residing in her apartment. She told him, while weeping, that Mrs. Müller had been arrested the same evening she pushed Švejk in his wheelchair to join the military. The old woman had been tried by the military courts. Since they couldn't prove anything against her, they had taken her to the concentration camp in Steinhoff. Her cousin had received a post card from her.

Švejk slowly read the only evidence that remained of her domestic existence:

Dear Aninko!

We have it really good here. We are all healthy. The neighbor on the bed next to me has spotted XXXXX and there are here also cases of small XXX. Other than that, everything is all right.

We have plenty of food and we collect potato XXXXX for soup. I have heard that Mr. Švejk already XXXX. So, somehow search out where his body is at so that, after the war, we can have his grave decked with sod. I forgot to tell you that in the attic, in the right corner, there is a little pincher doggie, a puppy in a box. But it's been I don't know how many weeks that he hasn't gotten anything to eat. Since the time when they came for me for XXXXXXX. So I think it's too late and that the doggie is also in the truth XXXXXXXXXXX.

And stamped across the whole card in pink letters was:

Zensuriert. K. k. Konzentrationslager Steinhoff. Censored. I&R Concentration Camp Steinhoff.

"And yes, the little dog was already dead," sobbed Mrs. Müller's cousin. "Also, you wouldn't even recognize your apartment. I have seamstresses renting there. And they've turned it into a ladies salon. There are pictures from fashion magazines all over the walls and flowers in the windows."

Constantly weeping and wailing, Mrs. Müller's cousin was not to be consoled.

She finally expressed her fear:

Švejk had run away from the military and wanted to bring tragedy upon her by corrupting her. In the end, she began to speak to him as if he was a degenerate adventurer.

"This is very funny," said Švejk. "I'm really enjoying it. Just so that you know, Mrs. Kejřová, you are absolutely right that I am a deserter. I had to kill 15 sergeants at arms and master sergeants. But don't tell anybody . . ."

So Švejk left the home that no longer accepted him, declaring:

"I've got some collars and shirt-fronts at the laundry, Mrs. Kejřová. Pick them up so that, when I come back from the military, I'll have something to wear as a civilian. Also, watch out for moths, so they don't eat into my clothes in the wardrobe. And give my greetings to those little ladies who are now sleeping in my bed."

Švejk decided to check out the Chalice. When Mrs. Palivcová saw him, she declared that she wouldn't serve him because he had probably run away from the army.

"My husband was so careful," she said, spewing the same old story all over again. "He's sitting there, the poor soul, locked up for nothing whatsoever. And such people as you are roaming the world, running away from military service. They were in here again last week looking for you.

"We were more careful than you," she proclaimed, "and we're in a mess. Not everybody is as lucky as you."

An older man, a locksmith from Smíchov, was there listening to the conversation. He went up to Švejk and said:

"Please, sir, wait for me outside. I have to talk to you."

Once in the street, he explained to Švejk that he also believed him to be a deserter. He told Švejk that he had a son who had also run away from the military and was now at his grandma's at Jasenná near Josefov.

Though Švejk kept assuring him that he was not a deserter, the old man pressed a ten into his hand.

"That's first aid," he said, as he brought him to the wine-bar at the corner. "I understand you. You don't have to fear me."

Švejk returned to the Field Chaplain's house late that night. Katz was not home yet. It was almost dawn when he did arrive, woke Švejk up, and told him:.

"Tomorrow we're going to serve a field Mass. Start making black coffee with rum. Or, better yet, start making grog."

11

ŠVEJK RIDES WITH THE FIELD CHAPLAIN TO SERVE A FIELD MASS

I

The preparations for putting people to death have always taken place in the name of God or some other supposedly higher being humankind has created in its imagination.

Before the old Phoenicians would cut the throat of some prisoner of war, they would perform a grand divine service of worship.

Several thousand years later, new generations would do likewise before they went to war and exterminated their enemies with both fire and sword.

The cannibals of the Guinea islands and Polynesia sacrifice to their gods before they festively devour their prisoners of war, or other useless people, like missionaries, explorers, the agents of various commercial firms, and people who are simply curious about them. Beforehand, they perform the most varied religious acts.

Because the culture of the chasuble has not penetrated as far as where they live, they decorate their buttocks with wreaths made with the colorful feathers of forest birds.

Before the Holy Inquisition burnt its victims at the stake, the grandest of divine services, the holy High Mass, with singing, was performed.

Priests have always played a role during the executions of the guilty, annoying the delinquent with their presence.

In Prussia, a pastor leads the poor condemned soul to the ax. In Austria, a Catholic priest leads him to the gallows, in France, it's to the guillotine, in America, it's to the electric chair. And, in Spain, the priest leads him to a chair where he is strangled by an ingenious apparatus. And, in Russia, a bearded Orthodox *pop*, leads the revolutionary to his death, and so forth.

In all these places, during such occasions, the priests waved the crucifix in their hands as if they wanted to say:

We will only chop your head off, or hang you, or strangle you, or run 15,000 volts through you. But, behold what did this Crucified One have to suffer!

The great slaughter of the World War could not proceed without a priestly blessing. Field chaplains of all armies prayed and served field Masses for the victory of the side whose bread they were eating.

A priest would appear during the executions of mutinous regular army soldiers. And, during the executions of Czech Legionnaires,[15] one could also see a priest.

Nothing has changed since the time when the highwayman Vojtěch, to whom they gave the moniker "Saint," played his role. With his sword in one hand and his cross in the other, he killed and annihilated the Baltic Slavs.

People in the whole of Europe have always been slaughtered like cattle. They were led to the slaughter by butcher emperors, kings and other potentates, and by military leaders. In addition, in the Great War, they were led by priests of all denominational confessions, blessing them and having them falsely swear their allegiance that "on earth, in the air, at sea, and so forth . . ."

Field Masses would be served twice: first when a detachment was going away to take a position at the front, and then again near the front line, before bloody clashes or a big slaughter. I remember that once during such a field Mass an enemy airplane dropped a bomb right on the field altar. Nothing was left of the Field Chaplain but some bloody rags.

They wrote about him as a martyr, while our airplanes were preparing similar glory for the field chaplains on the other side.

We had a crude sort of fun with it. On the improvised cross marking the buried remnants of the Field Chaplain, this sign appeared overnight:

---

[15] The Czech colony in Russia recruited Czech prisoners of war to fight with them against Austria. However, after the Bolshevik revolution, Czech Legionnaires were trapped deep in the interior of the new Soviet Union. In a series of heroic battles, the legions were forced to fight their way out of Russia and into the pages of history. After the war, these men became lionized in the First Czechoslovak Republic.

What can befall us, that is what befell you also..
You who kept promising the sureness of heaven to us, old boy,
Then it fell on you from heaven during the Holy Mass
Only a stain is left of you on this spot.

II

Švejk made his famous grog, surpassing the grogs of the old sailors. A grog such as this, could satisfy even the pirates of the eighteenth century.

Field Chaplain Otto Katz was elated.

"Where did you learn to cook such a good thing?" he asked.

"In Bremen, where I wandered years ago," answered Švejk. "I learned to make it from a degenerate sailor. He used to say that grog has to be so strong that if somebody falls overboard into the sea, he must be able to swim across the width of the English Channel. After drinking a weak grog, he would only drown like a puppy."

"After drinking such grog, Švejk, we'll have an easy time serving field Masses," mused Otto Katz.

"I think I should say a few words of parting beforehand. A field Mass is not as much fun as serving a Mass in the garrison prison and preaching to those hoodlums. In this case, one really has to have all his five senses together. Now, we do have a field altar. It's a collapsible, pocket edition . . .

"Jesusmaria, Švejk!" he grabbed himself by the head. "We are dumb oxen! I've got to tell you! Do you know where I hid that collapsible altar? In the sofa we sold!"

"Yes, that is a tragedy, Field Chaplain, sir," said Švejk. "I do know that trader in old furniture. But, the day before yesterday, I ran into his wife. She told me he's now doing time on account of some stolen wardrobe. She also told me that he sold our sofa to a teacher in the Vršovice neighborhood. There is gonna be a problem with that field altar. It will be best if we drink up the grog and try chasing it down. Obviously, without a field altar, the Mass cannot be served."

"All we're really missing is the field altar," the Field Chaplain said broodingly. "Other than that, everything is ready at the training ground. The carpenters have already made a platform there. The

Břevnov Monastery will lend us the monstrance. I'm supposed to have my own chalice, but where is it now . . ."

He started thinking:

"Let's say that I've lost it. – Then we'll have to get the sports trophy-cup from Lieutenant Witinger from the 75th Regiment. He used to run races years ago, and he won the cup running the Sport-Favorit. He was a good runner. He always brags to us that he used to do the 40 kilometers, Vienna to Mödling, in 1 hour 48 minutes. I already made a deal with him yesterday. I'm a dumb beast because I always postpone everything until the last moment. What a blockhead! Why didn't I take a look into that sofa."

Once under the influence of the grog Švejk made from the degenerate sailor's recipe, Otto Katz started deriding himself with the worst of curses. He expressed himself with the most colorful and varied statements as to where it was that he really belonged.

"Then, we should be looking for the field altar now," Švejk challenged. "It's already morning."

"I still have to put on my uniform and drink one more grog," Katz replied.

Finally, they set off to see the wife of the trader in old furniture. On the way, the Field Chaplain was telling Švejk that he had won a lot of money the day before. By the grace of God, he said, if all turned out well, he would redeem the upright piano from the pawn shop.

His oath was something akin to those of pagans promising their gods some future sacrifice.

They woke up the wife of the used furniture trader. Sleepily, she told them the address of the new owner of the sofa, a teacher in Vršovice. The Field Chaplain displayed unusual generosity. He pinched her cheek and tickled her under the chin.

Otto Katz said that he needed to stroll in the fresh air to freshen his thoughts. So they walked to Vršovice.

Once there and in the apartment of the teacher, a religious old man, they were unpleasantly surprised. Having found the field altar in the sofa, the old gentleman figured it was a divine occurrence. He had bestowed it upon the local church as a gift for its sacristy. He had secured a provision that they would add an inscription on the reverse side of the altar:

"Bestowed as a gift to honor and praise God, by Mr. Kolařík, teacher, Anno Domini 1914."

Now, caught in his underwear, he was showing a great reluctance to cooperate. It was apparent from the conversation that he thought finding the altar was a miracle and an instruction from God. When he bought the sofa, he said, some inner voice told him:

"Look in the sofa. In the drawer." He supposedly also saw some angel in a dream, who outright ordered him:

"Open the drawer of the sofa." He obeyed.

When he first saw the miniature collapsible three-part altar, with a built-in recess for the tabernacle, he knelt in front of the sofa and prayed fervently for a long time. He exalted God and viewed his discovery as an instruction from heaven to enhance the church in Vršovice.

"We're not interested in that," said the Field Chaplain. "That thing didn't belong to you. You should have turned it over to the police and not donated it to some damn sacristy."

"On account of this miracle," added Švejk, "you may have some difficulties. You bought a sofa but not an altar. *That* belongs in the military inventory. Such an instruction from God can cost you dearly. You shouldn't have listened to any angels.

"A man in Zhoř, tilling a field once, dug up a chalice. It was booty from a sacrilegious theft. It was hidden there for better times, when the theft would be forgotten. This farmer also thought he was instructed by God. So, instead of melting the chalice down, he went to the parish priest with it, saying that he wanted to bestow it on the church as a gift.

"The parish priest thought pangs of conscience had stirred in the farmer, so he sent for the mayor. The mayor sent for the cops. He was sentenced, though innocent, for sacrilegious theft. All because he kept blathering something about a miracle. He wanted to save himself, and so he kept talking about an angel. Even though he dragged in the Virgin Mary, he got 10 years.

"The best you can do is to come with us and ask the local priest to return this government property. A field altar is no cat or sock you can bestow as a gift on anybody you want."

As he dressed, the old man's body shook and his teeth chattered:

"I have not really had, nor entertained, any evil or wrong intent. I thought that, through such a divinely guided occurrence, I might help to adorn our poor temple of the Lord in Vršovice."

"At the expense of the military inventory, of course," Švejk said, toughly and harshly. "Thank God for these divinely guided occurrences. Some guy named Pivoňka from Chotěboř also thought it was a divine dispensation, when a halter with somebody else's cow attached wandered into his hand."

The poor old man was so confused by all of these pronouncements that he stopped defending himself altogether. He dressed up as fast as possible and was in a hurry to dispense with the whole matter.

The Vršovice parish priest was still asleep. They made a lot of noise to wake him. He started to thunder. He was still half asleep and thought that he was being called to go out and give someone the last sacrament.

"They should leave me in peace and forget that extreme unction," he growled, as he dressed up unwillingly. "These people decide to die when I am in my best sleep."

The representative of the Lord God among civilian Catholics in Vršovice met in the hallway with the representative of the Lord God on Earth of the military inventory. And they began to haggle over money. Basically, though, it was a dispute between a civilian and a soldier.

The parish priest claimed that the field altar did not belong in a sofa. The Field Chaplain asserted that it belonged even less in the sacristy of a civilian church.

Švejk remarked that it had been all too easy to enrich a poor church at the expense of the military's inventory. With the inflection of his voice, Švejk put the word "poor" into quotes.

In the end, they went to the sacristy of the church. The parish priest reluctantly gave up the field altar but demanded this receipt:

> I received a field altar which was acquired
> accidentally by the temple of Vršovice.
>   [Signed,]
>   The Field Chaplain Otto Katz

This glorious field altar was from the Jewish firm Moritz Mahler of Vienna. They made all kinds of Holy Mass accessories as well as other religious objects, like rosaries and the pictures of saints.

The altar consisted of three sections. It was elaborately appointed with false gild, just like the entire glory of the Holy Church.

The field altar had pictures painted on all its sections. Without the help of a good imagination, it was impossible to find out what they actually represented. One thing was certain. It was an altar which could be used equally by some pagans on the Zambezi, or by a shaman of the Buriats, or even by the Mongols.

Because it was painted in loud colors, from afar it looked like those charts used to detect color-blind people at the railroad.

Only one figure stood out: a naked man with a halo and a greenish body like the bishop's nose on a goose that already reeks from decay.

Nobody was doing anything to that saint. Quite to the contrary. He had two winged creatures on both sides of him that were supposed to represent angels. However, the viewer had the impression that the naked saint was screaming with fright because of the company that surrounded him. The angels looked like fairy-tale monsters, something between a winged wildcat and an apocalyptic monster.

Opposite the saint was a picture that was supposed to represent the Trinity of God. There was nothing about the dove the artist could, generally speaking, screw up. He painted some bird that could have been either a dove or a White Wyandotte hen.

On the other hand, God the Father looked like a Wild-West robber who was being introduced to the audience by some blood-and-gore adventure movie.

On the other hand, the Son of God was a merry young man with a nice tummy, covered by something that looked like a swimming suit. Altogether, it created the impression that he was an athletic jock. He held a cross in his hand with much elegance, as if it were a tennis racket.

From a distance, it all blended impressionistically creating the image of a train rolling into the railway station.

It was altogether impossible to appreciate the third picture, or to figure out what it represented. Soldiers were always trying to decipher this picture-puzzle, and arguing about possible solutions. Somebody even thought that it was a landscape depicting Posázaví, the region around the Sázava River.

There was, however, a caption underneath that read:

Heilige Maria, Mutter Gottes, erbarme unser. Holy Mary, mother of God, have mercy on us.

Švejk was barely able to load this colorful field altar into a cab. It took so much room that Švejk had to sit on the driver's box next to the cabman. However, the Field Chaplain stretched out and rested his feet comfortably on the Trinity of God.

Švejk began talking with the driver about military service.

The cabman was a rebel. He made various disparaging remarks about the victory of Austrian arms, like:

"They sure fixed it so you soldiers got rocked back on your heels in Serbia," and so forth.

When they crossed the food-tax line, the attendant asked what they were carrying. Švejk and the Field Chaplain both answered:

"The Trinity of God and the Virgin Mary."

In the meantime, the marching companies had been waiting impatiently for the Field Chaplain for a long time at the training ground. That is because Švejk and Katz were still in the process of fetching the sports "chalice" at Lieutenant Witinger's. They had already stopped at Břevnov Monastery for the monstrance, ciborium and other appurtenances, including a bottle of consecrated wine for the Mass. All of this shows that it is not that easy to serve a field Mass.

"We do it any which way we can," Švejk explained to the cabman.

And he was right.

They finally reached the training ground and were standing by the platform with the wooden railing, waiting for the field altar to be set up. Suddenly, it became apparent that the Field Chaplain had forgotten to bring along an altar-boy.

An infantryman from the regiment had always served as the altar boy. This time, however, he had preferred to have himself transferred and sent to the front.

"It doesn't matter, Field Chaplain, sir," said Švejk. "I can perform these duties."

"Do you know how to be an altar-boy?"

"I've never done it," answered Švejk. "But all things must be attempted. Nowadays, there is a war. And, in war, people do things they hadn't even dreamt of before. I can easily manage to put together some silly *'et cum spiritu tuo'* for your *'dominus vobiscum'*. And it shouldn't be that hard to pace around you like a cat around a bowl of hot porridge. Or, to wash your hands for you and pour wine from little jugs . . ."

"All right," agreed the Field Chaplain. "Just don't pour me any water. Better pour the wine from the second little jug right away. And, I'll always tell you whether you're to go right or left. If I whistle faintly once, that means to go to the right. Twice means go to the left. You don't have to bother to drag the missal around much either. This will be fun, after all. You don't have stage fright do you?"

"I'm not afraid of anything, Field Chaplain, sir. Not even of serving as an altar-boy."

The Field Chaplain was right when he said the field Mass would be fun.

Everything went tremendously smoothly.

The Field Chaplain's sermon was very terse.

"Soldiers! We've gathered here before your departure to the battle field, to turn our hearts to God, so that he will give us victory and preserve us in good health. I won't be delaying you long and wish you all the best."

"*Ruht*. At ease," an old colonel hollered on the left flank.

It is called a field Mass because it is subject to the same military principles as military tactics are in the field. For instance, during the long maneuvers of troops during the Thirty Years War, the field Masses, too, were unusually long.

With modern tactics, the movements of the troops are quick and smart, so field Masses must also be quick and smart.

This particular field Mass had been underway just ten minutes when those near the altar began to wonder why the Field Chaplain was whistling here and there in the midst of the Mass.

Švejk had the signals down really sharp. He'd walk to the right side of the altar, then to the left, and kept saying nothing but *"et cum spiritu tuo"*.

It looked like an Indian dance around a sacrificial rock. But it made a good impression and alleviated the boredom of the sad, dusty training ground. There was a double row of plum trees in the back. Their scent, combined with the smell of the latrines, created a fragrance which easily substituted for the mystical frankincense of the old, Gothic cathedrals.

All were tremendously entertained. The officers around the colonel were telling one another jokes, so everything went along in absolute order. The words, "Give me a drag," could be heard here and there among the troops.

Blue puffs of tobacco smoke floated above the troops like a sacrificial cloud. When the NCOs saw that even the colonel was smoking, they lit up, too.

At last the words *Zum Gebet*, To prayer, rang out. A swirl of dust arose as the huge gray rectangle of uniforms bent its knees before the sports chalice of Lieutenant Witinger, the cup he had won for winning the Sport-Favorit race from Vienna to Mödling.

Švejk filled the sports trophy-cup chalice with wine. The Field Chaplain swirled the wine around the cup, then drank it all down.

"Wow, he sure slurped that up!" was the general consensus that swept through the ranks.

Otto Katz repeated this act twice. Then once again. After one final, "Let us pray," the band played "Preserve us, Oh Lord," for good measure.

Finally the words, "Fall in formation! March!" rang out, and the field Mass was over.

The Field Chaplain pointed to the field altar and told Švejk:

"Pick up that and those *monatky* – those monthlies. So that we can take it all back to where it belongs!"

Their cabman drove them back along their route. And they returned everything honestly, except for the bottle of consecrated wine.

When they got home, they pointed the unhappy cabman in the direction of Command Headquarters to collect his fare for the long trip. Švejk then formally addressed the Field Chaplain:

"I dutifully report, Field Chaplain, sir. Does an altar-boy have to be of the same faith as the one he serves?"

"Of course," answered the Field Chaplain. "Otherwise the Mass wouldn't be valid."

"Then, Field Chaplain, sir, there's been a big mistake," said Švejk. "I'm without any religious faith. I just have such bad luck."

Otto Katz looked at Švejk, silently for a while. Then he patted him on the shoulder and said:

"You can drink up the consecrated wine that's left in the bottle, and think that you've joined the Church again."

12

A RELIGIOUS DEBATE

Sometimes, it would happen that Švejk did not see the nurturer of military souls for days at a time. The Field Chaplain performed his duties between carousing, and would come home only very rarely. When he did, he was dirty and unwashed, like a meowing tomcat tramping across the rooftops.

Once home, if he was able to express himself coherently, he would sit and chat with Švejk, talking about lofty goals, zeal, and the joy of thinking.

Sometimes he'd try to speak in verse and quote Heine.

Švejk served another field Mass performed by the Field Chaplain. It was celebrated for the sappers. It is their job to dig saps, long, narrow trenches that are dug to approach and undermine enemy positions. They are formally known as the Corps of Engineers.

The sappers had mistakenly invited yet another field chaplain to perform the field Mass. He was a former catechism teacher, an unusually pious man. He looked at his colleague in amazement when Otto Katz offered him a swig of cognac from Švejk's field flask, something the latter always carried to perform such religious acts.

"It's a good brand," said Otto Katz. "Have a drink and go home. I'll take care of it myself because I need to be under the open sky. I have a huge headache today."

The religious Field Chaplain left, shaking his head. As usual, Otto Katz acquitted himself very well in his role.

This time the blood of the Lord was changed into a wine spritzer. The sermon was better and longer. And every third expression he used was "and so forth" or "certainly."

"Soldiers, today you will be going to the front, and so forth . . Do turn to God now, and so forth, . . . Certainly, you don't know what will happen to you, and so forth and so on. . .and certainly. . ."

These words continued thundering from the altar and so forth and certainly, alternating with God and all the Saints.

In his zeal and lofty rhetoric, the Field Chaplain even tried to pass off Prince Eugene of Savoy as a saint who would protect those putting together bridges over rivers.

Nevertheless, in the eyes of all participants, the field Mass ended without scandal. It all went pleasantly and entertainingly. The trench engineers had a very good time.

On the way back, the conductor wouldn't allow them on the street car with the collapsible altar.

"I'll whack you over your head with this saint," Švejk threatened.

When they made it home at last, they discovered that they had lost the tabernacle somewhere along the way.

"It doesn't matter," said Švejk. "The first Christians used to serve the Holy Mass without a tabernacle. If we were to report it, an honest person finding it would want a reward from us. If we had lost money, then no honest person would come forward. Although there are still some people like that.

"There was a soldier at the regiment in Budějovice. He was such a good-natured, dumb beast. He once found 600 crowns in the street and turned them in at the police station. They wrote him up as an honest person in the newspaper. It brought him such shame. Nobody wanted to talk to him. Everybody yelled at him: 'You dumbbell, you! What sort of silliness did you do? Com'on! If you have a bit of honor left in your body, you will regret it until you die.'

"He had a girl. She stopped talking to him. When he came home on leave and went dancing, his friends threw him out of the pub on account of it. He started to mope about and take it too seriously. In the end, he let himself be run over by a train.

"Another time, a tailor found a golden ring on our street. People warned him not to turn it in at the police station. But he wouldn't let them talk him out of it. The police welcomed him unusually kindly. They said that there had already been a loss of a golden ring with a cut diamond reported. But when they looked at the stone, they said: 'Man, this is glass, not a cut diamond. How much did they give you for the diamond? We know all about honest finders like you.'

"In the end, it was revealed that another man had lost a golden ring with a fake diamond, some family memento. But the tailor did time, nevertheless. He sat for three days, because he insulted a cop in the excitement.

"Because that junk was worth only 12 crowns, he got the lawful reward of 10 percent: 1 crown and 20 halers. He threw the lawful reward into the rightful owner's face and sued him for insulting his honor. For that, they added a 10-crown fine, to boot. After the incident, he would tell everyone that any honest person who turned in what he found deserved 25 lashes and to have his ass kicked until he turns blue. He added that such a person should be roughed up thoroughly in public. That way people would remember all this and act accordingly.

"I don't think that anybody will bring back our tabernacle, even though it has the mark of our regiment on the back. That's because nobody wants anything to do with the military. They would rather throw it in the water somewhere, just to avoid any difficulties with the authorities.

"Yesterday, I spoke with a man from the country at the Golden Wreath pub. He is 56 years old. He went to the county administrator's office in Nová Paka to ask why they had requisitioned his gig. On the way back, after they threw him out of the county chief's office, he saw a supply convoy that had just arrived and stopped in the square. A young man asked him to watch his horses, because they were bringing food for the troops. The young man never showed up again.

"When the convoy got moving again, the man left watching the horses was forced to go with them. He made it all the way to Hungary where he then asked somebody else to stand by the wagon. That was the only way he saved himself. They would have dragged him all the way to Serbia. He came back all dumbfounded and never again will have anything more to do with military matters."

In the evening, they received a visit from the pious Field Chaplain who had wanted to celebrate the field Mass for the combat engineers that morning. He was a fanatic who wanted to get everybody closer to God.

When he had been a catechist, he developed a religious sense in the children by slapping their heads. Once in a while, in various magazines, they'd publish brief items about him, calling him:

"A brutal catechist." And, "A catechist who slaps heads."

He was convinced that a child would internalize catechism best with the help of the switch system.

He limped a bit with one leg. This was because the father of one of his pupils, whom the catechist had slapped a few times across the back of the head, had come after him. The pupil had been manifesting a few doubts about the Trinity of God. He had received three head slaps: one for God the Father, the second one for God the Son, and the third for the Holy Ghost.

Today, he had come to steer his colleague, Otto Katz, onto the right path, and to speak to his soul. He began with these remarks:

"I'm amazed that there's no crucifix hanging around here. Where do you pray your divine office? Do you even have a breviary, a priestly prayer book? Not even one picture of a saint adorns the walls of your living room. And, what is that hanging over your bed?"

Katz smiled:

"That is Susanna in the bath. The naked broad underneath is my old flame. On the right is a Japanese decorative artifact, representing a sexual act between a geisha and an old Japanese samurai. Isn't it really original? My breviary is in the kitchen. Švejk, bring that prayer book here and open it to the third page for me."

Švejk left. The sound of a cork being pulled out of a bottle of wine rang out three times in quick succession from the kitchen.

The pious catechist was obviously distraught when the three bottles appeared on the table.

"It's a lighter, consecrated wine, my dear colleague," explained Otto Katz. "It's a Riesling of very good quality. It is similar in taste to Moselle."

"I'm not drinking," the pious chaplain said in a stiff-necked tone. "I came to talk about your soul."

"In that case, dear colleague, you will get very dry in the throat," said Katz. "Have a drink and I'll listen. I am a very tolerant man and capable of listening to opinions other than my own."

The pious chaplain took a gulp and his eyes bugged out.

"The Demon's grade of good wine! Isn't that true, dear colleague?" asked Katz.

The fanatic replied harshly:

"I see that you swear."

146

"That's habit, answered Katz. "Sometimes I even catch myself and realize that I'm blaspheming. Pour another for the chaplain, Švejk. I can assure you, dear colleague, that I also say *Himmel-herr-gott,* Heavenly-lord-god, and crucifix and *sakra,* or damn.

"I think that when you have served in the military as long as I have, you'll get the hang of it, too. It is not at all hard or difficult. To us spiritual shepherds, it is very familiar: heaven, God, the cross and the exalted sacrament. Doesn't that sound nice and expert? Drink up, dear colleague."

The former catechist sipped mechanically. It was apparent that he would have liked to say something, but couldn't. He collected his thoughts.

"Dear colleague," Katz continued, "keep your head up. Don't sit there looking so mopey and sad, as if they were about to hang you in five minutes. I heard that once you ate a pork chop on Friday by mistake, because you thought it was Thursday. And that you went into the bathroom and stuck a finger down your throat so that it would come out. You thought that God would blot you out for that pork chop. Well, I'm not afraid to eat meat during a fast. I'm not even afraid of hell. Oh, pardon me. Take another sip. There, you must feel better already.

"Or is it that you have a progressive view of hell and go along with the spirit of the times and with the reformists? Then you must believe that, in place of the old common cauldrons with boiling sulfur, that today there are pressure cookers for some sinners. And that others of the damned fry in margarine, while still others, they say, are turned on electrically driven spits. Do you believe that millions of other wretched sinners are smashed by road-building steam rollers?

"Or, do you believe, that the sinners' gnashing of teeth is provided by dentists with special apparatus? That their wailing is being captured by the gramophones and that the record plates are then sent up to paradise for the amusement of the righteous?

"Perhaps, in paradise, they engage cologne sprayers to counter the stench. And, perhaps, the philharmonic plays Brahms for so long that you might prefer being in hell or purgatory instead. Who knows? The cherubs might have airplane propellers up their butts, so that they don't have to toil so hard with their wings.

147

"Yes, drink dear colleague. Švejk, pour him a cognac. It seems to me that he's not feeling so good."

When the pious chaplain had recovered from Katz' salvo, he whispered:

"Religion is a rational speculation. He who doesn't believe in the existence of the Holy Trinity . . ."

"Švejk," Katz interrupted him. "Pour the Field Chaplain one more cognac, so that he will come to his senses. Tell him a story, Švejk."

"I dutifully report, Field Chaplain, sir," said Švejk "that there once was a dean near Vlašim. His old lady ran away with a boy and all his money. So he got himself a cleaning woman. In his old age, this dean started studying St. Augustine, a saint they say belongs among the Holy Fathers. He read in his studies that a person who believes in the existence of antipodes is to be cursed.

"So he called in his cleaning woman and said to her: 'Listen, you told me once that your son is a machinist who left for Australia. That would mean that he is among antipodes. And St. Augustine said that anybody who believes in the antipodes will be damned.' 'Gentle sir,' replied the woman. 'My son sends me letters and money from Australia.' 'That is a Satanic deceit,' retorted the dean. 'Australia does not exist according to St. Augustine. The Anti-Christ is seducing you.'

"On Sunday, he publicly cursed them both and hollered to everyone that Australia didn't exist. They drove him from the church straight to the madhouse. If you ask me, there are a few more who belong there.

"In the convent of the little Ursulanies, they have a vial containing the milk with which the Virgin Mary nursed the baby Jesus. And, in the orphanage near Benešov, they brought in water from Lourdes and the orphans got the runs from it like the world has never seen before."

The pious chaplain now had black spots dancing before his eyes.

He was only revived with another shot of cognac. The cognac went straight to his brain.

The pious catechist squinted his eyes at Katz and asked:

"You don't believe in the Immaculate Conception of the Virgin Mary. You don't believe that the thumb of John the Baptist, being preserved and protected at the Piarists' Monastery, is genuine. Do you? Do you believe in the Lord God, at all? And if you don't, why are you a field chaplain?"

"Dear colleague," answered Katz, slapping him on the back in a familiar manner. "As long as the State judges it proper that soldiers, before they set out to die in battle, have the need of God's blessing, the position of field chaplain is a fairly well remunerated job in which one doesn't overwork oneself. For me, it was better than running around the training grounds, or going off on maneuvers . . . In those days, I received orders from my superiors. Today, I do what I want. I represent somebody who doesn't exist and I play the role of God myself. If I don't want to forgive somebody his sins, then I don't forgive them. Even if they beg me on their knees to do so. However, of those, one would find damn few."

"I love the Lord God," the pious chaplain said, beginning to hiccup. "I love him very much. Ah, give me a little wine . . . I respect God," he continued. "I respect Him very much and honor Him. I don't respect anybody as much as Him."

He banged his fist on the table so hard, the bottles hopped across it:

"God is an exalted character, something unearthly. He is honest in His matters. It is a radiant phenomenon. Nobody can uproot that belief in me. I hold St. Joseph in esteem, as well. In fact, I hold all the Saints in esteem. With the exception of Saint Serapion. He has such an ugly name."

"He should apply for a name change," remarked Švejk.

"I even like St. Ludmila," continued the former catechist. "And St. Bernard. He saved many pilgrims in St. Gotthard. He's got a bottle of cognac around his neck and he searches out people buried in the snow."

This entertaining discourse then took off in another direction. The pious chaplain started talking nonsense:

"I honor the innocent pups. Their holy day is December 28th. Herod, I hate . . . When the hens sleep, then you can't get fresh eggs."

He started laughing and began to sing, "Holy God, Holy Mighty."

However, he interrupted his song almost immediately, got up, turned to Katz, and asked him sharply:

"You don't believe that August 15th is the holy day of the Assumption of the Virgin Mary. Do you?"

The merriment was now going at full throttle. Still more bottles appeared, and every so often Katz would threaten:

"Say that you don't believe in the Lord God, or else I'm not going to pour another for you."

It seemed that the times of the first persecuted Christians were returning. The former catechism teacher sang a song about martyrs in the Roman arena, and then screamed:

"I believe in the Lord God. I won't deny Him. Keep your wine. I can send out for my own."

When he was about to pass out, they deposited him in bed. Before he fell asleep, he raised his right hand for an oath and declared:

"I believe in God, the Father, the Son, and the Holy Ghost. Bring me my priestly breviary!"

Švejk stuck a book laying on the bedside table into his hand. And so the pious chaplain fell asleep, clutching a copy of the *Decameron* by G. Boccaccio.

13

ŠVEJK GOES TO PROVIDE THE LAST RITES

The Field Chaplain Otto Katz sat lost in thought, musing over a circular he had just brought from the garrison office. It was a classified memorandum from the Ministry of Military Affairs:

"The Ministry of Military Affairs is abolishing, for the duration of the war, the regulations which are in force regarding the provision of the last rites for the enlisted men of the Army. The following rules for military clergymen are hereby established:

Article 1: The last rites are abolished for soldiers at the front.

Article 2: Seriously ill or wounded soldiers will not be allowed to return to the rear to receive the last anointing. Military clergymen are obligated to turn over such people immediately to the proper authorities for further prosecution.

Article 3: It will still be possible to administer the last anointing to soldiers as a group, in military hospitals in the rear. However, this will be allowed only if, on the basis of the expert opinion of military physicians, the last rites don't create any bother for the given military institution.

Article 4: In exceptional cases, the Command of Military Hospitals in the rear can allow individuals to receive the last anointing.

Article 5: Military clergymen are obligated, when requested by the Command of Military Hospitals, to administer the last rites to those being nominated by the Command."

The Field Chaplain read the regulation one more time, knowing that he had been ordered to go to the military hospital in Karlovo Square the next day to provide the last rites for two seriously wounded soldiers.

"Listen, Švejk, isn't that swine filth?!" shouted the Field Chaplain. "As if I were the only field chaplain in the whole of Prague. Why don't they send that pious priest that slept over here the other day? We're going to provide the last rites at Karlák, and I've already forgotten how it is done."

"Then, we'll buy a catechism book, Field Chaplain, sir. It will all be in there," said Švejk. "It's like a foreigner's guide for spiritual shepherds.

"In the Emmaus Monastery, there was a gardener's helper. He wanted to join the order of laymen to get a frock, so he wouldn't have to rip his own clothes when he worked.

"He had to buy a catechism and learn how a sign of the cross is made and who was the only one spared from original sin. He also had to learn what to do to have a clean conscience, and other such trifles. Then, one day, he sold half the cucumbers from their monastic garden on the sly, and left the monastery in shame. When I next ran into him, he told me: 'I could have been selling those cucumbers even without buying a catechism.'"

When Švejk brought the Field Chaplain the catechism he had purchased, Katz paged through it and said:

"See, the last anointing can be administered only by a priest, and only with oil sanctified by a bishop. So you see, Švejk, you yourself cannot provide the last anointing. Read me the part about how the last anointing is given."

Švejk read:

"It is administered in this way: The priest anoints the sick man at the points of his individual senses, praying concurrently: 'Through this holy anointing and His exceedingly gracious mercy, God has forgiven you whatever sins you have committed by sight, hearing, smell, taste, speech, touch and walk.'"

"I would like to know, Švejk, what sins a man can commit by touch. Can you explain that to me?"

"Many things, Field Chaplain, sir. You can touch the inside of somebody else's pocket. Or, at dancing parties . . . I'm sure you understand what spectacles can take place there."

"And by walking, Švejk?"

"When you start hobbling to make people feel sorry for you."

"And by smell?"

"When you don't like some stinking sonofabitch."

"And by taste, Švejk?"

"When you've got the taste for somebody's blood."

"And by speech?"

"That belongs with the hearing, Field Chaplain, sir. When somebody blabs a lot and another is listening to him."

After these gems of philosophical contemplation, Otto Katz stopped and said:

"Then we need oil sanctified by a bishop. Here are 10 crowns. Go out and buy a vial. They apparently don't have such oil at the army supply store."

So, Švejk set out on a journey for oil sanctified by a bishop. Such a search is worse than looking for the life-giving water in the fairy tales written by Božena Němcová.

He went to several drug companies. As soon as he would say, "I'd like a vial of oil sanctified by a bishop, please," some of them would start to laugh. Elsewhere, when they saw the unusually serious look on Švejk's face, they would hide under the counter, frightened stiff.

He then decided to try his luck at pharmacies. In the first, they had him escorted out by the pharmacist's assistant. In the second, they threatened to phone the security station. But, in the third one, the head pharmacist told him that a firm named Polák, a purveyor of oils and lacquers on Dlouhá Boulevard, would certainly have the desired oil in stock.

Polák was indeed an agile firm. It didn't let any buyer go without having satisfied his every wish. Should he want copaiba balsam, they poured him turpentine, and that did just as well.

So, when Švejk came and expressed a desire for 10 crowns worth of oil sanctified by a bishop, the boss told his shop clerk:

"Mister Tauchen! Pour him ten decagrams of hemp oil number three."

While wrapping the vial in paper, the shop clerk told Švejk, in a strictly business-like tone:

"This is top quality. Should you want brushes, lacquers or varnish, do turn to us. We will take care of you reliably, honestly and thoroughly."

In the meantime, the Field Chaplain was brushing up on his catechism. What he had learned in the seminary had not stuck in his memory. He really liked some of the unusually brilliant sentences in the booklet, some of which made him laugh:

"The term 'last anointing' originates in the fact that this anointing is usually the last of all anointments that the Church gives to a man."

Or:

"Any Catholic Christian can receive the last anointing when he has fallen dangerously ill and come to his senses. Such a person is to receive the last anointing, if possible, while still in possession of a good memory."

An army messenger then came with a package. In it, the Field Chaplain was informed that members of the "Association of Noblewomen for the Religious Education of Soldiers" would be present the next day at the hospital while he administered the last rites.

This Association consisted of hysterical nags who distributed holy pictures among soldiers in the hospitals. They also passed out a story book about Catholic enlisted soldiers dying for the Lord Emperor. On the cover of the book was a picture, in color, of a battle ground. The carcasses of people and horses, turned-over munition wagons, and cannons with their barrels pointing up, were strewn around everywhere. On the horizon, a village was burning and shells were bursting. In the foreground lay a dying soldier with his leg ripped off. Above him was an angel bending over and giving him a wreath with this inscription on the ribbon: "This very day you will be with me in paradise." The dying man smiled blessedly, as if they were bringing him ice cream.

After Otto Katz read through the contents of the package, he spat and thought: "Tomorrow is gonna be one of those days."

He knew these nagging dames, the rabble, as he called them, from the temple of Saint Ignatius. Years ago, he used to give sermons to the troops there. Back then, he still put a lot into his sermons. The shrews of the Association would sit behind the colonel. Two longish females, who were wearing black dresses and carrying rosaries, once approached him after a sermon. For two hours, they lectured him about the religious education of soldiers. Finally, he got ticked off and told them: "Forgive me ladies, the captain's waiting for me to join him for a game of ferbl."

"Well, we have the oil," Švejk said festively upon his return from the agile firm of Polák. "Hemp oil number three. Top quality. We can grease the whole battalion. It's a solid firm. They also sell varnish, lacquers and brushes. But, we still need a little bell."

"What do we need a little bell for, Švejk?"

154

"We have to ring it on the way, Field Chaplain, sir. It's so people will take their hats off to us. We will be on a holy mission, walking alongside the Lord God, with that hemp oil number three. That's the way it's done. There have already been a lot of people locked up because they didn't take off their hats, even though they didn't realize what was happening.

"In the Žižkov neighborhood, a parish priest once beat up a blind man because he didn't take his hat off on such an occasion. The blind man was locked up on top of it, because in court they proved that he wasn't deaf and dumb, but only blind, so he must have heard the tinkling of the bell. They said he caused everyone to feel offended, although it happened at night.

"It is like on the holy day of Corpus Christi. At other times, people wouldn't even notice us. But now, they'll be taking their hats off to us. If you don't have anything against it, Field Chaplain, sir, I'll get one right away."

Having received permission, Švejk procured a little bell in half an hour's time.

"I took it from the gate of Křížek's, that roadside inn," he said. "It cost me five minutes of fear. I had to stall, because people kept trickling in and out."

"Švejk, I'm going to the coffee house. If anybody comes, let them wait here for me."

In about an hour, a graying, older gentleman, with stern, piercing eyes and an erect body posture knocked at the door.

His whole appearance reeked of belligerent tenacity and anger. He looked as if he had been sent by fate to destroy our miserable planet and obliterate its traces in the universe.

His speech was rough, dry and stern:

"Not at home? He's gone to some coffee house? I'm to wait? Fine. I'll wait until morning. He's got money for some coffee house, but not to pay his debts? Priest, phooey! Get away from me, demon!"

He spat on the kitchen floor.

"Sir, don't spit in our house," warned Švejk, watching the stranger with concern.

"I'll spit one more time. See? Like this . . ." The stern gentleman spat on the floor for a second time. "How come the Field Chaplain's not ashamed? Military spiritual shepherd? For shame!"

"If you are an educated man, then quit spitting in somebody else's apartment," Švejk said, putting him on notice. "Or, do you think that, because there's a world war, you can dare to do anything? You must behave properly here, and not like a bum. You are going to act gently and speak decently and not carry on like a rascal, you civilian jerk, you!"

The stern gentleman got up from the chair, started shaking with agitation and screamed:

"How dare you say that I am not a decent man! What am I, then? Talk . . ."

"You are a little shithead sonofabitch, that's what you are," answered Švejk, looking straight into his eyes. "You're spitting on our floor as if you were in a streetcar, or on a train, or in some other public place. I've often wondered why they hang those signs everywhere that say spitting is forbidden. Now I know that it's on account of you. They must know you very well everywhere."

The stern gentleman's face started changing colors. He answered with a flood of epithets aimed at both Švejk and the Field Chaplain.

After a while, Švejk had heard enough of phrases like: "Both of you are hoodlums," and, "So the master, so also is his knave."

"Are you done with your name-calling?" Švejk asked calmly. "Or do you want to say more before you are thrown down the stairs?"

The stern gentleman had exhausted himself to such an extent that no valuable epithet came to his mind. He therefore fell silent. Švejk decided that waiting for further addenda would be in vain. So, he opened the door and placed the visitor in the doorway facing the hall. He then gave him such a kick that even the best player on an international championship soccer team would not have been ashamed to claim it.

Švejk's voice followed the stern gentleman's body down the staircase:

"The next time you go somewhere to be among decent people, visiting, I suggest you behave correctly."

The stern gentleman paced under the windows for a long time. He was still waiting for Otto Katz. Švejk opened the window and observed him.

In the end, the visitor's patience paid off. The Field Chaplain came home and escorted the stubborn man into the living room. Katz sat down in a chair opposite him.

Švejk brought in a spittoon and placed it in front of the guest.

"What are you doing, Švejk?"

"I dutifully report, Field Chaplain, sir, that there has already been a slight unpleasantness with this gentleman on account of his spitting on the floor."

"Leave us, Švejk. We are resolving something just between the two of us."

"I dutifully report, Field Chaplain, sir, that I'm leaving you."

Švejk went into the kitchen. Meanwhile, a very interesting conversation began to take place in the living room.

"You came for the money to cover the draft, if I'm not mistaken?" Otto Katz asked of his guest.

"Yes, and I hope . . ."

The Field Chaplain let out an audible sigh.

"A man comes often into a situation where all he has left is hope. How beautiful is that little phrase: 'to have hope.' It's part of that three-leafed clover which elevates man from the chaos of life: faith, hope, and love."

"I hope, dear Field Chaplain, that the amount . . ."

"Honorable sir," interrupted Otto Katz. "Must I repeat one more time that the words 'to hope' strengthen man in his struggle with life? Even you are not losing hope. How beautiful it is to have a certain ideal, to be an innocent, pure creature. You are someone who lends money against a draft and has the hope that it will get repaid on time. You hope, incessantly hope, that I will pay you the 1,200 crowns, when I have less than 100 in my pocket."

"Then you . . .," stuttered the guest.

"Yes, I then . . .," answered Otto Katz.

The face of the guest regained the belligerent, tenacious and angry expression it had displayed earlier.

"Sir, this is fraud!" he said, getting up.

"Calm down, honorable sir . . ."

"This is fraud!" the guest bellowed stubbornly. "You have taken advantage of my trust."

"Sir," Otto Katz observed, "you could certainly benefit from a change of air. It is too stuffy in here. -- Švejk!" he yelled into the kitchen. "This gentleman wishes to be out in the fresh air."

"I dutifully report, Field Chaplain, sir," rang out from the kitchen, "that I have already thrown the gentleman out once."

"Repeat!" the Field Chaplain ordered.

Švejk executed this directive quickly, smartly and roughly.

"It's a good thing, Field Chaplain, sir," Švejk said as he returned from the hallway, "that we got rid of him before he committed some other breech of the peace. There was once a pubkeeper in Malešice, an avid reader of the Scriptures. He had quotes from the Holy Writ for everything. When he had to whack somebody with a blackjack, he always said: 'He who spares the rod hates his son. But he who loves him, chastens him in time. --- I'll show you to fight in my pub!'"

"You see, Švejk, that's how it ends up with a man who doesn't honor a priest," the Field Chaplain said with a smile. "Saint Jan Goldenmouth, you know, John Chrysostom, said: 'He who honors the priest, honors Christ. He who persecutes the priest, persecutes Christ the Lord, whose representative happens to be that very priest.' -- Let's get well prepared for tomorrow. Let's make fried eggs and ham and cook up some Bordeaux punch. Then, let's meditate. As it says in the evening prayer: 'All the snares of the enemies of this dwelling are turned away by the mercy of God.'"

There exist some very resilient people in this world. Among them was the man who had already twice been thrown out of the Field Chaplain's apartment. Just when dinner was ready, the door bell rang. Švejk went to the door, then came back and reported:

"He's here again, Field Chaplain, sir. I've locked him in the bathroom, for the time being, so that we could dine to our satisfaction."

"That's not right, Švejk," Otto Katz said. "When a guest comes into the house, God comes into the house. During the feasts of ancient times, they amused themselves with mutant freaks. Bring him in here, and let him entertain us."

Švejk returned in a while with the amazingly persistent man, who only stared morosely off into the distance.

"Sit down," the Field Chaplain invited kindly. "We're just finishing our dinner. We had lobster and salmon. And, now, we're having fried eggs and ham, to boot. It's easy for us to feast when people lend us money."

"I hope that I'm not here to be the butt of jokes," the man said sullenly. "I'm here for the third time, already. I hope that now we can discuss this problem."

"I dutifully report, Field Chaplain, sir," remarked Švejk. "He's almost the perfect diehard. He reminds me of this guy Boušek from Libeň. One night, they threw him out of Exner's pub 18 times. And, each time, he got back in, saying that he had forgotten his pipe. He crawled in through a window, then through a door, and once through the kitchen. Finally, he came into the pub over a wall, sneaking through the cellar and into the tap-room. He'd have dropped in down the chimney had the firemen not picked him off the roof. He was so persistent that he could have become a government minister, or a member of parliament. They tried everything they could to keep him out."

The persistent man didn't seem to mind what was being said. He just stubbornly repeated:

"I want everything to be clear, and I wish to describe my predicament."

"That will be permitted of you," Otto Katz said. "Speak, honorable sir. Speak as long as you want. We will, in the meantime, continue our feast. I hope that it won't hinder your narration --- Švejk, bring more to the table!"

"As you know," said the persistent man, "a war is raging. I lent you that money before the war. And, if it were not for the war, I wouldn't insist that it be paid up. But I've had sad experiences."

He pulled a notebook from his pocket and continued:

"I have it all written down. Lieutenant Janata owed me 700 crowns. Then, he had the audacity to fall in battle at the Drina River. First Lieutenant Prášek was captured on the Russian front. He owes me around 2,000 crowns. Captain Wichterle owed me the same amount and was killed by his own soldiers near the Russian Ráva railway junction. Lieutenant Machek was taken prisoner in Serbia. He owes me 1,500 crowns.

"There are lots more people like that. This one falls in the Carpathians with my debt unpaid, while that one is taken into captivity. Another drowns on me in Serbia, someone else dies in a hospital in Hungary. Now, I hope you can understand my fears. This war will ruin me if I am not energetic and inexorable. You might raise the objection that, in your case, no direct danger looms. Well, look at this entry."

He stuck his notebook under the Field Chaplain's nose.

"Look at this. Here's a field chaplain named Matyáš from Brno. He died in an isolation hospital a week ago. I could pull my hair out. He doesn't pay me my 1,800 crowns. Yet, he goes into some quarantined building to give the last rites to a man with cholera who was none of his business."

"That was his duty, dear sir," said the Field Chaplain. "Tomorrow, I'm also going to administer the last rites ."

"And in a choleric building, too," remarked Švejk. "You should come with us, so that you can see what it's like to sacrifice yourself."

"Field chaplain, sir," the tenacious man said, "believe me, I'm in a desperate situation. Is the World War being fought in order to wipe all of my debtors off the face of the earth?"

"When they draft you in the military and march you into the field," Švejk again remarked, "then the Field Chaplain will celebrate a Holy Mass, asking heavenly God to make sure the first grenade thrown at you blows you up."

"Sir, this is a serious matter," the perfect diehard said to the Field Chaplain. "I ask that your servant not mix into our affairs, so that we can immediately resolve our problem."

"You may order me, Field Chaplain, sir," said Švejk, "to not mix into your affairs. Otherwise, I'll keep defending your interests as is proper for a real soldier. That gentleman is completely right, if he wants to leave here under his own power. I, too, don't like nasty scenes. I'm a social man."

"Švejk, this is beginning to bore me," Otto Katz said, as if not noticing the guest's presence. "I thought that this man would entertain us, would tell us some jokes. But, here he is demanding that I order you not to mix in it, although you already had to deal with him twice.

"Here he is, bothering me with some asinine story about a miserable 1,200 crowns. He's turning me away from searching my conscience, away from God. He does this on the evening before an important religious act, when I'm supposed to turn all of my senses to God. He wants me to tell him, one more time, that I won't give him any money. I don't want to talk to him any longer, lest this sacred evening be spoiled. You tell him, Švejk: The Field Chaplain won't give you anything."

Švejk fulfilled the order, yelling loudly into the guest's ear.

The persistent guest, however, remained seated.

"Švejk," Otto Katz challenged, "ask him how long he thinks he's going to sit there with his mouth hanging open?"

"I won't move from here until I am reimbursed," the perfect diehard asserted stubbornly.

Otto Katz stood up, went to the window and said:

"In that case, I am relegating him to you, Švejk. Do with him what you will."

"Let's go, sir," said Švejk, grabbing the unpleasant guest by the shoulder. "Three times lucky."

Švejk repeated his earlier performance quickly and elegantly, while the Field Chaplain drummed a dirge with his fingers on the window pane.

The rest of the evening was devoted to meditation and went through several phases. The Field Chaplain drew closer to God so piously and ardently that, at twelve o'clock at night, the sound of his singing could still be heard coming out of his apartment:

> *When we were marching,*
> *all the girls were weeping . . .*

Singing along with him was the good soldier, Švejk.

Two men in the military hospital desired the last anointing. One was an old major and the other was a reserve officer, who was also a bank manager. They both had caught a bullet in the belly in the Carpathian mountains and were laying in a ward next to each other. The reserve officer felt it was his duty to have the last rites because his superior strongly desired he have a last anointing. He believed he would be insubordinate if he did not have the last anointing. The pious major was doing it out of smart calculation, thinking that an act of faith might heal a sick man.

However, the night before their last anointing, they both died. When the Field Chaplain and Švejk arrived in the morning, they were laying under bed sheets with their faces turned black, like all those who die of asphyxiation.

Švejk was angry when they were informed at the office that the two would no longer need the last rites.

"We were in our glory, Field Chaplain, sir. And, now they've spoiled it for us."

It was true that they had been in their glory. As they rode to the hospital in a cab, Švejk had constantly rung the bell. The Field Chaplain had held the vial of oil in his hand, wrapped in a cloth napkin. He solemnly blessed any passers-by, who took off their hats, with the oil.

It's true there weren't many of them, although Švejk attempted to create a huge racket with his bell.

Several innocent children ran behind the cab. One of them sat down on the back bumper. His cohorts cried out in unison:

"Follow the cart! Follow the cart!"

Švejk had rung his bell in the midst of it all, while the cabman slashed his whip to the back, trying to discourage the kids. On Vodičkova Street, some resident custodian, a member of a Marian congregation, ran to catch up with the cab. She had herself blessed while jogging. She crossed herself, then spat:

"You're carrying the Lord God, but riding as if all the demons were driving the cab! I could catch T.B. trying to keep up!" Then, she returned, out of breath, to her old spot.

The mare pulling the cab was the creature most disturbed by the sound of the bell. It must have reminded her of something from the past, because she kept turning and looking back. Once in a while, she'd even attempt to do a dance on the cobble stones.

This was the great "glory" Švejk was talking about.

The Field Chaplain followed him into the office to take care of the financial side of the canceled last anointing. He had already calculated a bill for the accounting master sergeant. The military owed him about 150 crowns for the journey and the sanctified oil.

A dispute then followed between the officer in command of the hospital and the Field Chaplain. The Field Chaplain banged his fist on the desk several times and expressed himself in these words:

"Don't think, Commander, that last anointings are free of charge. When an officer of the dragoons, of heavily armed cavalry, is ordered to a stud farm to be with his horses, his per diem has to be paid to him anyway. I am really sorry that these two didn't live to get the last anointing. It would have cost you 50 crowns more."

In the meantime, Švejk waited down at the guard house with the vial of sanctified oil, which stirred real interest among the soldiers.

One was of the opinion that the oil might well be used to clean their rifles and bayonets.

A very young soldier from somewhere in the Czech-Moravian Highlands begged they not talk about such things. He still believed in the Lord God and said not to bring the Holy Mysteries into the conversation. There is still hope, he said, for the Christian tradition.

An old reservist looked at the greenhorn and said:

"Nice hope that is! That shrapnel will tear your head off. They're trying to bamboozle us. Once some member of the Parliament came and told us about God's peace spreading over the Earth. And, how the Lord God doesn't want war and desires that everybody live in peace and tolerate one another like brothers.

"As soon as the war broke out, they were praying for the success of arms in all the churches. And now, they speak of the Lord God like he's a chief of the general staff who directs and conducts the war. Well, you dope, I've already seen too many burials out of this hospital. And they cart away the cut-off legs and arms from here by the wagon load."

"They bury the soldiers naked," another soldier said. "So, they can dress another live one up in that uniform. And so it goes, non-stop."

"Until we win," remarked Švejk.

"This old pipe wants to win something," said a sergeant in a corner of the room. "To a front-line position with you! Into the trenches! Let you be chased with bayonets for all it's worth. Onto the barbed wire, into the mortars and through the land mines. Laying around in the rear, anybody can handle that. Nobody wants to fall."

"I think that it might be very nice to get run through with a bayonet," said Švejk. "And, it's not so bad to get a round in the belly. It's still nicer yet, when a grenade rips a man up and he sees that his legs and belly are somehow detached from him. He becomes fascinated that he will die before somebody can explain it to him."

The very young soldier sighed sincerely. He was feeling sad about his own young life, that he was born in such a stupid century, to be cut down like a cow at slaughter time.

Why?

As if he were reading his thoughts, one of the soldiers, a teacher by profession, remarked:

"Some learned men explain war by the emergence of spots on the sun. As soon as a spot emerges, then something terrible always happens. The conquest of Carthage . . ."

"Keep your educated bullshit," the sergeant interrupted. "Go and sweep out the room. It's your turn. What do we care about some idiotic sun spot? If I had even twenty of them, I wouldn't be able to buy anything with them."

"The spots on the sun have a really great significance," Švejk piped up. "There once emerged such a spot on the very same day I got beaten up at Banzets' joint in Nusle. Since then, whenever I go somewhere, I always search in the newspaper to see whether another spot has emerged. As soon as I know it has, good-bye, Mary! I don't go anywhere and just wait it out.

"When that volcano called Mont Pele destroyed the whole island of Martinique, a professor wrote in the *Národní politika*, National Politics, that he'd been long alerting his readers to a large spot on the sun. But, the *Národní politika* didn't arrive to the island in time. So, over there on Martinique, they really paid for it."

In the meantime, Otto Katz was meeting in the office upstairs with a member of "The Association of the Noblewomen for the Religious Education of Soldiers." She was an old, unpleasant nag. Since early that morning, she had been going around the hospital, giving out pictures of the saints. The sick and wounded soldiers had already pitched them into the spittoons.

During her rounds, she had upset everybody with her stupid prattle. She said that they should feel sincerely sorry for their sins and truly repent. That way, after they died, God would give them eternal salvation.

She was pale when she spoke to the Field Chaplain. She noted that the war, instead of ennobling the soldiers, turned them into animals. She said that, downstairs, the patients had stuck their tongues out at her and told her that she was a phony ogre and an unearthly goat. "*Das ist wirklich schrecklich, Herr Feldkurat, das*

164

Volk ist verdorben. That is really horrible, mister Field Chaplain. The people have turned coarse."

She started speaking of her vision of the religious education of the soldier. Only when he fights courageously for his Lord Emperor and believes in God, and has religion, only then is the soldier not spooked by death. She explained that this was because he then had the knowledge that paradise was waiting for him.

This motor-mouth kept spewing similar idiocies. It was apparent to Otto Katz that she was determined not to let him go. So, he excused himself bluntly and without elegance.

"We're going home, Švejk!" he called into the guard house.

They were not in their "glory" on the return trip home.

"Whoever wants to, can go next time to provide the last rites," said the Field Chaplain. "It's almost as if a man has to haggle over money for each soul he wants to save. All they care about is their accounts, the riffraff."

Spotting the vial of "sanctified" oil in Švejk's hand, he frowned: "The best we can do, Švejk, is to have you shine our shoes with it."

"I'll try to grease the lock with it, too," added Švejk. "It screeches terribly when you come home late at night."

Thus ended the last anointing that never took place.

14

ŠVEJK AS A MILITARY SERVANT TO LIEUTENANT LUKÁŠ

I

Švejk's good luck and happiness was not of long duration. Merciless fate tore the fabric of his friendly relationship with the Field Chaplain asunder. Up until now, Otto Katz has been presented as a nice and appealing person. But, the act he will now commit has the potential to strip him of what might be an otherwise appealing general impression.

The Field Chaplain sold Švejk to Lieutenant Lukáš. Or, said better, he actually lost him playing cards, much in the same way they used to sell serfs in Russia in earlier times. The end came so suddenly.

It all simply began as a nice social gathering at Lieutenants Lukáš' place. The game played was 21.

When Otto Katz had lost his entire stake, he said:

"How much are you going to lend me against my military servant? He's an astounding numskull and an interesting figure. He's something unsurpassed. Never have you had such a military servant."

"I will lend you 100 crowns," offered Lieutenant Lukáš. "If I don't get repaid by the day after tomorrow, you'll send me this rarity. My spotshine, my *putzfleck,* is an irritating man. He constantly mopes and writes letters home. And, all the while, he steals everything he comes across. I have already beaten him, but it's of no use. I slap him across the head every time I run into him, but it doesn't help. I knocked out several of his front teeth, but still haven't managed to straighten the guy out."

"Then it's a deal," Otto Katz said nonchalantly. "Either I repay the 100 crowns the day after tomorrow, or you get Švejk."

He lost the 100 crowns and left for home.

"I could have easily asked for 200 crowns," he mused petulantly.

However, he knew with certainty, and doubtlessly was certain, that by the day after tomorrow, he wouldn't be able to chase down the 100 crowns. He began to realize he had done something really lousy and deplorable. He had sold Švejk. While changing to the street car line which would carry him home, he was attacked by feelings of recrimination and sentimentality.

"This is not humane of me," he thought to himself, as he rang the doorbell of his own apartment. "How will I be able to look into this good-natured blockhead's eyes?"

"Dear Švejk," he said shortly after his arrival. "Today something unusual happened. I had extremely bad luck in cards. I bet everything because I had an ace in my hand. You know, I hopped it. Then, I got a 10, for a total of 21. The banker had a boy, a jack in the hole. But, he, too, dragged his total up to 21. Several times during the game I licked off an ace or a 10. But, I always seemed to draw the same count as the banker. I blew all my money."

He paused. "In the end. I lost you in the game. I borrowed 100 crowns against you. And, if I don't repay it by the day after tomorrow, you won't belong to me anymore, but to Lieutenant Lukáš. I'm really sorry about it . . ."

"I still have 100 crowns," Švejk offered. "I can lend them to you."

"All right, then give them to me," the Field Chaplain said, suddenly revived. "I'll take them to Lukáš right away. I really wouldn't like saying goodbye to you."

Lukáš was very surprised to see the Field Chaplain so soon.

"I'm coming to pay my debt," the Field Chaplain said triumphantly. "Deal me in."

"I'll hop it," the Field Chaplain said when it was his turn.

He lost the hand and announced:

"I was over only by an eyeball."

"I'll hop it again," he said the second time around.

"I'll hop ---- blind."

"Twenty takes," the banker announced.

"I'm just short of 19," the Field Chaplain meekly proclaimed. He then gave the banker the last 40 of the 100 crowns that Švejk had lent him to buy himself out of his new serfdom.

Returning home, the Field Chaplain became convinced that nothing could save Švejk, that it was foreordained that he serve Lieutenant Lukáš. This was indeed the end.

"All is in vain, Švejk," he said when Švejk opened the door for him. "Nobody can defend himself against fate. I lost you in the first game. And now, I've lost those 100 crowns of yours, too. I did everything in my power, but your fate was stronger than me. It has cast you into the talons of Lieutenant Lukáš. The time will soon come that we will have to part."

"Was there a lot in the bank?" Švejk asked calmly. "Or was it that you were only seldom the forehand and given the first card of the game? When the cards are not falling, it can be very bad. But, sometimes, it's just as lousy even when the game goes your way too well.

"In Zderaz, there lived a plumber named Vejvoda. He always played *mariáš* in a pub behind the Centennial coffee house. Once, the card demon whistled in his ear, too. 'And how about playing a little 21? You know, some onezie, for just a nickel a hand.' So, they played nickel onezie and he held the bank. They all kept getting busted. So, the ante grew to a tenner. Old Vejvoda wanted to let the others win a little, too. He kept saying: 'Little one, bad one, going home.' You cannot imagine the bad luck he had. A little one, a bad one, would not come. The bank grew to 100 crowns. None of the players had enough to hop it. So, Vejvoda began to sweat. All you could hear was this: 'Little one, bad one, going home.'

"They kept upping the stakes by a tenner and the tenners always fell in the bank. A master chimney sweep got ticked off and went home to get more money. There was already 150 in there, and he had bet it all. Vejvoda just wanted to get rid of the bank. Later, as he told the story, he wanted to get his hand up to maybe 30, just so that he wouldn't win. Instead, he got two aces. He acted as if he had nothing and purposefully said: 'Sixteen takes.' The master chimney sweep had only 15. Isn't that rotten luck?

"Old Vejvoda was all pale and unhappy. They were already bitching and whispering that he was cheating. Although he was the most honest player, they gossiped that he'd once been beaten up for stacking the deck. They poured one little crown in there after another. The bank was up to 500 crowns.

"The pubkeeper couldn't stand just watching any longer. He had put money aside to pay the brewery. So, he grabbed that cash, took a seat, threw in 200 crowns, squinted his eyes, turned the chair around for good luck and said:

"'I'm betting it all! I'm hopping the bank! And let's play,' he added sternly, 'with all our cards face-up, on the table.'

"Old Vejvoda would have given anything, just then, to lose the bank. They all marveled when he turned a seven and kept it. The pubkeeper's mouth smiled under his mustache, because he had twenty-one. Old Vejvoda was dealt a second seven, and he kept that one, too.

"'Now, you will get an ace or a ten,' the pubkeeper said with malicious pleasure. 'I'm betting my neck, Mister Vejvoda, that you go bust.' There was an astounding silence. Vejvoda gingerly turned the next card over. And what comes up, but a third seven!

"The pubkeeper turned pale as chalk. That was his last money. He went into the kitchen. After a little while, a boy, his apprentice, runs in yelling that we should go and cut the pubkeeper down. He had hung himself from the window handle. So we cut him down, revived him, and the game went on.

"By now, nobody but Vejvoda had any money. Everything was in the bank in front of him and he kept saying: 'Little one, bad one, going home.' I swear to the Living God, all he wanted was to go bust. However, because he had to turn his cards over and lay them on the table, he couldn't cheat and go over on purpose. More than 2000 crowns were piled up in front of the old plumber. They were all completely dazed over his good luck.

"Since they didn't have anymore money, they just kept putting in their markers. This lasted for several hours. The master chimney sweep already owed the bank a million. A coalman from Zderaz owed almost another million. The custodian from the Centennial cafe owed 800,000 crowns, and a doctor over two million. The *pinka*, the players fee-cup, held another 300,000 in IOU's, all on little scraps of paper.

"Old Vejvoda tried to lose every which way he could. He kept going to the washroom and giving his hand to somebody else to stand in for him. When he would come back, they would report to him that he had gotten another 21. They sent out for new cards, but

170

it was in vain. When Vejvoda would stop at 15, the next closest player would have 14.

"They all looked at old Vejvoda with outrage. The one bellyaching the most was a paver who had put in all of eight crowns in cash. He openly proclaimed that a man such as Vejvoda shouldn't be walking the face of the Earth. He should be kicked into a squirming ball, he said, and drowned like a puppy. You cannot imagine old Vejvoda's desperation.

"Finally, he got an idea. 'I'm going to the washroom,' he said to the chimney sweep. 'Take over for me.' And just like that, without a hat, he ran out of the pub and right to Myslíkova Street to get the police. He found the patrol and informed them that there was a hazardous card game taking place in the pub. The cops asked him to go up ahead. They said that they would follow right away.

"When Vejvoda returned, the other players explained to him that the doctor had lost over two million and the custodian more than three. They said the *pinka* now had markers for 500,000 crowns.

"A little while later, the cops burst in. The paver yelled out 'Save yourself, if you can!' But, it was too late. They confiscated the bank and led everyone to the police station. The coalman from Zderaz resisted, so they locked him in the drunkards' cart. There were IOU's for 150 billion in the bank, but cash money of only 15 crowns.

"'I've never seen anything like it,' the police inspector said when he saw such dizzying amounts. 'This is worse than Monte Carlo.'

"They all had to stay in jail until morning, with the exception of old Vejvoda. They let him go. Since he was the informer, they promised he'd get the customary legal reward, one third of the confiscated bank. That would have been more than 160 million crowns. However, by morning, he had gone mad and was walking around Prague ordering burglar-proof safes by the dozen. That's what you call bad luck at cards."

Švejk then went into the kitchen to make grog. Later that night, when Švejk finally managed to transport the Field Chaplain to bed, Otto Katz shed a tear and whined:

"I've sold you, buddy. Shamefully sold you. Curse me. Beat me. I'll hold myself steady. I threw you to the lions to be devoured. I can't look you in the eyes. Scratch me and scrape me, bite me, destroy me. I don't deserve anything better. Do you know what I am?"

Otto Katz buried his tear-stained face into a pillow and said quietly, with a gentle, soft voice:

"I am a scoundrel without principles." He then fell dead asleep.

The next day, the Field Chaplain avoided Švejk's gaze. He left early in the morning and returned late at night with a fat infantryman.

"Show him, Švejk," he said, again avoiding his eyes, "where everything is, so that he can orient himself. And teach him a lesson in how to cook that grog. In the morning, report to Lieutenant Lukáš."

Švejk and the new man pleasantly cooked grog for most of the night. Toward the morning, the fat infantryman was barely able to stand on his feet. He hummed a strange medley of national folk songs, which he got mixed up:

"Around Chodov, a little water runs . . . my most beloved draws red beer there . . . Mountain, mountain, you are high . . . maids were strolling down the road . . . On the White Mountain a little farmer is plowing."

"I don't worry about you," said Švejk. "With talent like yours, you'll last a long time with the Field Chaplain."

So, that morning, Lieutenant Lukáš saw the honest and sincere face of the good soldier Švejk for the first time. He saluted and said:

"I dutifully report Lieutenant, sir, that I'm Švejk, who was lost by the Field Chaplain playing cards."

II

The institution of military servants is of ancient origin. It seems that Alexander the Great of Macedonia had a *putzfleck*. In feudal times, the knights' mercenaries fulfilled this role. What was Sancho Panza to Don Quixote? I am surprised that the history of military servants has not yet been written. If there were such a history, we

172

would find the story of the starving Duke of Almavira, who ate his military servant during the siege of Toledo. And he ate him without any salt. The duke himself writes about this in his memoirs, saying that his servant's meat was delicate, tender, and supple. The taste, he says, was similar to something between chicken and donkey.

In an old Swabian book on the military arts, we find detailed guidelines for military servants. The *putzfleck* of old times was to be pious, virtuous, truthful, modest, valiant, courageous, honest, and diligent. In short, he was to be the paradigm of a man. In this new era, a lot has changed pertaining to this archetype.

The modern *putzfleck* is now sometimes simply called a "pipe."[16] Today, he isn't usually pious, or virtuous, or truthful. He lies, bamboozles his master, and often turns the life of his officer into a genuine hell. He is a sly slave, thinking up the most varied, insidious tricks to make his master's life more bitter. A self-sacrificing creature who would let himself be eaten by his master without salt, as the Duke of Almavira's noble Fernando did, cannot be found among this new generation of *putzflecks*.

On the other hand, we see that today's officers, wrestling for life or death with these servants of the new era, use the most diverse means to hold onto their authority. They tend to rule with a certain type of terror. In the year 1912, there was a trial in the Styrian Gratz. The leading role was played by a captain who had kicked his *putzfleck* to death. He was freed because it was only the second time he had murdered one.

Obviously, to these gentlemen, the life of a *putzfleck* has no worth. He is merely an object. In many cases, he is a punching bag, a slave, a servant to perform any and all jobs. It's no wonder then, that such a position demands that this slave be crafty and sly. His position on our planet can be compared only to the suffering of the waiter apprentices of old times, who were trained to be conscientious by constant slaps to the head, and torture.

However, there are cases when a *putzfleck* rises to become an officer's favorite. In such cases, he becomes the terror of the company, or even of the battalion. He decides the soldiers' leaves.

---

[16] Named for the long curved pipes most of them smoked. "Pipe" was also used to denote any older man: i.e., an "old goat," or an "old geezer."

Or he can put in a good word, so that at command report a case will turn out well. Consequently, all the NCOs try to bribe him.

During the war, these favorites were awarded large and small silver medals for courage and gallantry.

I knew several of them in the 91st Regiment. One *putzfleck* got a large silver medal only because he was an excellent cook of the geese he stole. Another one got a small silver medal because he received beautiful shipments of food supplies from home. While the regular troops were starving, this *putzfleck*'s master overstuffed himself so much that he couldn't walk.

His master wrote this recommendation for his medal:

"For the fact, that in battle, he shows extraordinary courage and gallantry. He disregards his own life and doesn't abandon his officer for even one second while under the heavy fire of the charging enemy."

Actually, he was somewhere in the rear plundering hen-houses. The World War has changed the relationship of the *putzfleck* to his master. It has made him the most hated creature among the troops. The *putzfleck* always had a whole can of food when only one was being issued to feed five men. His field flask was always full of rum or cognac. This creature chewed on chocolate, munched on his officers' sweet biscuits, and smoked his officer's cigarettes all day long. He baked and cooked for entire hours and had an extra uniform blouse.

The officer's servant was in intimate contact with the official army messenger. He granted him plentiful left-overs from his table, and other favors.

Completing this triumvirate of company privilege was the accounting master sergeant. This threesome, living in immediate contact with their officer, knew all troop movements and war plans.

A platoon whose sergeant was the buddy of the officer's servant was always the best informed.

For instance, if the word came down:

"At two-thirty-five, we'll be hauling our ass out of here and trying to save it." Then, sure enough, at exactly two-thirty-five, the Austrian soldiers would disengage from the enemy.

The officer's servant also had the most intimate of relationships with the field kitchen. He gladly hung around the cooking cauldron.

He ordered food for himself as if he were at a restaurant and had a menu in front of him.

"I want a rib," he'd tell the cook. "Yesterday you gave me a tail. Also, add a piece of liver to the soup for me. You know that I don't feed on spleen."

The *putzfleck* was at his most magnificent when he created panic. During a bombardment of the positions, his heart would drop into his pants. At that time, he would take his master's luggage to the safest shelter. He would then hide his head under a blanket believing that a grenade couldn't find him. He had no greater wish than for his master to be wounded. He would then get to follow him to the rear, and fade into the really deep background.

He constantly cultivated panic with certain secretiveness.

"It seems to me, that they are breaking down the telephones," he would relay confidentially among the ranks. He was even happier when he could say:

"They've already broken them down."

Nobody liked to retreat as much as the *putzfleck* did. At that moment, the pipe would forget that the swishing above his head was the sound of grenades and shrapnel. He would retreat tirelessly to the staff headquarters, hauling the luggage. There, horse-drawn transport wagons were waiting. He loved to ride in the Austrian military supply convoys. In the worst cases, the *putzfleck* was known to even seize two-wheeled ambulance gigs. When he had to go on foot, he was devastated. In such cases, he left his master's luggage in the trenches and would only drag his own possessions to safety.

When it happened that his officer ran away, but that he, himself, was captured, the officer's servant never failed to drag his master's luggage into captivity, as well. It became his property and he clung to it with his soul.

An officer's servant, who had been captured, once walked from Dubno all the way to Dárnice, on the other side of Kiev. In addition to his backpack and the backpack of his officer who had run away, he was lugging five hand suitcases of various shapes, two blankets and a pillow, aside from some luggage he carried on his head. He complained that he originally had two more suitcases, but Cossacks had stolen them.

I'll never forget the man who was killing himself dragging his baggage through the whole Ukraine. He was like a live shipping-wagon. I cannot see how he could have managed to carry such an ungodly weight for so many hundreds of kilometers. He rode with his baggage all the way to Tashkent. He died looking after it. He perished on his pile of luggage, from spotted typhoid, in a prisoner-of-war camp.

Nowadays, officers' servants are dispersed throughout this whole Republic of ours. They tell yarns of their heroic deeds. They charged the enemy at Sokal, Dubno, Niš, and Piava. Every one of them is a Napoleon:

"I told our colonel to call the staff headquarters, that the battle can now be started."

Most of the pipes were just reactionaries. But, some were informers and the troops hated them. For these *putzflecks*, it was a special pleasure to stand by and watch when somebody they had snitched on was being tied up.

They evolved into a special caste. Their selfishness knew no limits.

III

Lieutenant Lukáš was the archetypal active duty officer of the decrepit Austrian monarchy. The cadet school prepared him well to be an amphibian. He spoke German when in public. He wrote in German, but read Czech books. When he taught at the one-year volunteer school, his pupils were all Czechs. He'd tell them in confidence:

"Let us be Czechs, but nobody has to know about it. I also am a Czech."

He viewed being Czech as if it were some sort of secret society that it is better to detour far around.

Otherwise, he was a kind man who didn't fear his superiors. He took good care of his company during maneuvers, as is decent and proper. He'd always deploy the company comfortably in barns. Often, he'd buy a barrel of beer from his modest pay and have them roll it out for his soldiers.

He liked when the soldiers sang songs on the march. He made them sing both to and from their exercises. Walking alongside his company, he would sing along with them:

And when it was midnight,
The oats would jump from the sack.
Zhoom-tar-ee-ah, Boom!

He was popular with the troops, because he was unusually just. And, it was not his habit to torture anybody.

The NCOs trembled before him. He could make a genuine lamb out of the most brutal master sergeant in a month.

It's true that he knew how to scream, but he never swore. He used choice words and sentences.

"Boy, I really don't like punishing you," he'd say. "But, I have no choice, because the capability and prowess of the troops depends on discipline. Without discipline, the army is a reed swaying in the wind. If you don't have your uniform in order, if the buttons are not sewn on well, or are missing, then, it becomes apparent to me that you've forgotten your obligations to the army.

"It might seem incomprehensible to you. You might ask, 'Why should I be locked up merely because yesterday, during uniform inspection, I was missing one button on my blouse?'

"Such a tiny, minuscule thing is totally overlooked in civilian life. But, in the military, neglect of your appearance must be punished immediately. And why? It is not a question of the mere fact that you were short a button. It's because you must get used to order. Today, you might not sew on a button. You start being lackadaisical.

"Then, tomorrow, it might seem too difficult for you to disassemble your rifle and clean it. The day after tomorrow, you'll forget your bayonet in a pub somewhere. In the end, you'll fall asleep at your post. And just think, you started to live the life of a slouch and it all started with that unfortunate missing button.

"That's the way it is, boy. And, that's why I'm punishing you. It's so that I can spare you even worse punishment for acts that you might commit later. You would slowly, but surely, forget your duties. So, I'm locking you up for five days. I hope that, on bread and water, you will think about this punishment, not as revenge, but as a means of education. It's purpose is the reformation and improvement of the punished soldier."

He should have been promoted to captain a long time ago. And, his carefulness regarding the nationalities question didn't help him because he approached his superiors with real directness. He refused to be servile on the job.

These traits were what was left of his character, nurtured on the farm where he was raised in the Czech south. He was born in a village in the midst of black forests and ponds.

Though he was just toward his troops and didn't torment them, there was a peculiar negative trait in his character. He hated his servants. It was partly because he always had the bad luck to get the most irritating and vile of *putzflecks*.

He'd hit them in the mouth and slap them on the head. He tried to improve them by talking to them, by his good example, and by not regarding them as soldiers. He wrestled with them hopelessly for a number of years. He replaced them constantly, but he knew it was hopeless. In the end, he would just sigh:

"Again, I've been assigned a wretched, dumb beast." He viewed his military servants as a lower species of animal life.

However, he liked other animals to an unusual degree. He had a Harz canary, an Angora cat and a stable pincher. All his servants treated his animals as badly as he treated them when they did something despicable.

They'd torment the canary by starving it. One servant even knocked one of the Angora cat's eyes out. The stable pincher was viciously beaten on sight by most of them. In the end, one of Švejk's predecessors led the poor creature to a carrion dealer in Pankrác, where he had him put to sleep. And the *putzfleck* did not regret putting up 10 crowns for the job out of his own pocket. He simply informed the Lieutenant that the dog had run away from him during a stroll. The next day, the Lieutenant had him back on the training ground, marching with the company.

When Švejk came to check in with Lukáš and report for duty, the Lieutenant led him to the living room and said:

"You were recommended by Field Chaplain Katz. I hope that you don't disgrace his reference. I've already had a dozen servants and none has even stayed long enough to be broken in. I'm letting you know that I am strict and that I horribly punish every vile deed and every lie. I want you to always speak the truth and carry out all my orders, without grumbling. If I say: 'Jump into the fire,' then, into that fire you must jump, even if you don't feel like it. What are you staring at?"

Švejk had been staring at the canary in a cage hanging on the wall.

He swiveled his good-natured eyes to the Lieutenant and answered him in a pleasant, good-natured tone:

"I dutifully report, Lieutenant, sir. I was looking at that Harz canary over there."

Švejk knew he had interrupted the flow of the Lieutenant's speech. So, he stood in true military fashion, without blinking, and gazed straight into the Lieutenant's eyes.

The Lieutenant wanted to say something sharp. But after observing the innocent expression on Švejk's face, he only said :

"The Field Chaplain recommended you as an astounding numskull. And I think that he was not mistaken."

"I dutifully report Lieutenant, sir, that the Field Chaplain really wasn't mistaken. When I was on active duty, I was discharged for idiocy, and notorious idiocy at that. They let two of us from the regiment go on that account, myself and Captain von Kaunitz. Please forgive my description, Lieutenant, sir. But, when the captain walked down the street, he would concurrently dig into the left nostril of his nose with a finger of his left hand. And with a finger of his right hand, he'd dig in the right nostril. When he came with us to army exercises, he would always stand us in a parade-march formation and say: 'Soldiers, eh, remember, eh, that today is Wednesday, because tomorrow will be Thursday, eh.'"

Lieutenant Lukáš shrugged his shoulders like a man puzzled and unable to immediately find the words to express a certain thought.

He went from the door to the window on the side opposite Švejk, and back again. Švejk, reacting to where the Lieutenant then happened to be located, was doing eyes-right and eyes-left with such a decidedly innocent face that the Lieutenant lowered his gaze. He looked at the carpet. Then, he said something that had no bearing on Švejk's remark about the idiotic captain: "Yes, I've got to have order and cleanliness. And I must not be lied to. I love honesty. I hate a lie and I punish it mercilessly. Do you understand me?"

"I dutifully report, Lieutenant, sir, that I do understand. Nothing is worse than when a man lies. Once he starts getting entangled, then he's lost.

"In a village on the other side of Pelhřimov, there was a teacher named Marek. He was going after the daughter of a gamekeeper named Špera. And, the gamekeeper let Marek know through somebody else, that if he met his daughter in the forest, he would shoot him in the butt with bristles and salt.

"The teacher sent Špera a message that what he'd heard wasn't true. However, once again, he went to meet the girl. The gamekeeper was waiting and wanted to shoot him in the butt. The teacher was trying to talk himself out of trouble, saying that he was there gathering flowers. He added that he was also trying to catch some beetles. He was getting further and further entangled. He kept babbling and finally said that he was there just to lay down snares for the hares.

"So, the gamekeeper packed him up and led him to the police station. From there, they went directly to court. The teacher almost went to jail. If he had only told the bare truth, he would have just been shot in the ass with the bristles and salt.

"I am of the opinion that it is always best to confess, to be open. When something has already happened and when I've done something I just come out and say: 'I dutifully report that I've done such and such.' Honesty is always a very nice thing. A man always gets the farthest with it.

"Like when they have speed-walking races. As soon as they start cheating by running, they're disqualified. That happened to my cousin. An honest man is held dear. He is honored everywhere. He is happy within himself and feels born again. When he goes to sleep, he can say: 'Today, I was honest.'"

During this talk, Lieutenant Lukáš sat on the chair. For a long time, he stared at Švejk's shoes. He thought to himself:

"My God! I, too, spout such idiocies. The only difference is the form I serve them up in." But he did not want to lose his authority. So, when Švejk finished, he said:

"Under my command, you have to shine your shoes and have your uniform in order. Your buttons must be sewn on correctly. You must have the appearance of a squared-away soldier, and not some civilian bum. It is curious that none of you *putzflecks* can carry on as a military man. Of all the military servants I've had, only one had a combat appearance. And, in the end, he stole my dress uniform and sold it in the Jewtown market."

He paused and then explained to Švejk all his duties. He didn't fail to stress the fact that he must be loyal. And he must not tell anyone, anywhere, about what was going on at home.

"There are ladies who visit me," he pointed out. "Sometimes, when I'm not on duty in the morning, one of them will stay overnight. In such cases, when I ring, you will bring us our coffee in bed. Do you understand?"

"I dutifully report, that I understand, Lieutenant, sir. If I were to come near the bed unexpectedly, then it could perhaps be embarrassing to a lady. I once brought a young lady home and just as we were having great fun, my cleaning woman brought coffee to my bed. She panicked and drenched my whole back. But, she still politely said: 'May God give you a good morning.' I know what is decent and proper when a lady sleeps over."

"Yes, Švejk, we always have to maintain unusual tact concerning the ladies," said the Lieutenant. He was getting into a better mood because the talk had turned to a favorite subject. The ladies filled his free time between the garrison, the training ground and playing cards.

Women gave his apartment a soul. They created a home for him. There were several dozen and many of them would try to decorate his apartment with various nick-knacks during their stay.

The wife of a coffeehouse owner lived with him for two whole weeks before her husband came for her. She embroidered a charming cloth table-runner. She monogrammed all of his underwear with his initials. She would have even finished embroidering the wall-hanging if her husband hadn't destroyed their idyll.

One young lady's parents came for her after a three-week stay. She tried to turn his bedroom into a ladies's boudoir. She scattered various trinkets, and little vases, everywhere. Over his bed she hung the picture of a guardian angel.

From all the corners of the bedroom and dining room you could sense the touch of a female hand. It even penetrated into the kitchen. There you could find the most varied kitchen tools and implements. These were magnificent gifts from Mrs. Factory-owner. Besides her passion, she brought along an apparatus for cutting kitchen vegetables, including cabbage. She gave him gadgets for grating buns and scraping liver. She brought pots, baking pans, frying pans, wooden mixing spoons and god-knows what else.

However, she left a week later, because she couldn't reconcile herself to the thought that the Lieutenant had about 20 other lovers, besides her. They all had evidently left certain imprints on the performance of the noble stud in uniform.

Lieutenant Lukáš also kept up a wide correspondence. He had an album of pictures of his lovers and a collection of various relics. For the past two years, he'd exhibited a tendency toward fetishism. So, he had collected various female items. Among them were: four charming pairs of female panties with embroidery, several stockings, some batiste kerchiefs, several garters, three fine, see-through, ladies' negligees, and even a corset.

"I'm on duty today," he told Švejk. "I'll be home only at night. Look after everything and put the apartment in order. My last servant, due to his villainy, was sent off to the front with a march company."

He gave Švejk still more instructions, regarding the canary and the Angora cat. And, while in the doorway, he still found the time to rattle off a few more words about honesty and order.

After his departure, Švejk put everything in the apartment in the best of shape. When Lieutenant Lukáš returned home at night, Švejk was able to say:

"I dutifully report, sir, that everything is in order. However, the cat got into mischief and devoured your canary."

"How?" thundered the Lieutenant.

"I dutifully report, Lieutenant, sir. I know that cats don't like canaries and that they mistreat them. So, I wanted to get them mutually acquainted, because I like animals very much. I wanted the beast to learn how she was supposed to behave toward a canary. If she made one false move, I intended to dust her fur so hard that she'd never forget it for the rest of her life.

"A hat maker lives in my building. His cat ate three canaries before he'd trained her to leave them alone. Now, a canary can even sit on her. I wanted to try it, too. I pulled the canary out of the cage and gave the bird to her to sniff. And, the monkey, before I could stop her, she bit its head off. I really didn't expect such a dirty, low-down thing from her.

"Lieutenant, sir, if it were a sparrow, I would say nothing. But such a nice canary, a Harz canary. And how eagerly she devoured him, feathers and all. The whole time, she purred with pure joy. It is said that cats do not appreciate music and can't stand it when a . canary is singing. I really gave that cat a piece of my mind. But God forbid, I didn't do anything to her. I waited for you to decide how to punish the mangy bitch."

Švejk had looked sincerely into the Lieutenants' eyes while telling his story. Lukáš had at first stepped up to him with brutal intention. Now, however, he backed away, sat down on a chair and asked:

"Listen, Švejk, are you really one of God's dumb beasts?"

"I dutifully report, Lieutenant, sir," Švejk answered festively. "I am! – Since I was little, I have had such bad luck. I always want to do good, or to fix something. But, it never works out. Some unpleasantness always results. For me and the people around me. I really wanted to have the two get acquainted. So they would understand each other. It's not my fault that she devoured him and ended their relationship. Years ago, in the Štuparts' building, a cat devoured a parrot, because it was laughing at her and meowing like her. Cats have a tough life, too, Lieutenant, sir. But, if you order me to execute her, then I'll have to slam the door on her and yank her by the tail, otherwise she might never die."

All the while, Švejk maintained his most innocent face and a likable, good-natured smile. Then Švejk began to expound about methods of executing cats. The content would certainly have driven anyone from the association against tormenting animals into the madhouse.

However, as he did so, he exhibited some expert knowledge. This prompted Lieutenant Lukáš to forget his wrath and ask:

"You know how to handle animals? Do you love animals and have a feel for them?"

"I love dogs best of all," said Švejk. "It is a lucrative trade for someone who knows how to sell them. I couldn't do it well, because I've always been honest. People would come after me because I had sold them some half-dead wimp instead of a healthy, pure-blooded dog. People think that all dogs have to be pure-blooded and healthy. Everybody wants a pedigree. So, I had to have pedigrees printed up. I had to make some mutt in Košíře, that was born in a brick yard, into the most pure-blooded nobleman. I gave him a pedigree from a Bavarian dog kennel named Armin von Barheim.

"People were so glad to have a pedigreed dog at home, and that I was able even to offer a spitz from Vršovice as a basset. They only marveled: 'Why, such a rare dog! It's come all the way from Germany. It's hairy and doesn't have crooked legs.' And that's the way it's done in all the kennels.

"Lieutenant, sir, if you could only see the fraud that is perpetrated with pedigrees in the big kennels. Few dogs could say of themselves: 'I'm a pure-blooded creature.' Either the mother forgets herself with some mutt, or his grandmother did. Or, he had more than one daddy and inherited something from each of them: from this one, the ears; from that one, the tail; from another, the hair on his snout; from the third one, the nose; from the fourth, a gimpy leg; and from the fifth one, his size. And when a dog has had twelve or more fathers, Lieutenant, sir, then you can imagine what such a dog looks like.

"Once, I bought such a dog, a bowser. He had so many fathers and was so ugly, that all the other dogs avoided him. So, I bought him out of pity. He was so forlorn. And, he would constantly sit at home in a corner and be sort of sad. Finally, I sold him as a stable pincher. Changing his color to salt-and-pepper was the hardest part of the job. Now, he's with his master in Moravia, and I haven't seen him since."

Lieutenant Lukáš became very interested in this exposition of canine science. So, Švejk continued without interruption:

"Dogs can't color their hair by themselves, the way the ladies do. That always has to be taken care of by whoever wants to sell him. When a dog is such an old man that he's all white-haired, you might want to sell him as a year old puppy, or even try to pass this grandpa off for a nine-month old. Then you have to buy cracking-silver, dissolve it, and paint him black, so that he looks like new. In order for him to gain strength, you feed him like a horse with arsenic. His teeth, you clean with sand paper. The kind that they clean rusty knives with.

"And before you take him on a leash to sell to some buyer, you pour slivovitz into him, so the dog will be a little drunk. Right away, he is alert and happy. He barks joyously and makes friends with everybody like a drunken, city council member.

"Lieutenant, sir, the main thing is this: people have to be talked to. Talked to for so long that the buyer is totally baffled into a stupor. If you don't have anything at home but some hunting dog, and somebody wants to buy a miniature pincher, you must be able to talk the man into changing his mind. Instead of the miniature pincher he's got to take away that hunting dog. And if, by chance, you only have a miniature pincher, and a customer comes to buy a mean, German mastiff as a watchdog, you must confuse him so much, that he will walk away with that midget pincher in his pocket, instead of a mastiff.

"Once, when I used to trade animals, a lady came saying that her parrot had flown away into the garden. Just then, some little boys were playing Red Indians in front of her villa and they caught the parrot for her. They pulled out all his tail feathers. They adorned themselves like Austrian cops with plumes on their hats. The parrot fell sick from shame because he had no tail. The veterinarian finished him off with some kind of pills. So, the lady wanted to buy a new parrot. Some decent one, she said, not a vulgar one that only knows how to swear. What was I supposed to do? I had no parrot and knew of none to buy. I only had a mean bulldog, who was totally blind.

"So, Lieutenant, sir, I had to talk to her from four o'clock in the afternoon until seven in the evening. Finally, she bought the blind bulldog instead of a parrot. It was worse than some kind of a diplomatic situation. When she was leaving, I yelled after her: 'Just let the boys try to pull his tail out!' I've never spoken to her again, because, on account of that bulldog, she had to move out of Prague. He had bitten everyone in a whole apartment building. Do you believe, Lieutenant, sir, how hard it is, to get a proper animal?"

"I like dogs very much," the Lieutenant said. "Some of my buddies at the front have dogs with them. They wrote me that in the company of such a loyal and devoted animal, the war passes well and quickly for them. You know all the kinds of dogs very well. I hope, that if I get a dog, you would take care of him right. What kind, in your opinion, is the best? I have in mind to have a dog as a companion. I once had a stable pincher, but I don't know . . ."

"In my opinion, Lieutenant, sir, the stable pincher is a very pleasant dog. True, not everybody likes them because they've got such bristles. The hair is so hard on their snout, that they look like recently released penitentiary inmates. They are so ugly, that they're beautiful. And at the same time, they're smart. There's no comparison with some dimwit St. Bernard clawing the pavement trying to catch up with them. The pincher will have nothing to do with him. He's even smarter than a fox-terrier. I used to know one . . ."

Lieutenant Lukáš looked at his watch and interrupted Švejk's conversation:

"It's late. I have to sleep because tomorrow I'm on duty again. So, you can devote the whole day to finding us a stable pincher."

He went to sleep. Švejk went in the kitchen. He laid himself down on a bench to read the newspaper that the Lieutenant had brought from the garrison office.

"There you go," Švejk said to himself, reading with interest the digest of the day's events. "The Sultan decorated Emperor Wilhelm with a war medal, and I still don't even have a small silver one."

He was immersed in thought, but suddenly jumped up:

"I have almost forgotten . . ."

Švejk went into the bedroom and woke the Lieutenant, who had already fallen into a deep sleep:

"I dutifully report, Lieutenant, sir, that I don't have any order regarding the cat."

The Lieutenant was half asleep and in a dream-like state. He turned over to the other side of the bed and growled:

"Three days of confinement to the barracks!' Then, he went back to sleep.

Švejk quietly left the room and pulled the unlucky cat from underneath the sofa.

"You have three days of confinement to the barracks, he told her. "*Abtreten*! Fall out!"

The Angora cat crawled under the sofa again.

IV

Švejk was just getting ready to go look for a stable pincher, when a young lady rang the doorbell saying she wished to speak to Lieutenant Lukáš. Next to her lay two heavy suitcases. Švejk caught a glimpse of the cap of a helper descending the stairs.

"He's not home," Švejk said toughly. But, the young lady was already in the hallway and categorically ordered:

"Carry the suitcases into the bedroom!"

"I can't do that without the permission of the Lieutenant," said Švejk. "He ordered me never to do anything without him."

"You've gone mad!" exclaimed the young lady. "I have arrived to visit the Lieutenant."

"I know absolutely nothing at all about that," answered Švejk. "The Lieutenant is on duty. He'll return tonight. And he gave me an order to find a stable pincher. I know nothing of any suitcases or of any lady. I'm leaving the apartment now, so I beg you kindly to leave. I've been told nothing. I can't leave a stranger, a person that I don't know, in the apartment.

"Once, they left a man behind in the confectioner Bělčický's apartment on our street. He robbed the wardrobe and fled. – I don't˙ mean for that story to reflect anything about you," Švejk added when he saw that the young lady had a desperate look on her face and was beginning to weep.

"But you definitely cannot stay here. You've got to recognize that. The whole apartment has been entrusted to me, and I am responsible for every little trinket. Therefore, I'm asking you very kindly, one more time, not to exert yourself for nothing. As long as I don't get an order from the Lieutenant, I don't even know my own brother. I am really sorry that I have to speak to you like this. But, in the military, there has to be order."

In the meantime, the young lady had calmed down a little bit. She pulled a calling card out of her purse. She wrote several lines in pencil, inserted them into a small envelope and said dejectedly:

"Take this to the Lieutenant. I'll wait here for an answer. Here's five crowns for the trip."

"That idea holds no promise," Švejk answered, offended by the intransigence of the unexpected guest. "Keep your five crowns. I'll put them here on the chair. If you want, come along with me to the garrison and wait for an answer. I'll deliver your little note and bring you his answer. But, you definitely can't wait here in the meantime."

After those words, he pulled the suitcases into the hallway. He rattled the keys like a chateau warden, and announced formally by the door:

"I'm locking up."

The young lady walked hopelessly out into the hall. Švejk closed the door and went up ahead. The visitor pitter-pattered behind him like a little doggie. She caught up with him only when Švejk went into a tobacco shop to buy cigarettes for himself.

Now, as she walked alongside him, she attempted to establish a conversation:

"You will be sure to give it to him?"

"I will. I already said I would."

"And, will you be able to find the Lieutenant?"

"That I don't know."

They walked side by side, reticently. Only after a while did his female companion start talking again:

"You think that you won't be able to find the Lieutenant?"

"I didn't say that."

"Where do you think he could be?"

"I'm not sure."

Again, there was a lull in the conversation for a considerable time. It was reestablished with a question posed by the young lady:

"Have you lost the letter?"

"I haven't lost it, so far."

"Then, you'll be certain to turn it over to the Lieutenant?"

"Yes."

"And will you find him."

"As I've already said, I'm not sure of that," Švejk answered. "I'm always surprised when curious people constantly ask about only one thing. It is as if I were to stop every other man on the street and ask him what date it is."

Her attempt to talk, and to reach an understanding with Švejk, was thereby finished. The rest of the journey to the garrison went by in total silence. When they reached the garrison, Švejk told the young lady to wait.

He started talking to the soldiers at the gate about the war. The young lady surely must have derived an absolutely tremendous joy from this, because she began pacing nervously on the sidewalk. She appeared to be very unhappy, watching Švejk continue his long expositions. He wore such a stupid expression. The same look can also be seen in a photograph published at that time in the *Chronicle of the World War*. A caption under it reads:

"The Austrian heir to the throne is seen conversing with two pilots who have shot down a Russian airplane."

Švejk sat down on a bench at the gate and was explaining how the army's offensives had failed on the Carpathian battle front. He said that though their commander at Přemyšl, General Kusmanek, had reached Kiev in Russia, and, in the south the army had left 11 bridgeheads behind them in Serbia, he believed the Serbians wouldn't be able to keep running after Austria's soldiers for long.

He then delved into a critique of all the currently known battles individually. He said he had discovered a military El Dorado: that a platoon, when it is besieged on all sides, must indeed surrender.

When he felt he'd talked enough, he judged it appropriate to walk out and tell the desperate lady not to leave or go anywhere, that he'd be right back. Then, he went upstairs to the office. There he found Lieutenant Lukáš deciphering a trench schematic for another lieutenant. He was admonishing the other officer, telling him that he couldn't draw and had no idea whatsoever of geometry.

"See, this is the way to draw it. For a given straight line, we draw another, perpendicular straight line. We have to draw it so that it forms a right angle with the first. Do you understand? If you do this, you'll construct the trenches correctly and you won't let them stray toward the enemy. You'll stay 600 meters away from him. But the way you were drawing it, our position would penetrate the enemy line. You'd stand with your trenches perpendicular above the enemy and you need an obtuse angle. That's so simple, isn't it?"

The lieutenant was a reservist, the treasurer of some bank in civilian life. He stood desperately over the plans for the trenches. He didn't really understand anything Lukáš was saying. He sighed with relief when Švejk stepped up to the Lieutenant:

"I dutifully report, Lieutenant, sir, that some lady has sent you this note and is waiting for an answer." As he spoke, he winked meaningfully and confidentially at Lukáš.

What he read did not impress the Lieutenant favorably:

Lieber Heinrich! Mein Mann verfolgt mich. Ich muss unbedingt bei Dir ein paar Tage gastieren. Dein Bursch ist ein grosses Mistvieh. Ich bin unglücklich. Deine Katy. Dear Heinrich! My husband is persecuting me. I absolutely must visit you and stay a couple of days. Your servant is a vulgar, dumb beast. I am unhappy. Your Katy.

Lieutenant Lukáš sighed loudly, led Švejk next door to an empty office, closed the door and started pacing among the desks. When he finally stopped near Švejk, he said:

"This lady writes that you are a dumb beast. What have you done to her?"

"I have done nothing to her, I dutifully report, Lieutenant, sir. I have behaved very decently. But, she wanted to settle in the apartment right away. And because I had not received any order from you, I would not leave her behind in the apartment. On top of it, she arrived with two suitcases, as if she was coming home."

The Lieutenant sighed loudly again, and Švejk loudly echoed him.

"Why did you do that?" the Lieutenant yelled menacingly.

"I dutifully report, Lieutenant, sir, that it is a hard case. Two years ago, in Vojtěšská Street a young lady moved in to the upholsterer's apartment. He couldn't drive her out. He was forced to kill them both with gas and the fun was over. Women are a bother. I can see through them."

"A hard case," Lieutenant Lukáš said, echoing Švejk. And never had he uttered such a bare truth. Dear Heinrich was certainly in an ugly situation. A wife persecuted by her husband decides to visit him for a few days. Why did this have to happen just when Mrs. Micková from Třebon was supposed to come? She was scheduled to visit him soon, to repeat for three glorious days that, which she so generously provided every quarter of the year, when she came to Prague to shop. Even more urgently, the day after tomorrow another young lady was supposed to visit. She had already promised to let herself be seduced. She had taken all week to make up her mind, because, in no less than a month, she was supposed to marry an engineer.

190

The Lieutenant sat down on the table with his head bowed. He quietly wracked his brain, but could think of no solution. Finally, he took a seat at the table, seized an envelope and paper with an official letterhead, and wrote:

Dear Katy! I'm on duty until 9:00 PM. I will come home at ten. Please feel as if you were in your own household. As regards Švejk, my servant, I have already given him orders to oblige you in everything you should desire. Yours, Heinrich.

"You will give this letter to the gentle lady," said the Lieutenant. I'm ordering you to behave toward her deferentially, and with tact. And, you must fulfill all her wishes. That is an order. You must behave gallantly and serve her honestly. Here is 100 crowns, which you'll be accountable for. She may send you out for something. You'll order lunch and dinner for her, and so forth. Then, you'll buy three bottles of wine, and a pack of Memphis cigarettes. That's all. Nothing more for the time being. You can go. And take this to heart, Švejk, you have to do everything for her that you see in her eyes."

The young lady already had lost all hope that she would see Švejk again. Therefore, she was very surprised when she saw him walk out of the garrison and come toward her carrying a letter.

He saluted, handed her the letter and reported:

"According to the order of the Lieutenant, I am to behave toward you deferentially, gentle lady. I am to serve you with tact and honesty. And I am to do everything for you that I see in your eyes. I am to feed you and buy you anything you wish. I got 100 crowns from the Lieutenant. But, out of that, I'll have to buy three bottles of wine and a pack of Memphis cigarettes."

When she read the letter, her decisiveness returned to her. She expressed it by ordering Švejk to get her a cab. When that was fulfilled, she ordered him not to ride in the coach, but to sit next to the driver.

They were driven home. Once they were in the apartment, she played the role of the lady of the house to the hilt. First, Švejk had to carry the suitcases to the bedroom. Then, he had to beat the carpets dust-free in the yard. When she found a small cobweb behind the mirror, she flew into a state of great wrath.

191

Everything seemed to suggest that she wanted to install herself for a long time. After all, she had been forced to fight for her position.

Švejk was sweating. After he finished beating the carpets, she decided, out of the blue, that the curtains had to be taken down and shaken out. Then, he was ordered to wash all the windows in the bedroom and kitchen. Following that, she began ordering him to move the furniture around. She did this nervously. When Švejk was done dragging it all from corner to corner, she would decide she didn't like it there, and think up a new arrangement.

She turned everything in the apartment inside out. However, her energy for rearranging the nest became slowly depleted and finally came to an end.

She took clean linen out from the chest of drawers and changed the pillow and feather-down comforter cases by herself. It was apparent that she was doing this with a great longing for the bed, an object that induced her to sensuously flare her nostrils.

She sent Švejk to fetch wine and lunch. Before he returned, she changed into a see-through morning-gown, which made her especially seductive and attractive.

During lunch, she drank up a bottle of wine and smoked up a lot of the Memphis cigarettes. She then lay down in the bed. Švejk was in the kitchen enjoying his commissary ration of bread by dunking it in a sweet liqueur.

"Švejk!" She called out loudly from the bedroom. "Švejk!"

He opened the door and saw the young lady gracefully arranged in an alluring position on the pillows.

"Come on in!"

He walked over to the bed. With a peculiar smile, she took the full measure of his husky figure and strong thighs.

She slowly pulled away the fine fabric that had been hiding her feminine treasures. Then, she said sternly:

"Take off your shoes and pants. Come on!"

So it happened that, when the Lieutenant returned from the garrison, the good soldier Švejk could truthfully report to him:

"I dutifully report, Lieutenant sir, that I fulfilled all the wishes of the gentle lady, and served her honestly according to you order."

"Thank you, Švejk," said the Lieutenant. "Did she have a lot of those wishes?"

"About six," answered Švejk. "But, now she's sleeping as if she were dead to the world, as if she'd been killed by the ride. I did everything for her that I saw in her eyes."

V

Meanwhile, masses of troops were pinned down in the forests by the Dunajec and Ráb rivers and absorbing a heavy rain of grenades. Big caliber guns were ripping up whole companies and pounding them into the Carpathians Mountains. The fires of burning villages and towns lit the horizon on all the battlefields.

Yet, Lieutenant Lukáš and Švejk had other concerns. They were stuck in an unpleasant idyll. They were living with a dame who had run away from her husband, but who had now assumed the role of "the Lady of the house," in Lukáš' apartment.

When she left for a stroll, the Lieutenant called Švejk to a war council session to plan how they might get rid of her.

"It would be best, Lieutenant, sir," said Švejk, "if that husband she ran away from knew where she was. Then, he could just come and get her. As it said in the note from her that I brought you, he *is* looking for her. Why don't you send him a telegram, telling him that she's here? He could either send for her, or come and pick her up.

"There was such a case last year at a villa in Všenory. But, at that time, the hussy herself sent the telegram to her husband. He came for her and slapped both of them around. They were both civilians. But in this case, he wouldn't dare to strike an officer. After all, you are absolutely not a bit guilty, because you didn't invite anybody. When she ran away, she did it on her own. You'll see. Such a telegram will serve your purpose very well. If any blows should be thrown . . ."

"He is very intelligent," Lieutenant Lukáš interrupted. "I know him. He trades hops wholesale. I definitely have to talk to him. I will send the telegram."

The telegram he sent was very terse and business-like: "The current address of your spouse is . . . " The address of Lieutenant Lukáš' apartment followed.

So it happened that Katy was unpleasantly surprised when her husband, the trader in hops, barged through the door. He acted both judiciously and carefully when Katy introduced them to each other:

"My husband, meet Lieutenant Lukáš."

She had not lost her balance for a moment. However, nothing more to say came into her mind.

"Please sit down, Mister Wendler," Lieutenant Lukáš offered affably. He pulled a cigarette case out of his pocket. "Would you like to have one?"

The intelligent trader of hops politely took a cigarette. When he exhaled the smoke out of his mouth, he said deliberately:

"Will you be going to a front-line position soon, Lieutenant?"

"I have requested a transfer to the 91st Regiment in Budějovice. From there, I'll probably go to the front as soon as I'm done teaching in the One-year Volunteer School. We need a whole lot of officers. Nowadays, we have a sad phenomenon. Young people, who have a legitimate right to become one-year volunteers, don't claim that right. They would rather remain common infantrymen, than strive to become cadets."

"The war has greatly damaged the hops trade. I didn't think that it would last this long," remarked the trader, looking alternately at his wife and the Lieutenant.

"Our situation is very good," said Lieutenant Lukáš. "Nowadays, no one doubts that the war will end with the victory of the Central Powers. France, England and Russia are too weak in comparison with the Austro-Turko-German granite. True, we've suffered slight setbacks at some fronts. However, as soon as we break through the Russian front between the Carpathian ridge and the central Dunajec, there's no doubt whatsoever that it will mean the end of the war.

"And, the French are threatened with losing the whole of eastern France. Soon, German troops will invade Paris. It is absolutely certain. Besides that, our movements in Serbia are continuing very successfully. The departure of our troops is, in fact, a shift in deployment. Many are interpreting that altogether differently. However, war demands absolute cool-bloodedness. We will soon see that our calculated movements in the southern theater of war will bear fruit. Please take a look . . ."

Lieutenant Lukáš gently took the hops trader by the shoulder and led him over to a map hanging on the wall that displayed the theater of war. He showed him the individual places and expounded:

"The eastern Beskydy Mountains are an excellent base for us. In sections of the Carpathians, as you can see, we have great support. A mighty blow on this line, and we won't stop until we are in Moscow. The war will be over before we know it."

"And what about Turkey?" asked the hops trader. He was trying to think of a way to get to the crux of the matter for which he had come.

"The Turks are holding themselves well," answered the Lieutenant, leading him back to the table. "The Chairman of the Turkish Parliament, Hali Bej, and Ali Bej, have arrived in Vienna. Marshall Liman, the nobleman of Sanders, was appointed supreme commander of the Turkish Dardanelles army. Goltz Pasha has come to Berlin from Constantinople. And, Enver Pasha, Vice-Admiral Usedom Pasha, and General Dževad Pasha were decorated by our Emperor. That is a lot of decorations in a relatively short time."

They all sat for a while staring at each other. Finally, the Lieutenant judged it fitting to interrupt the embarrassing silence with these words:

"When did you arrive, Mister Wendler?"

"Today, in the morning."

"I am very glad that you found me at home, because I am on night duty. I always go to the garrison in the afternoon. I was able to offer your Mistress hospitality, because the apartment is really empty all day long. Nobody is bothering her during her stay in Prague. For the sake of old acquaintance . . ."

The hops trader coughed:

"Katy is certainly a strange dame, Lieutenant. Please accept my most heart-felt thanks for everything that you have done for her. She decides to go to Prague out of the clear blue. She says that she has to cure her nervousness. I'm on the road. I come home and the house is empty. Katy is gone."

Trying to affect the most pleasant demeanor, he shook his finger at her threateningly. Smiling forcibly, he asked his wife:

"You probably thought that, since I was on the road, that you could travel, too? But, it didn't cross your mind . . ."

Lieutenant Lukáš, seeing that the flow of the conversation was veering into unpleasant difficulties, again led the intelligent hops trader to his map of the battle ground. He pointed to the underlined places and said:

"I forgot to alert you to one very interesting circumstance. Here, at this big southwest-facing arch, this group of mountains forms a great bridgehead. This is where the offensive of the allies is focused. By closing the rails that connect this bridgehead with the main defense line of the enemy, we can sever the contact between the right flank and the Northern Army on the Visla River. Is that clear to you now?"

The hops trader answered that everything was clear to him. Fearing that he might be viewed as less than tactful, he returned to his place and mentioned:

"Due to the war, our hops have lost their markets abroad. We've lost the export to France, England, Russia, and the Balkans. We're still shipping hops to Italy, but I'm afraid that Italy will get mixed up in it, as well. But, when we finally win the war, we can dictate the prices for our goods to all."

"Italy is maintaining a strict neutrality," consoled the Lieutenant. "It is . . ."

"Then, why don't they admit that they are bound by the Triple Alliance treaty with Austria-Hungary and Germany?" The hops trader had become instantly enraged. Suddenly, all his troubles flooded into his head --- his hops, his wife, the war:

"I expected that Italy would march into the field against France and against Serbia. Then, the war would already be over. The hops in my warehouses are already rotting on me. Domestic closed trades are few. My exports equal zero.

"And, Italy is maintaining neutrality. Why did Italy, as late as 1912, renew the Triple Alliance with us? Where is the Italian foreign minister, the Marquis of San Giuliano? What is that gentleman doing? Is he sleeping or what? Do you know the sales revenue I had before the war and what I have today? Do not think, that I'm not following the events," he continued, watching the Lieutenant furiously.

Lukáš was calmly releasing rings of cigarette smoke from his mouth. One smoke ring would catch up with another and smash against it. Katy watched with great interest.

"Why did the Germans go back to the border? When they were near Paris already? Why are there artillery battles raging between the Maas and the Moselle? Do you know that near the Marche in Combres and Woëwre, three breweries were burnt out? That I had been sending over 500 bales of hops to them, annually? In Vosges, the Hartmansweiler brewery burnt down. The huge brewery in Niederaspach near Müllhausen is leveled to the ground. Right there, my company lost the annual sale of 1,200 bales of hops."

He could speak no longer because he was upset. He stood up, marched over to his wife and said:

"Katy, you're going home with me immediately. Dress up. – All those events upset me so."

After a while he said in an apologetic tone:

"I used to be completely calm at one time."

When she'd left to put on her coat, he said quietly to the Lieutenant:

"It's not the first time she's acted up. Last year, she went with a substitute teacher. I found them in Zagreb. On that occasion, I closed a deal at the municipal brewery in Zagreb for 600 bales of hops. Yeah, to the south it was altogether a gold mine. Our hops used to go as far as Constantinople. Today, we're half ruined. If the government limits production of beer in this country, that will be the last blow."

He lit the cigarette Lukáš offered, and said desperately:

"Warsaw alone used to take 2,370 bales of hops. The biggest brewery there is the Augustinian. Their representative used to visit me every year. It is enough to drive one to desperation. Thankfully, I don't have any children."

This last logical conclusion, combined with a description of the annual visits of the representative of the Augustinian brewery from Warsaw, caused the Lieutenant to smile gently. The hop trader caught it and continued talking:

"The Hungarian breweries in Sopron and Gross-Kanisza used to buy, on average, 1,000 bales from my company. They bought them for their export beers which they shipped as far as Alexandria. Today, they refuse to order anything on account of the blockade. I'm offering them hops at 30% cheaper, and they still won't order even one bale. Stagnation, downturn, and misery. And, I've got domestic woes on top of it."

The hops trader fell silent. The silence was interrupted by Katy, who was ready to leave:

"What are we going to do with my suitcases?"

"They will come for them, Katy," the hops trader said contentedly. He rejoiced that everything had ended without an outburst, or a scene that would have given rise to feelings of offense. "If you still want to take care of some shopping, it is high time that we went. The train leaves at two-twenty."

They both said their friendly good-byes to Lieutenant Lukáš. The hops trader was so glad that it was all over with that he told the Lieutenant while parting in the hallway:

"God forbid, should you get wounded in the war, come to us to recuperate. We would take the most diligent care of you."

Having returned to the bedroom where Katy had dressed for the journey, the Lieutenant found 400 crowns and this note on the dresser:

Mister Lieutenant! You did not stand up for me in front of that monkey, my husband, an idiot of the first order. You allowed him to drag me away like some "thing" he had forgotten at the apartment. And, you dared to make the remark that you had offered me hospitality. I hope that I didn't cause you any larger expenses than the 400 crowns enclosed. I beg you share this money with your servant.

Lieutenant Lukáš stood for a while with the note in his hand. Then, he slowly ripped it into pieces. He smiled and looked at the money. He laid it on the sink. He noticed that, being upset, she had forgotten a decorative comb. It lay on the vanity where she had fixed her hair in front of the mirror. He deposited it among his fetishistic relics.

Švejk returned after noon. He had been looking for a stable pincher for the Lieutenant.

"Švejk," said the Lieutenant, "you're lucky. The lady staying with me is already gone. Her husband took her away with him. For all the services you extended to her, she left 400 crowns for you. You have to thank her nicely. Or rather, her husband, because it was his money she took with her on the trip. I will dictate the letter for you."

He dictated:

"Most Honored Sir! Condescend to relay my most heart-felt thanks for the 400 crowns your wife bestowed on me as a gift for the services I extended to her during her visit in Prague. Everything I did for her, I did willingly. Therefore, I cannot accept this sum and I am sending it . . . Well, just go on writing, Švejk. Why are you fidgeting so? Where did I stop?"

"I am sending it," Švejk said with a voice trembling with sorrow at this unfolding tragedy.

"All right, then let's continue: I am sending the money back with the assurance of my deepest respect. Respectful greetings and a kiss for the gentle lady's hand. Josef Švejk, officer's servant of Lieutenant Lukáš. Done?"

"I dutifully report, Lieutenant, sir. The date is still missing."

"December 20, 1914. Now, write the address on the envelope, take the 400 crowns to the Post Office, and send them to this address."

Lieutenant Lukáš began merrily whistling an aria from the operetta *The Divorced Lady*.

"One more thing, Švejk," the Lieutenant said as Švejk was departing for the Post Office. "What's with the dog that you went to look for?"

"I've got one in mind, Lieutenant, sir. He's a tremendously pretty animal. But, it will be hard to get him. Nevertheless, I hope to bring him here tomorrow. He bites."

VI

Lieutenant Lukáš didn't really catch that last word. Yet, it was so important. The sonofabitch was biting everything like there was no tomorrow. Švejk wanted to repeat it one more time. But, in the end, he thought to himself:

"What business of the Lieutenant's is it, really? He wants a dog, so I'll get him one."

It isn't a light matter to say: "Bring me a dog!" Owners are very careful about their dogs. And it doesn't have to be exactly a pure-blooded dog, either. Their owners love them and won't let anybody hurt them --- even a mutt that doesn't do anything else, except warm the feet of some dear old woman.

A dog has to have the instinct that one beautiful day he will be stolen from his master, especially if he's pure-blooded. He lives in constant fear that he will be stolen, that he *has* to be stolen.

For example, a dog will get a certain distance away from his master during a walk. At first, he is merry and frolicking. He plays with other dogs, climbs on them immorally, and they on him. He sniffs cornerstones. He raises his little leg at every opportunity, even over the grocer-woman's basket of potatoes. In short, he has such a joy of life that the world seems to him to be beautiful. That doggie is as happy as an adolescent boy after his successful high-school graduation.

Suddenly, you notice his cheerfulness is diminishing. The dog is beginning to get the feeling that he's lost. Now, a genuine despair comes over him. He runs, horrified, up and down the street. He sniffs everything and whines. In absolute desperation, he puts his tail between his legs, aims his ears toward his butt, and zips down the middle of the street to some unknown destination.

If he could talk, he'd be screaming:

"Jesusmaria! Somebody is going to steal me!"

Have you ever been in a kennel and seen these poor, frightened, canine apparitions? All of them have been stolen. The big city has bred a peculiar species of thieves who make a living exclusively by stealing dogs. There are small breeds of parlor doggies. They are midget size: tiny, miniature pinchers, no bigger than a small glove. They fit into the pocket of an overcoat, or in a lady's muff, where they are carried along. Even from there, these thieves can snatch the poor things.

At night, they will even steal a mean German spotted mastiff that is furiously guarding a villa in some suburb. They'll steal a police dog from right under a detective's nose. While you're leading your dog on a leash, they will cut it. Before you know it, they're gone with your dog and you're left staring like a dunce at the empty leash.

Fifty percent of the dogs that you pass in the street have changed masters several times. Often, years later, you'll buy back a dog that was stolen from you as a puppy, when you'd taken it out for a walk. The greatest danger looms for dogs when they're taken out to perform their physical needs, number one and two. Most of them disappear during the latter. That's why every dog looks around carefully all during this act.

There are several systems for stealing dogs. The first is the direct method, sort of in the manner of a pick-pocket. Another method is fraud, by enticing the unlucky creature to come to you. They say the dog is a loyal animal, but that is only true in a classroom reader or in a natural science textbook. Let even the most loyal dog sniff fried horsemeat sausage, and he's doomed. He'll forget all about the master alongside him. He'll turn and follow you, with saliva drooling from his jaws. He'll wag his tail affably with the joyful premonition of eating the horsemeat sausage. His nostrils will flare like those of the most high-spirited stallion being led to a mare.

*

One day, in the Small Side of Prague, down by the Chateau Stairway, two men sat in a small tap-room, passing the twilight hours. One was a soldier and the other a civilian. They leaned close to each other and whispered mysteriously. They looked like conspirators from the times of the Venetian Republic.

"Every day at eight o'clock," whispered the civilian to the soldier, "the maidservant walks with him to the corner of Havlíčkovo Square, then continues toward the park. But, he is a real sonofabitch. He bites like there's no tomorrow. He won't let you pet him, not even once."

Leaning still closer to the soldier, he whispered in his ear:

"He won't even take a sausage from you."

"Not even a fried one?" asked the soldier.

"Not even a fried one."

They both spat.

"What, then, does this sonofabitch eat?"

"God knows what. Some dogs are spoiled and pampered like an archbishop."

The soldier clanked steins with the civilian. The civilian whispered again:

"I needed to get a black spitz for a kennel above the Klamovka area. He wouldn't take a sausage from me. I kept trying for three days. I couldn't stand it anymore. So, I asked the woman that took the dog for a stroll what the dog eats, because his coat is so pretty. The lady was flattered and said that he likes pork cutlets best.

"So, I bought a schnitzel for him, thinking that was even better. But that stinking dog didn't even notice it, because it was veal. He was used to pork meat. So, I had to go back and buy him a pork cutlet. I let him sniff it, and I ran. The dog ran after me. The lady screamed: 'Spot! Spot!' But, dear Spot paid no attention. He ran all the way around the corner after the cutlet. I slipped a chain around his neck. The next day he was in the kennel above Klamovka. Under his neck, he had a tuft of white hairs. They painted them black and nobody ever recognized him.

"But, all the other dogs I've ever gone after went for the fried horsemeat sausage. And, let me tell you, there were lots of them. You can do it, too. Just ask her what that dog prefers to feed on the most. You are a soldier. You are well-built. She is likely to tell you.

"I've already asked her. But, she looked at me like she wanted to run me right through with a blade. She just yelled: 'What is it to you?!' She's not too pretty. In fact, she's a monkey. But, she'll talk to a soldier."

"Is it a real stable pincher? My Lieutenant wants nothing else."

"A dandy stable pincher. Salt-and-pepper. And really pure-blooded. Just as you are Švejk, and I am Blahník. After I lure him away with his favorite food, I'll bring him to you."

The friends clinked their steins again. Before the war, when Švejk was still making his living selling dogs, Blahník was his chief supplier. He was an experienced man. It was rumored that he bought questionable dogs from a carrion collector and then resold them. He had even caught rabies. He had been in the Pasteur Institute in Vienna so often, it was like his second home. Now, he viewed it as his duty to selflessly help the good soldier, Švejk. He was knowledgeable about all the dogs in the whole city of Prague, and its vicinity.

He spoke quietly. He did not want to reveal himself to the pubkeeper. He had tucked the pubkeeper's puppy under his coat half a year ago, and stolen him. It was a dachshund. He gave it milk to suck out of a baby bottle. The stupid puppy apparently took him for its mommy and didn't as much as breath under his coat.

As a matter of principle, he stole only pure-blooded dogs. He knew his dogs and could easily serve as an expert witness in court. He supplied kennels and private persons in any way he could. When he was walking down a street, most of the dogs would growl at him. After all, he had stolen most of them, at least once.

Often, if he were to stand by a shop window, some vengeful dog would raise its little leg and sprinkle on his pants.

*

The next day, at eight o'clock in the morning, the good soldier Švejk could be seen pacing at the corner of Havlíčkovo Square and the park. He was waiting for the maidservant to walk by with the stable pincher. At last, his waiting was rewarded. A bearded dog flew past him. His sharp hair was bristled up and he had wise black eyes. Like all dogs that have just finished doing their business, he frolicked for a while. Then, something caught his attention and he rushed toward a group of sparrows breakfasting on horse dung in the street.

Švejk walked past the maidservant. She was older. Her hair was braided neatly into a little wreath. She was whistling at the dog while twirling a chain and an elegant whip.

Švejk addressed her:

"Pardon me, miss. Can you tell me how to get to the Žižkov neighborhood?"

She stopped and looked closely at him, to see whether he was sincere. Švejk's good-natured face convinced her that this soldier really did want to go to Žižkov. The expression on her face softened and she told him willingly how to get there.

"I've only recently been transferred to Prague," Švejk said. "I'm not a local person. I'm from the countryside. You are not from Prague, either. Are you?"

"I'm from Vodňany."

"Then, we're from places not far from one another," answered Švejk. "I'm from Protivín."

His knowledge of the topography of the Czech south, gained while once on maneuvers in that region, filled the heart of the maidservant with the warmth of local fellowship.

"So, you must know the butcher, Pejchar, in the square in Protivín?"

"How could I not know him."

"He is my brother."

"Everybody likes him very much," said Švejk. "He is very nice and helpful. He's got good meat and weighs it honestly."

"Aren't you Jareš' son?" asked the girl, beginning to sympathize with the anonymous soldier from the countryside.

"I am."

"And which Jareš? The one from Krč, near Protivín, or the one from Ražice?"

"From Ražice."

"Is he still delivering beer?"

"Still."

"But, he's got to be way over 60?"

"He was 68 this year in the spring," Švejk replied calmly. "Now, he's got himself a dog and really enjoys his route. The dog sits on the wagon. He's just like that dog over there that's chasing the sparrows. A nice doggie, very nice."

"That's ours," explained his new acquaintance. "I work for the master colonel. Don't you know our colonel?"

"I do. He's really *some* intellectual," said Švejk. "We had a colonel like him in Budějovice."

"Our master is strict. When people were saying that they really beat us up in Serbia, he came home rabid and knocked all the plates down in the kitchen, and wanted to fire me."

"So, that is your doggie," Švejk interrupted her. "It's a pity that my Lieutenant can't stand dogs. I like dogs very much." He paused, then suddenly said:

"Yet, each is different. Some won't eat anything you feed them."

"Our Fox is terribly picky," she replied. "One time he stopped eating meat at all. But, now he eats it again."

"What does he like best to eat?"

"Liver, cooked liver."

"Veal or pork?"

"It's all the same to him." Švejk's fellow countrywoman smiled, because she viewed his last question as an unsuccessful attempt at a joke.

They strolled for a little while. Soon, they were joined by the stable pincher. She attached him to a chain. He behaved toward Švejk in a very familiar way and tried to at least rip his pants with his muzzle. He jumped up playfully on Švejk. Then, all of a sudden, as if he sensed what Švejk was thinking, he stopped jumping and became sad and looked stunned. He stared at Švejk as if he wanted to ask:

"So, is it the sad fate of abduction that awaits me, too?"

The maidservant told him that she walked the dog every evening at six o'clock, as well. She said she didn't trust any men from Prague. She said she had advertised herself in the newspaper once. The only one who answered was a locksmith proposing marriage. He talked her out of 800 crowns for some invention and disappeared. In the countryside, she said, people are much more honest. If she were to marry, she would accept only a country man for a husband. And, she would marry only after the war. She explained that she viewed wartime weddings as stupidity, because such brides usually ended up as widows.

Švejk led her to believe that he would come back at six. Then, he hurried to inform his friend Blahník that the pincher would eat liver of any kind.

"I'll treat him to beef liver," Blahník decided. I already hooked a St. Bernard with beef liver. He belonged to that factory owner, Hydra. And, he was a tremendously loyal animal. Tomorrow, I'll get you that dog in short order."

Blahník kept his word. In the morning, when Švejk was done tidying up the apartment, he heard barking at the door. Blahník dragged the stable pincher into the apartment. He was resisting and his hair stood on end, even more than nature had bristled him up. He rolled his eyes wildly. He glowered like a hungry tiger in a cage at the zoo with a fat visitor standing before him. He snapped his teeth and growled, as if he wanted to say: I'll rip you apart and devour you.

They tied the dog to the kitchen table and Blahník described the theft.

"I passed him by on purpose, holding the cooked liver wrapped up in paper. He started sniffing and jumping up on me. I didn't give him anything and kept going. The dog came after me. I made a turn by the park into Bredovská Street. There, I gave him the first piece. He was devouring it while we were underway. He didn't want to lose sight of me. I turned the corner into Jindřišská Street, where I gave him a new portion. When he got his fill, I put him on a chain. I dragged him all across Wenceslaus Square to the Vinohrady Quarter, and then all the way to the Vršovice neighborhood. On the way, he came up with some wonderful tricks. When I crossed the street-car tracks, he laid down and wouldn't move. Perhaps, he wanted to get himself run over.

"Oh, and Švejk, I've brought a blank pedigree with me. I bought it at Fuchs, the stationer. I know you know how to fill out pedigrees."

"It must be written in your handwriting, Švejk answered. "Write down that he comes from Leipzig, from the von Blow kennel. The father will be Arnheim von Kahlsberg. The mother, Lemma von Trautensdorf, after her father, Siegfried von Busenthal. Put down that the father received the first prize at the Berlin exhibition of stable pinchers in the year 1912. The mother was decorated with the gold medal by the Nüremberg society for the breeding of thoroughbred dogs. How old do you think he is?"

"By his teeth, about two years."

"Write down that he's one and a half."

"He's not been clipped right, Švejk. Look at his ears."

"That can be fixed. We'll trim him when he's used to us. Doing it now would just make him more angry."

The stolen dog growled rabidly, panted and writhed. Finally, he laid down with his tongue sticking out. He was tired and waited to see what would happen to him next.

Slowly, he grew calmer. But, once in a while, he would give out a sad whimper.

Blahník handed over the rest of the liver and Švejk put it in front of him. He wouldn't even peek at it. He gave them that hard-to-get look, then glared at both of them with an expression that seemed to say: I've already been tricked once. Eat it yourselves.

He laid there in resignation and pretended that he was dosing. All of a sudden, something got into his head. He got up, stood on his hind legs, and started begging with his front paws. He was capitulating.

This touching scene had no effect on Švejk.

"Down!" he shouted at the dog. The pincher laid down again, whining sorrowfully.

"What name should I put down on the pedigree?" asked Blahník. "They called him Fox. Something similar would be good. So that he'd understand it right away."

"Maybe we should call him Max," Švejk said. "Look, Blahník. He's perking up his ears. Up, Max!"

The unfortunate stable pincher, whom they had robbed of both home and name, stood up and awaited further orders.

"I think I'll untie him," Švejk decided. "We'll see what he does."

When he was untied, his first trip was to the door. He barked three short times at the door handle, as if asking them to open it. Apparently, he was relying on the magnanimity of these larcenous people who had just stolen him. Seeing that they had no sympathy for his desire to leave, he made a little puddle by the door. He was convinced that they'd throw him out, as they used to when he was young. The colonel had trained him brusquely. He had been *zimmerrein*, housebroken, in the military style.

Švejk remarked to Blahník:

"He's a smart one. He's got a big chunk of the Jesuit in him."

He struck him with his belt and stuck his snout quickly into the puddle, so he couldn't lick himself clean fast enough.

He whined over the humiliation and started running around the kitchen, sniffing desperately at his own trail. Then, clear out of the blue, he went to the table and gobbled up the rest of the liver on the floor. Finally, he laid down by the stove and fell asleep.

When he was saying goodbye to him, Švejk asked Blahník:

"What do I owe you?"

"Don't even talk about it, Švejk," Blahník said softly. "I'll do anything for an old friend, especially when he's serving in the military. God be with you, boy. And, don't ever take that dog across Havlíčkovo Square. Some tragic accident could happen. Should you ever need another dog, you know where I live."

Švejk let Max sleep for a long time.

Meanwhile, he went out and bought him a quarter kilo of liver at the butcher's. He cooked it and waited until Max woke up. He put a piece of the warm liver next to his nose .

Max started licking himself in his sleep. He stretched, sniffed the liver, and gobbled it up. Next, he went to the door and repeated his attempt to draw attention to the door handle.

"Max!" Švejk yelled at him. "Come to me!"

He came, but with distrust. Švejk took him in his lap and patted him. Max wagged the remnant of his clipped tail in a friendly way.

Then, he gently snatched Švejk's hand, held it in his mouth, and looked at him wisely. It was as if he wanted to say: There is nothing more to be done here. I know that I have lost.

Švejk continued to pet him and started telling him in a tender voice:

"There once was a doggie. His name was Fox and he lived with a colonel. The maidservant would take him for a stroll. And a man came and stole Fox. Fox ended up in the military and came to be owned by a Lieutenant. They gave him the name Max.

"Max, give me your paw! There. You see, you dumb beast. We will be good buddies. If you behave and are obedient. Otherwise, your military service will be as tough as a leather belt."

Max jumped down from Švejk's lap. He started to merrily nibble at his hand. By the time Lukáš returned from the garrison that evening, Švejk and Max were the best of friends.

Looking at Max, Švejk thought philosophically about the entire situation. One way to look at it is this, he thought:

"When you look at it from all sides, every soldier, too, is stolen from his own home."

Lieutenant Lukáš was very pleasantly surprised when he saw Max. The dog also exhibited great joy upon seeing a man with a saber again.

When asked questions about where he got the dog, and how much he cost, Švejk informed Lukáš, with absolute calm, that the dog had been given to him as a gift by a friend who had just been drafted.

"That's great, Švejk," said Lukáš, playing with Max. "You'll get 50 crowns from me on the first of the month for the dog."

"I can't accept your money, Lieutenant, sir."

"Švejk," the Lieutenant said sternly, "when you started working for me, I explained to you that you have to obey my every word. When I tell you that you'll get 50 crowns, then you have to take them and drink them up. So, what will you do with the 50 crowns, Švejk?"

"I dutifully report, Lieutenant, sir, that I will drink them up as ordered."

"And, should I perhaps forget Švejk, I order you to remind me that I am to give you 50 crowns for this dog. Understand? Does the dog have fleas? Better give him a bath and brush him down.

Tomorrow, I've got duty. But, the day after tomorrow, I will take him out for a walk."

While Švejk was bathing Max, his former owner, the colonel, was at home cursing up a storm. He screamed that whoever stole his dog would stand in front of a military court. Angry swearing thundered from his apartment. It was so loud, the windows shook. The colonel bellowed that he would have the thief shot, hanged, locked up for 20 years, and chopped to pieces.

"*Der Teufel soll den Kerl buserieren!* Let the demon from hell torment this bum! *Mit solchen Meuchelmördern werde ich bald fertig!* I'll soon be finished with such assassins!"

A catastrophe loomed ominously, over both Lieutenant Lukáš, and the good soldier, Švejk.

15

CATASTROPHE

Colonel Bedřich Kraus also carried the title of von Zillergut. His title reflected his family's dominion over a small village in the Salzburg area, which his forefathers had picked clean and frittered away in the 18th century. He was remarkably asinine. When relating a story, he would say only positive things. All the while, he would ask all present if they understood the most primitive expressions.

"For instance, a window, gentlemen. Yes, a window. Do you know what a window is?"

Or:

"A path which has a ditch next to it is called a road. Yes, gentlemen. Do you know what a ditch is? A ditch is an excavation on which more than one person works. It is a depression. Yes. The work is done with hoes. Do you know what a hoe is?"

He suffered an explanation mania. He would indulge in it with spirited animation, like some new inventor talking about his life's work.

"A book, gentlemen, is made of multiple, variously cut paper sheets, with differing formats, which are imprinted and assembled together, bound and glued. Yes. Do you know, gentlemen, what glue is? Glue is an adhesive."

He was so blatantly stupid that officers avoided him at all costs. They didn't want to hear him say things like:

"A sidewalk runs parallel to a roadway. It is an elevated, paved lane alongside the front of the house. And, the front of the house is that part which we see from the street, or from the sidewalk. We cannot see the back part of the house from the sidewalk. We can ascertain that immediately by stepping into the roadway."

He was willing to demonstrate that interesting point right away. As luck would have it, he was run over when he stepped from the sidewalk into the roadway. Since that time, he's become an even greater boor. He stops officers and gets them into endlessly long conversations about omelets, the sun, thermometers, doughnuts, windows and postage stamps.

It is really amazing that such an idiot was able to advance relatively quickly. He had very influential people behind him. His sponsor, a commanding general, always kept his fingers crossed because he knew of von Zillergut's total military incompetence.

On maneuvers, he would execute some genuine spectacles with his regiment. He never made it anywhere on time and would lead his regiment in columns against machine guns. Once, years ago, during imperial maneuvers in the Czech south, he got totally lost with his regiment. He led them all the way into Moravia. He walked his troops about for several days, until long after the maneuvers were over. The other soldiers were already laying around, back in the garrison barracks. Amazingly, he got away with it.

His friendly relations with the commanding general, and other no-less-idiotic military bigwigs of old Austria, brought him several decorations and orders of merit. Having received these unusual honors, he viewed himself as the best soldier under the sun. He also considered himself to be a superior theoretician of strategy and a master of all the military sciences.

During regimental parade reviews, he would talk to the soldiers and always ask them the same question:

"Why is the rifle adopted by the military called a 'manlicher gun'?"

Consequently, the regiment had nicknamed him *manlichertrot,* the manlicher idiot. He was unusually vengeful and destroyed subordinate officers he didn't like. When they wanted to get married, he would send bad recommendations up the chain of command to sabotage them.

He was missing half of his left ear, which an antagonist had cut off in his youth. It was the result of a duel about his opponent's simple statement of the truth:

"Bedřich Kraus von Zillergut is a primordial numskull of a man."

Should we analyze his mental abilities, we would conclude that Zillergut's faculties were not unlike those that brought infamy to that notorious idiot, the bulldog-faced Hapsburg, František Josef.

They had the same rhythm to their speech, and the same inventory of utter naiveté. Once, at a banquet in the officers' casino, the talk turned to Schiller. Out of the clear blue, Colonel Kraus von Zillergut, though the talk was about Schiller, proclaimed:

"Listen to this, gentlemen. Yesterday, I saw a steam plow, driven by a locomotive. Imagine, gentlemen, a locomotive. Not one, but two locomotives. I saw the smoke and went to get closer. And, there was a locomotive. And, on the other side was another. Tell me, gentlemen, isn't that laughable? Two locomotives, as if one wouldn't be enough."

He fell silent. After a while, he added:

"Should the gas run out, the automobile must stop. I saw that yesterday, too. Then, they keep blathering about inertia, gentlemen. It's not going. It's standing there. It won't move. It has no gas. Tell me, isn't it laughable?"

Though dull, he was unusually religious. He had a domestic altar in his home. He'd often go to confession and communion at St. Ignatius. Since the outbreak of the war, he prayed for the success of Austrian and German arms. He mixed Christianity with his dreams of German hegemony. God would help them appropriate the wealth and territory of the vanquished.

He always got terribly upset when he read in the newspaper that they had brought in prisoners of war.

He would say:

"Why bring in prisoners of war? They all should be mowed down by guns. Have no mercy. Dance among the corpses. We should burn up all the civilians in Serbia, down to the last one. Put the children to death with bayonets!"

He was no worse than the German poet Vierordt. He published verses during the war that encouraged Germany to hate and kill, with an iron soul, millions of French Devils:

All the way to the clouds and past the mountains tops
  Let us pile human bones and smoldering flesh . . .

*

After his day of teaching in the One-year Volunteer School, Lieutenant Lukáš decided to take Max out for a stroll.

"I take the liberty of bringing to your attention, Lieutenant, sir," Švejk began with concern, "you have to be careful with that dog. So that he won't run away on you. He might long for his old home. He could take off, if you were to untie him from the leash. Also, I wouldn't recommend you to take him to Havlíčkovo Square. There is a mean butcher's dog from the Marian Picture that walks there. He bites tremendously. If he sees a strange dog in his neighborhood, he immediately gets jealous, fearing the new dog will eat something of his. He is like that beggar from Saint Haštal."

Max merrily jumped around. He was getting under the Lieutenant's feet. He wrapped his leash around Lukáš' saber and expressed unusual joy to be going out for a walk.

They walked out into the street and Lieutenant Lukáš aimed the dog toward Příkopy Street. He was to meet a lady at the corner of Panská. He was absorbed in official thoughts. He was thinking about the lecture he would give the next day to the one-year-volunteers at the school. How should we state the height of a hill? Why do we always state the height as measured from sea level? From heights above sea level, how do we determine the simple height of a hill from its foot? Damn, why does the Ministry of Military Affairs put such things into the school program? Come on, this stuff is for the artillery. And, there are maps sent by the General Staff to every regiment with these calibrations on them. If the enemy is at spot elevation 312, it's not important to know what the height of the hill is from sea level. Or, even to calculate it yourself. We just look at the map, and we've got it. It's right there.

Just as he neared Panská Street, he was disturbed out of his thoughts by a stern "*Halt!*"

Simultaneously, Lukáš felt the dog trying to yank himself free from the leash. Max was barking joyfully. He broke free and threw himself at the man who had sternly called "*Halt.*"

In front of the Lieutenant stood Colonel Kraus von Zillergut. Lieutenant Lukáš saluted and snapped to attention, apologizing that he hadn't seen him.

Colonel Kraus was known among the officers for his passion for stopping and detaining soldiers for their failure to salute.

He felt Austria's success in the war depended on saluting.

Indeed, he felt all of military might was built on it.

"The soldier is supposed to insert his whole soul into saluting," he would say. It was a most beautiful example of drill-sergeant mysticism.

He cared deeply about receiving the honor of a salute from those of lower rank. Consequently, he executed this gesture according to army regulations, down to the subtlest detail, exactly and solemnly.

He laid in wait for all who passed him by. From lowly infantrymen, all the way to lieutenant colonels, none escaped him. Some infantrymen saluted on the fly, as if they were saying, "How's it going," while casually touching the bill of their caps. These, von Zillergut would bring to the garrison for punishment himself.

For him, the excuse, "I didn't see you," had no currency.

"A soldier," he would say, "must seek his superior out in a crowd and think of nothing else. He must meet his duties as prescribed for him in the *dienstreglamá*, the service regulations. When a soldier falls on the battlefield, he must salute before his death. He who doesn't know how to properly salute, or acts as if he doesn't see an officer, or salutes carelessly, is a beastly creature in my book."

"Lieutenant!" barked Colonel Kraus in a fearsome voice. "Lower ranks must always bestow honor on the higher ones! That rule hasn't been abolished! Secondly: Since when have officers become accustomed to walking down the promenade with stolen dogs? Yes, with stolen dogs. A dog which belongs to another, is a dog stolen!"

"This dog, colonel, sir . . ." objected Lieutenant Lukáš.

". . . belongs to me, Lieutenant," the Colonel interrupted him roughly. "That is my Fox."

And Fox, or "Max," remembered his old master well. He immediately and totally expelled this new master out of his heart. He tore himself loose and jumped up on the colonel. He expressed a level of joy only capable of being duplicated by a high-school sophomore in love, one who has just attained the mutual understanding of his idol, the object of his desire.

"Walking with stolen dogs, Lieutenant, is contrary to an officer's honor. Didn't you know that? An officer cannot buy a dog without having ascertained that he can buy him without repercussions," thundered Colonel Kraus, petting Fox-Max. Out of villainy, the pincher started growling at the Lieutenant and baring his teeth, as if the colonel had pointed to the Lieutenant and said:

"Get him!"

"Lieutenant," the colonel continued, "would you consider it right to ride a stolen horse? Haven't you read my ad in either the *Bohemie* or the *Tagblatt*? Alerting everyone that my stable pincher had disappeared on me? Why have you not read an ad that your superior has placed in the newspapers?"

The colonel clapped his hands together loudly.

"Really, these young officers! Where's the discipline? A colonel places ads, and a lieutenant doesn't read them!"

"If I could, you old fart, I would love to slap you a few times," Lieutenant Lukáš thought to himself. He stared at the colonel's sideburns and decided they reminded him of an orangutan.

"Walk with me for a minute," the colonel said. They walked along as if they were having a pleasant conversation:

"At the front, Lieutenant, a thing like this could not happen to you for a second time. And, walking with stolen dogs, here in the rear, must be very unpleasant. Yes! Here you are, parading with your superior's dog. At a time when we lose hundreds of officers daily on the battlefields. And, ads that go unread. If this were to continue, I could advertise for a hundred years that I lost a dog. Two-hundred years! Three-hundred years!"

The colonel blew his nose noisily, always a sign that he was greatly upset. Suddenly, he said:

"You can just keep on walking!"

He then turned around and walked away, cracking his riding whip angrily across the tip of his officer's overcoat.

Lieutenant Lukáš crossed to the other side of the street. He heard another loud "*Halt!*" The colonel had just intercepted an unfortunate infantryman, a reservist, who had been thinking of his mom at home, and not seen the colonel.

The colonel dragged the soldier, with his own hands, to the garrison for punishment, calling him a stupid sea-pig all the way there.

"What will I do to this Švejk?" Lukáš thought to himself. "I could break his face, but that's not enough. Even pulling narrow strips of skin off his body is not enough for that hoodlum.

"I'll kill him, that chicken-shit catchpole," he said to himself, while boarding a streetcar.

In the meantime Švejk had been engrossed in a conversation with a messenger from the garrison. The soldier had brought some papers for the Lieutenant to sign and was waiting for him to return.

Švejk treated him to coffee. Each was telling the other that Austria was sure to totally lose the war.

They spoke as if this was entirely self-evident. It was an endless stream of statements. Each word could certainly be cited in a court of law as high treason. They both could be easily hanged for their babble.

"The Lord Emperor must be stupid from it all," Švejk proclaimed. "He was never too bright, anyway. But, this war is sure to finish him off."

"He's an idiot," the soldier from the garrison chimed in with certainty. "He's as stupid as a log. He probably doesn't even know there *is* a war. Maybe, his lackeys were ashamed to tell him. If his signature is on that proclamation to those nations of his, then it must be a fraud. They surely printed it without his knowledge. His mind has got to be mush by now."

"He's finished," Švejk added expertly. "He craps in the seat of his pants and they have to feed him like a little kid. One of the guys in the pub says that he's got two wet nurses. He says the Lord Emperor is at the breast three times a day."

"If only this thing were done already," sighed the soldier from the garrison. "Our ass would be kicked and Austria, for once, would be left alone, at last."

They continued their conversation. Finally, Švejk condemned Austria for good with the words:

"Such an idiotic monarchy shouldn't even exist in this world."

He augmented this statement with a practical idea:

"As soon as I get to the front, I'll bolt and disappear on them."

They continued to exchange observations from the Czech point of view. The soldier from the garrison told Švejk what he had heard in Prague that day. He said that artillery could be heard near Náchod and that the Russian Czar would soon be in Krakow.

They talked about the fact that grain was being transported from the Czech lands to Germany. They bitched about how German soldiers got cigarettes and chocolate.

They recalled the times of ancient wars. Švejk seriously attempted to prove that, long ago, when they used to throw reeking stink-pots into a besieged castle, it was no bowl of honey to fight in such a stench. He had read how they had once laid siege to a castle somewhere for three years. The enemy had toyed daily with those under siege in this manner.

He would certainly have said something even more interesting and enlightening if their talk hadn't been interrupted by the return of Lieutenant Lukáš.

He cast a horrible, crushing look at Švejk. He signed the papers, dismissed the soldier, and beckoned Švejk to follow him into the living room.

The eyes of the Lieutenant emitted menacing lightning bolts. He sat down on a chair. He was pondering, while watching Švejk, when he should commence the massacre.

"First, I'll punch his face a few times," the Lieutenant thought to himself. "Then, I'll bust his nose and rip off his ears. The rest remains to be seen."

Across from Lukáš, Švejk stared at the Lieutenant sincerely and good-heartedly, with a pair of amiable, innocent eyes. He dared to interrupt the quiet before the storm with these words:

"I dutifully report, Lieutenant, sir, that you've lost your cat. She devoured the shoe polish and took the liberty to croak. I threw her into the neighbor's cellar. You'll never again be able to find such a well-behaved and pretty Angora cat."

"What *will* I do to him?" flashed through the Lieutenant's mind. "For-christ-the-lord, he has such a dumb expression on his face."

The good-hearted, innocent eyes of Švejk kept right on radiating softness and tenderness. He combined his gaze with a demeanor that suggested absolute mental balance. He acted as if everything was all right, that nothing unusual was happening at all.

Lieutenant Lukáš jumped up. But, he didn't hit Švejk, as he had originally intended. He waved his fist under his nose and hollered:

"Švejk! You have stolen a dog!"

"I dutifully report, Lieutenant, sir, that I know of no such recent case. And, I take the liberty, Lieutenant, sir, to remark, that you went with Max for a stroll right after lunch. Therefore, I could not have stolen him. I thought it was strange, right away, when you came home without the dog. I knew that something must have occurred. That's called a situation.

"In Spálená Street, there is a bag maker named Kuneš. He couldn't go with his dog for a walk, as he would be sure to lose him. Usually, he forgot the dog somewhere at a pub, or somebody stole the dog from him, or someone borrowed the dog and didn't return. . ."

"Švejk, you cattle swine! *Himllaudon*! Shut your trap! Either you're a cunning scoundrel, or you are a stupid camel and an idiotic dodo. You're all of these things. But, I'm telling you, don't play with me. Where did you get that dog from? How did you get him? Did you know that he belongs to our colonel, who took him back when we ran into each other by chance? Do you know that this is a huge scandal? So, tell the truth, did you steal the dog or not?"

"I dutifully report, Lieutenant, sir, that I didn't steal him."

"Did you know the dog was stolen?"

"I dutifully report, Lieutenant, sir, that I did know that the dog was stolen."

"Švejk! Jesusmaria! *Himelhergott*! Lord-god-in-heaven! I'll shoot you dead, you dumb beast! You ox! You shithead sonofabitch! Are you that idiotic?"

"I dutifully report, Lieutenant, sir, that you are right."

"Why did you bring me a stolen dog? Why did you plant that beastly creature in my apartment?"

"To make you happy, Lieutenant, sir."

Švejk's good-natured eyes looked tenderly at the Lieutenant's face. Lukáš sat down and groaned:

"Why is God punishing me with this dumb beast?"

The Lieutenant sat in his chair in quiet resignation. He not only didn't have the strength to give Švejk a slap on the head, he didn't even have the energy to roll himself a cigarette. Without knowing why, he sent Švejk for the *Bohemia* and the *Tagblatt*, so he could read the colonel's ad about the stolen dog.

Švejk returned with the newspapers already opened to the classifieds. He was beaming and joyously reported:

"It's in here, Lieutenant, sir. The Colonel describes the stolen stable pincher so nicely. It's just a pleasure to read it. On top of all that, he's giving a 100-crown reward to whomever recovers the dog for him. That is a very decent reward. Usually the reward is only 50 crowns.

"A man named Božetěch, from Košíře, made a living doing just that. He'd steal a dog, then look in the classifieds to see if the dog had been reported missing. He'd go over to claim the reward right away. Once, he stole a nice black spitz. But, the owner didn't run an ad in the classifieds. So, Božetěch placed an ad in the newspaper himself. He spent a whole tenner on advertising.

"At last, a gentleman reported that it was his dog. He had lost him and thought that it would be futile to look for him. The gentleman said that he didn't believe that people were honest anymore. He said that now, however, he was tremendously pleased that honesty could still be found, after all.

"He said it was against his principles to reward honesty, but that he had decided to give Božetěch a gift, a memento: his book on growing flowers at home and in little backyard gardens.

"Dear Božetěch took the black spitz by the hind legs and thrashed the gentleman over the head with it. Since that time, he swears that he will never advertise again. He would rather sell a dog to a kennel, when nobody wants to claim him, than run an ad in the classifieds."

"Go lay down, Švejk," the Lieutenant ordered. "You're capable of babbling until the morning."

Lukáš went to sleep, as well. That night, he had a nightmare. Švejk had stolen a horse from the heir to the throne and given it to him. During a parade review, Lieutenant Lukáš rode the horse at the head of his company. Unfortunately, the heir to the throne was there and recognized his horse.

The nightmare pursued Lukáš and jarred him awake. It weighed heavily on his mind. He had fallen back asleep toward the morning, exhausted by the horrible dream. Then, a persistent knocking on his door again woke him up. The good-natured face of Švejk emerged with a question:

"When am I supposed to wake you up Lieutenant, sir?"

The Lieutenant groaned from the bed:

"Out, you swine! This is something horrific!"

When he finally did wake that morning, Lieutenant Lukáš felt like he had been cracked on the back of his head a few times during a night of debauchery. Švejk brought him breakfast. The Lieutenant was shocked by Švejk's first question:

"I dutifully report, Lieutenant, sir. Would you like for me to procure a new doggie for you?"

"You know, Švejk, I'd like to send you to stand in front of a field court," said the Lieutenant with a sigh. "But, they would acquit you, because you are such a colossal dimwit. They would never have seen anything like you in their lives. Look at yourself in the mirror. Don't you get sick from the stupid expression on your face? You are the biggest mental freak-of-nature that I have ever seen. Well, tell the truth, Švejk. Do you like the way you look?"

"I dutifully report, Lieutenant, sir, that I don't like how I look in the mirror. I look somehow crooked or something. Well, of course, it is not a polished mirror.

"Once, at that Chinaman Staněk's, they had a convex mirror. When somebody would take a look at himself, then he would want to puke. The mouth was goofy, like this. The head was like a slop sink, the gut looked like something on a drunken canon. In short, the viewer cut a strange figure in that mirror. The regional governor passed by one day, took a look at himself, and they immediately had to take the mirror down."

The Lieutenant shook his head and turned away. He judged it more reasonable to deal with his coffee and milk, than with Švejk.

Švejk was already putzing around in the kitchen. Lieutenant Lukáš heard him singing:

Grenevil is marching through the
Powder Gate to take a stroll,
His sabers are flashing on him,
pretty girls are weeping . . .

Švejk soon enthusiastically began another song:

We soldiers, we are masters,
Us, the girls love on their own,
We get paid, we have a good life everywhere . . .

221

"You sure have it made, you knave," Lukáš said to himself and spat.

Švejk's head suddenly emerged in the doorway:

"I dutifully report, Lieutenant, sir, that there are two guys here for you from the garrison. You are to go immediately to see the colonel. There's also a messenger here."

Acting as if he were imparting confidential information, he added:

"Perhaps, it's on account of the doggie."

"I've already heard," said the Lieutenant, when the messenger in the hallway wanted to report to him.

He said it with true distress in his voice. As he left, he shot a devastating look at Švejk.

*

It was not just a report. It was something worse. When the Lieutenant entered his office, the gloomy colonel was sitting in an armchair.

"Two years ago, Lieutenant," the Colonel began, "you wanted to be transferred to the 91st Regiment in Budějovice. Do you know where Budějovice is? On the Vltava River. Yes, on the Vltava River. The Ohře, or something similar, flows into it. The town is very, I should say, friendly. And, if I'm not mistaken, it even has an embankment. Do you know what embankment is? It is a wall built above the water. Yes. However, that's beside the point. We had maneuvers there, once."

The colonel fell silent, and looked into his ink well. He quickly changed the subject:

"That dog of mine turned bad while you had him. He won't eat anything.

"There you go. There's a fly in the ink well. It is peculiar that, even in winter, flies fall into the ink well. What disorder."

"Spit it out already, you miserable old fart," the Lieutenant thought to himself.

The colonel stood up and walked across the office several times.

"I've been thinking it over for a long time, Lieutenant. And, I kept thinking: what should I actually do to you? What could I do so that this could never be repeated?

"Then, I remembered that you wished to be transferred to the 91st Regiment. Not long ago, the Supreme Command informed us that there's now a great shortage in the officers corps at the 91st Regiment, because the Serbians slaughtered them all. I guarantee you, with my word of honor, that within three days, you will be at the 91st Regiment in Budějovice. They're forming march battalions there. You don't have to thank me. The military needs officers who. . ."

Not knowing what really to say next, he looked at his watch and announced:

"It is ten-thirty. High time to go to the regimental report."

Thus ended their pleasant conversation. For some reason, the Lieutenant felt much better. He walked out of the office and went to the school for one-year volunteers. There, he spread the news that he would soon be going to the front, and that his going away party would be held at the Nekázanka.

When Lukáš returned home, he asked his military servant dramatically:

"Do you know, Švejk, what a march-battalion is?"

"I dutifully report, Lieutenant, sir, that a march-battalion is a march-batty, a marshka, or a march-gang. We always shorten the name to one of those."

"Then, Švejk," the Lieutenant said with a festive voice, "I am informing you, that you will soon be riding with me in a march-batty, since you like such nicknames. But, don't think that, at the front, you'll be able to act out your idiocies the same way that you do here. Does all this make you happy?"

"I dutifully report, Lieutenant, sir, that I am tremendously happy," answered the good soldier Švejk.

"It will be something truly exquisite when we both fall together for the Lord Emperor, and his family . . ."

AFTERWORD TO THE FIRST VOLUME: "IN THE REAR"

Having finished the first volume of this book, The Fateful Adventures of the Good Soldier Švejk (In the Rear), *I am announcing that two more parts will be issued in quick succession:* At the Front *and* In Captivity.[17] *In these next volumes, both soldiers and people will again speak and act as they do in reality.*

Life is no school of polished behavior. Everybody speaks as he is capable. The Master of Ceremonies, Doctor Guth, speaks differently than the pubkeeper Palivec does at the Chalice. This novel is not meant to be a text used to refine someone so he might enter the salons of society. Nor is this a book to inform socialites of which expressions they might use in polite society. It is but a historical snapshot of a certain time.

When there is a need to use a strong expression which was actually uttered, I do not hesitate to relay it in the very way it happened. I view the use of euphemisms, or the dotting out of a word, as the most asinine hypocrisy imaginable. These very words are even used in the world's parliaments.

It was said correctly, once upon a time, that a well-reared man could read anything. Only the biggest, dirty-minded swine, and other cunning vulgarians, stumble over that which is natural. In their most miserable, fraudulent, pseudo-morality, they refuse to grasp the true content. Instead, in frantic indignation, they throw themselves at individual words.

Years ago, I read a review of some novel. The critic was upset over the fact that the author wrote: "He blew and wiped his nose." He said this crass statement was contrary to everything esthetic and exalted, and to all that our literature is supposed to give to the nation.

That is just one little example of the vile, dumb beasts that are born under the sun.

---

[17] Jaroslav Hašek did, indeed, publish two more parts of the Švejk saga. The next was called "At the Front," as promised. The third, however, was called "The Glorious Thrashing." Jaroslav Hašek died on January 3rd, 1923, while writing his fourth book, "The Glorious Thrashing Continued." It is but a fragment, 80 pages long. In this last fragment, Švejk is near the front lines, but yet to fight a battle, or be captured.

People who become disconcerted over a strong expression are cowards, because it is really life that shocks them. And, such weak people are the very greatest agents of harm to both culture and character. They would have us be a nation of oversensitive folks, masturbators of false culture, of the type of Saint Alois. It is said in a book by the monk Eustach, that when Saint Alois heard how a man with flatulence released his winds, he began to weep. And, it was only by prayer that he consoled himself and found peace.

Such people say publicly that they are offended. However, they will make a circuit of public washrooms with unusual fondness, just to read the vulgar inscriptions on the walls.

By using several strong expressions in my book, I have simply demonstrated how people actually speak.

We cannot demand that the pubkeeper Palivec speak as gently as Mrs. Laudová, Doctor Guth, Mrs. Olga Fastrová, and a whole number of others. This group would love to make the whole Czechoslovak Republic a huge salon with parquet floors, where people would come in tails and gloves. Proper language would always be used, and salon manners would be exercised. Under this veil of sophistication, the salon's resident lions indulge themselves in the worst vices and eccentricities.

*

I use this opportunity to advise the reader that the pubkeeper Palivec is alive. He withstood the war by serving his sentence in a hard-labor prison. But, he has remained the same man as when he had the trouble over the picture of the Emperor František Josef.

When he read that he was in the book, he came to visit me. He bought over twenty copies of the first serial issue and has distributed them among his acquaintances, thereby helping to spread the book far and wide.

He is sincerely happy that I wrote about him and described him as a well-known foul-mouth.

"Nobody will ever muzzle me again," he told me. "I've spoken vulgar all my life. I spoke what was on my mind. And, I'll keep on talking like that. I won't, on account of some silly cow, put a gag over my trap. Today, I'm famous."

His self-esteem and confidence have really risen. His fame is based on several strong expressions. That is enough for him to be satisfied. Had I perhaps wanted to advise him that he shouldn't speak that way, I definitely would have offended this good man. But, that was not my intention. I reproduced his speech truthfully and correctly.

With his genuine language, he simply and honestly expressed the resistance of the Czechs to Byzantine ways. And, he himself didn't even know it. It was in his blood: that same disrespect for the Emperor, and for decent expressions.

*

Otto Katz is also alive. Though he could still cut a real fine figure as a field chaplain, he hung it all up on a nail after the change of the regime. He resigned from the Church. Today, he works as an executive at a factory that produces bronze and paints in northern Bohemia.

He wrote me a long letter. He threatened that he'd set things in order with me. A certain German paper published the translation of a chapter in which he is described as he really was. I visited him and it turned out very well. At two o'clock in the morning, he could not stand on his feet, but he was preaching and saying: "I am Otto Katz, Field Chaplain, and all of you are nothing but plaster heads."

Today, there are a great many people of the type of the late Bretschneider, the state detective of old Austria, still walking around this Republic. They are unusually interested in what is being said, and who is saying it.

*

I do not know whether I will manage, through this book, to achieve what I wanted. Just the fact that I heard one man cussing at another by saying: "You're as stupid as Švejk," does not very much attest to my success. However, should the word Švejk become a new epithet in the flowery wreath of defamation, I will have to be content with this as my contribution to the enrichment of the Czech language.[18]

Jaroslav Hašek

---

[18] Not only the name Švejk, but the verb **"to švejk"**, and the words **"švejking"** and **"švejkism"** became an integral part of the Czech language, culture, academic discourse, and even politics. For example: Gustav Husák, the General Secretary of the Czechoslovak Communist Party who replaced the Prague Spring reformer Alexandr Dubček in that post after the 1968 Warsaw Pact invasion and occupation of Czechoslovakia, and assumed the Presidency as well, exhorted the population in a speech during the 1970's period of "normalization" to **STOP ŠVEJKING!!!** The Czechs themselves speak of being **a nation of Švejks**. Švejk is for them a source of both great pride and shame. However, as you now know, there is some of Švejk in all of us.

About the Author

Jaroslav Hašek (b. April 30, 1883, Prague — d. January 3, 1923, Lipnice, Czechoslovakia.) Czech writer best known for *The Good Soldier Švejk*, considered one of the greatest masterpieces of satirical writing.

Hašek worked in Prague as a bank clerk, although at 17 he was already writing satirical articles for Czech newspapers. He soon abandoned business for literary career, and before World War I he published a volume of poetry, *Májové výkřiky*, (1903; "Shouts in May") and wrote 16 volumes of short stories, of which *Dobrý voják Švejk a jiné podivné historky* (1912; "Good Soldier Švejk and Other Strange Stories") is among the best known. From 1904-07 he was an editor of anarchist publications. Drafted into the Austrio-Hungarian Army, Hašek was captured on the Russian front during World War I and was made a prisoner of war. While in Russia he became a member of the Czech liberation army but later joined the Bolsheviks, for whom he wrote Communist propaganda. Upon returning to Prague, the capital of the newly created country of Czechoslovakia, he devoted himself to writing *Osudy dobrého vojáka Švejka za světové války* (1920-23; *The Good Soldier Schweik*, 1930). It was intended to be a six-volume work, but only four were completed by the time of his death.
Encyclopedia Britannica

One of Hašek's biographers, Emmanuel Frynta, writes:

"He was one of that generation which fully fought with the problems of the modern world. He was one of the artists at the start of the century who so splendidly cast light on the question of a live, valid, meaningful art worthy of the time. He was a curious, not easily understood person, too mobile and opaque for portrayal. As a creator, (he was) seemingly careless, natural, (and) spontaneous, . . . but, in reality (he was) sharply discerning and refined in his specific type of non-literariness . . . (he) was working farsightedly in the field of language and style, with something that was to become the shape of (the) speech of the century."

Hašek's life was much wilder and interesting than one can glean from the above excerpts. To learn more about the writer of the vastly popular *Good Soldier Švejk*, read the *Bad Bohemian: The life of Jaroslav Hašek* by Cecil Parrott (Bodley Head, London, 1978).

About the New Translation Team

Zdeněk K. Sadloň was born in 1953 in Czechoslovakia. He defected from the formerly communist country in 1972 shortly after graduating from an Electrical Engineering Secondary School.

He came to the U.S. a year later and worked as an electrician at Western Electric's Hawthorne Works in Chicago. While an undergraduate philosophy and political science major at the University of Illinois at Chicago, he worked as a busboy and waiter at the Old Prague restaurant in Cicero. He also has worked as an insurance underwriter for the Czechoslovak Societies of America fraternal insurance company, and was a typesetter, translator and a writer for the Czech *Denní Hlasatel* (Daily Herald) in Chicago.

As a college senior in 1978, he met his future wife in a U.S. foreign policy class and they married within the year. The following year he became a U.S. citizen.

Since 1986, he's been working as broadcaster and reporter for the Voice of America. He also works as a professional translator and interpreter. He has served a variety of clients, including President George Bush, Secretary of State James Baker, Chairman of the Joint Chiefs of Staff, Gen. Colin Powell, and many others. For eight years he was a U.S. Navy reservist, achieving the rank of Journalist Petty Officer Second Class.

Zenny lives in Cicero, Illinois, with his wife Mary and their six-year-old daughter, Lucille Zdenka.

Emmett Michael Joyce worked as a factory worker, dock hand, material handler, bartender and saloonkeeper before turning to journalism as a way to get off his feet. To that end, he earned BA and MA degrees from Northwestern University. Since then, he has written for the *Chicago Tribune* and *Chicago Daily News* and now works for the Voice of America as a radio reporter at its Midwest News Bureau in Chicago. He also co-authored a non-fiction novel entitled *Shoot to Miss* with writer John Whalen.

He lives in Crystal Lake, Illinois, with his wife, Demetra and two children, Jamie and Michael.